Praise for *Billions to Bust*

From post-communist Russia to Iceland's financial
meltdown, Thor Bjorgolfsson has lived six or seven
entrepreneurs' lives. His adventures – and his self-aware
reflections on them – offer powerful lessons to anyone
interested in developing the two essential qualities
for starting and running a business: perseverance and
adaptability.
> – Scott Galloway, Professor of Marketing at NYU's
> Stern School of Business, host of the Prof G podcast,
> co-host of the Pivot and Prof G Markets podcasts
> and a serial entrepreneur

A self-confessed deal junkie afloat on the turbulent seas of
global capitalism, Thor Bjorgolfsson's life story of triumph,
disaster and, it seems, redemption is in the finest tradition of
Viking sagas. He provides a gripping insider's perspective
on the causes of the financial crisis and its aftermath that you
won't read anywhere else.
> – Matthew Bishop, former globalisation editor of
> *The Economist* and co-author of *The Road From Ruin:*
> *A New Capitalism for a Big Society*

Thor Bjorgolfsson made $4 billion by the time he was 40 and
lost most of it by the time he was 41. His story has much to
tell about entrepreneurship, dogged ambition and the brutal
might of global markets.
> – Brent Hoberman, co-founder of Lastminute.com and
> creator of Founders Forum

Though the global financial crisis has spawned shoals of instant histories, mostly by small-fry journalists, there are precious few first-hand accounts of what it was like to be one of the big fish swimming in the treacherous economic seas of the past two decades. Now comes Icelandic entrepreneur Bjorgolfur Thor Bjorgolfsson with a gripping autobiography that describes not only his part in his homeland's banking blow-up but also his earlier career as a brewer in the 'Wild East' that was post-Soviet Russia. Anyone who wants to understand the animal spirits that propelled the world economy all the way underwater in 2008 – and then slowly raised it back the surface again – will relish *Billions to Bust*.

– Niall Ferguson, senior fellow at the Hoover Institute,
senior fellow at Harvard University and
writer and presenter of *The Ascent of Money*

About the authors

Thor Bjorgolfsson is a self-styled 'adventure capitalist' and was Iceland's first billionaire. Born in 1967, he made his first $100 million in 2002, from the sale of his Russian Bravo brewery business to Heineken. Over the following six years he grew this 40-fold, setting up the investment firm Novator as a platform for global investments ranging from generic pharmaceuticals to mobile telecoms.

Andrew Cave has written eight previous books on chief executives and leadership. He has been interviewing the world's leading business figures for more than 25 years, writing for the *Daily Telegraph* and *Sunday Telegraph* from London and New York.

BILLIONS TO BUST
– AND BEYOND

HOW I MADE, LOST AND REBUILT A FORTUNE, AND WHAT I LEARNED ON THE WAY

THOR BJORGOLFSSON
WITH ANDREW CAVE

Profile Books

This revised and updated edition published in Great Britain in 2025 by
Profile Books Ltd
29 Cloth Fair
London EC1A 7JQ
www.profilebooks.com

First published as *Billions to Bust – and Back* in 2014 by Profile Books Ltd

A CIP catalogue record for this book is available from the British Library.

Our product safety representative in the EU is Authorised Rep Compliance
Ltd., Ground Floor, 71 Lower Baggot Street, Dublin, D02 P593, Ireland.
www.arccompliance.com

ISBN 978 1 80522 023 7
eISBN 978 1 80522 024 4

Typeset in Palatino by MacGuru Ltd

Printed and bound in India by
Manipal Technologies Limited, Manipal

MIX
Paper | Supporting
responsible forestry
FSC
www.fsc.org   FSC™ C104740

CONTENTS

Prologue: On top of the world   ix
1 Billions to bust   1
2 A tale of two Thors: 1967–1986   12
3 Adventure capitalism in Russia: 1986–2002   36
4 Exceptional returns in emerging Europe: 1999–2008   71
5 Never go back: 2000–2007   98
6 The very public meltdown of God's frozen people:
   2008–2009   120
7 How to lose $4 billion in ten months: 2008–2009   143
8 Aftershock: 2009–2014   169
9 New horizons: 2014–2023   194
10 Adventure capitalism 2.0: 2014–2023   219
11 This time is never different?   243
Epilogue   267

Appendices
1 Timeline   273
2 Easy come, easy go   274
3 How banks shrink   275

Acknowledgements   277
Index   281

To my parents Thora and Bjorgolfur, who met, locked hands and remained together through hope and adversity for sixty years. Their love inspired everything I have achieved, and the safety and stability they provided was their greatest gift.

PROLOGUE

ON TOP OF THE WORLD

On my 40th birthday in March 2007, I was sitting on top of the world and only 250 people in it were richer than me. I lent my jet to presidents, mingled with Hollywood stars and media moguls, and was a celebrity in Iceland as the nation's first billionaire.

To celebrate, I decided to do something very special. My wife Kristin came up with this idea of not only celebrating the birthday but making it about something else as well. 'Thor, you can now do almost anything you want,' she said. 'Why don't you reflect on how you got there and share something unique with the friends and family who helped you get to this position?' Her comments struck a chord with me and we coined the idea of a kind of thank-you party. While I was a little nervous of making too big a deal out of a birthday, and uncomfortable with the kind of lavish parties that some people were throwing at the time, I started thinking about it differently. This was a chance for me to share the rich lifestyle I enjoyed with the people who I most valued and who were dearest to me, many of whom would never otherwise have the opportunity to experience it. Once I had become sold on the idea, the sky was the limit.

Kristin and I simply thought about the place where we had

the most magical memories, and which music we liked best, and we decided that we had to go to Jamaica. We also had the crazy notion that it should be a complete surprise party – for the guests instead of the birthday boy!

We hired a Boeing 767 furnished only with business class flatbeds and had two pick-up points, as people were coming in from all over the world. We told people to show up at Heathrow airport in London at 5 pm or in Reykjavik at 8 pm on the Thursday and get ready for a mystery trip to a faraway destination. The location was a closely guarded secret, and the 120 people on the plane had absolutely no clue as to where they were going, only that they would be returned back on Monday morning. I knew that there was a long flight ahead and that people were likely to start partying on the plane, but I needed them to have plenty of energy for the full programme we had planned. So I made sure that no alcohol was served on the flight and tried to get everyone to rest. That did not go down so well with everyone on board, but they had no choice. Everyone was an important friend to me, and most of the passengers would never have been able to afford to do something like that for themselves.

The guests didn't know anything about the party we had planned either. On the Saturday, we were all dressed up for dinner when suddenly a white screen dropped down, whereupon Kristin stood up, took hold of a microphone and announced that she had secretly made a short film about me and my life which she wanted to share with us. When the lights went off and the film started rolling I was amazed to find myself watching interviews with my family, my friends and the people I had been closest to at different periods in my life. Kristin had even sent a video crew to Russia to interview people from my time there and film the background there – all the interviewees were in the room, but no one had breathed a word to me. It was a documentary in which people described their impressions of me, and key moments from our relationship. Towards the end, there was even a personal greeting from my childhood James Bond idol Sean Connery, whom I had met twice. I simply could not believe it. The whole thing was one of the most surprising and moving experiences I have ever had. It left me completely speechless.

We had two sets on a beach, one with Jamiroquai and the other with Bob Marley's son Ziggy. Jamiroquai told me after his performance that this was the most beautiful setting he had ever performed in. He was at the top of his game and proceeded to party with us into the night. Then 50 Cent played on a purpose-built Hollywood-style set at our dress-up dinner in a white castle built in the 1920s in the middle of nowhere by a German eccentric. It was a hugely extravagant occasion.

As 50 Cent sang the line 'We're gonna party like it's your birthday', I would not have believed anyone if they had told me that within eighteen months I would have lost 99 per cent of my $4 billion fortune and would be pursued almost to the brink of bankruptcy by seven major banks. I would have found it impossible to contemplate that I would be treated like a pariah in my home country, saddled with $1 billion of debts and hated as a man who had supposedly almost single-handedly brought down an entire economy. But that is exactly what happened. How did I get from Caribbean hero to Icelandic zero? And how did I live to tell the tale? In 2014, I told that story – and detailed my recovery from that nadir – for the first time. Now I have updated it to add a subsequent Latin American journey that has also been an incredibly eventful ride.

1

BILLIONS TO BUST

And you may find yourself living in a shotgun shack
And you may find yourself in another part of the world
And you may find yourself behind the wheel of a large
automobile
And you may find yourself in a beautiful house, with a
beautiful wife
And you may ask yourself: Well, how did I get here?

Talking Heads, 'Once In a Lifetime'

My name is Bjorgolfur Thor Bjorgolfsson and I'm a deal junkie.
There, I've said it. But, just as when an alcohol abuser finally
makes the admission he has been denying for years, this
disclosure shouldn't come as any surprise. Business deals are
my fix. I have been addicted to them for most of my life and as
I became increasingly hooked, the temptation to borrow way
over my head to fund them became too much for me to resist.

Born into one of Iceland's most famous capitalist families, I
remember negotiating my earliest deal at the age of 10 when I
persuaded my father to lend me $80 to buy a stack of vintage
Marvel and *X-Men* comic books. I went into a 50–50 partnership with him. It was my idea and his money, which seemed
to be a good notion at the time. I never paid him back, but the

comics became a great investment. They have never been sold and are stored in a warehouse, accumulating value that will hopefully be passed on to my children.

A decade and a half later, I made my first fortune amid the Khrushchev-era concrete apartment blocks of Russia's hinterland following the collapse of the Soviet Union and fall of communism. I made my money from alcopops and beer, funding growth through my credit card, bank and private equity borrowings and working all the hours I could. Calculating that there were large profits to be made for the first outsider to successfully launch a premium beer brand in newly capitalist Russia, I set up shop in the Wild East and built the nation's biggest foreign-owned brewery start-up, selling out for hundreds of millions of dollars ten years later.

That's when the high life began for me as I moved in elite circles as an international business fixer, consorting with prime ministers and powerbrokers in privatisations in everything from telecoms to pharmaceuticals.

How did that feel? Much like a breaker wave appears to an experienced surfer who knows what it's like to be sucked under as the powers of nature overwhelm him but also loves the thrill of staying on his feet and figuring out a way of coming back out on top. It's dramatic imagery but for me, that was the sensation of being Iceland's first billionaire. I became a self-styled adventure capitalist who loved riding the storms of international business, never knowing exactly what economic, financial and political forces I would have to confront and having to calculate the risks and weave in and out of cycles, trends and the whims of the individuals I had to deal with.

I thrived on coping with the esoteric, the dangerous and the exotic in pursuit of a deal. From pharmaceuticals investments in Bulgaria at the time NATO was bombing Serbia to dismantling a top-heavy former nationalised telecoms giant in the Czech Republic, I discovered that a little capital and a lot of debt could multiply my initial wealth many times over. It peaked when I bought a Bulgarian telecoms group, BTC. My leverage on that deal was 95 per cent, meaning I only had to put up 5 per cent of the funds myself. I was hooked.

I had more money than I could have spent in a thousand years. *Forbes* estimated my wealth at $3.4 billion and put me on its cover. Steady increases in asset value kept adding to my fortune. It might just as well have been on autopilot. Doubts crept up on the periphery, but everything was moving too fast for me to process it clearly and objectively.

What does a deal-aholic think about when he wakes up in the morning with a dull thud in his head? I am not interested in financial architecture or in predicting the regulatory weather, nor do I rely on structural change. Economies and their markets, their regulators and their rules are constantly changing. A proficient surfer knows how to read the waves but cannot dictate what kinds of waves come in. The market is often wrong and it is those sorts of imbalances I make money from. I have made profits by accepting more risk than some other investors could stomach and then quickly de-risking through financial engineering before selling out to people with different risk appetites. Do I want a level playing field? No – no more than a surfer would like the sea to turn flat. In both instances, that course of events would just turn everything into a commodity.

I have always been interested in what I call special situations. I like to parachute into hairy situations, save them from getting worse, turn them around and make an exit. You could call it storm-riding financial markets. Such situations develop only when people are scared and do not understand the risks. I act like one of the advance guards who seeks to establish an entrenched advantage. I am not a mercenary. I am account-able. My personal reputation and wealth are at stake and my next deal depends on how I have entered and exited my last one. Publicly quoted corporations are normally not nimble or brave enough to put their balance sheets at risk in the same way that risk-taking individuals do. I can put myself on the line for what I am doing. People know who I am and what they see is what they get.

So what do they see? A deal junkie who constantly has his eye on the next stage of the plan? A financial manoeuvre that will turn the situation and open up the potential for profit? And what do I think of when I'm in the midst of such a plan? How I can tweak the shape of the business. What can be spun off, demerged or sold? What potential is there for mergers to create larger focused businesses, maybe specific to geographies or sectors? How much leverage can be put on the deal? What is the potential for stock or bond offerings? Which larger investors can be brought in for slices of the action? My eye is always on how I exit. I don't normally just buy something, hold it for a long time without changing the business and then just sell. What interests me is the evolution, the de-risking, and the stage-by-stage metamorphosis of a business into something that is simply inherently more profitable.

That has always been my investment approach. When the markets seized up and the appetite for risk diminished, my personal capacity to exploit opportunities became much more restricted. But a bit of cold turkey is not altogether a bad thing. It allows me to reflect on how I got here and where I go next. It has been, as they say, one hell of a ride.

In the boom years, along with countless others, I worshipped the god of leverage. In my best year, I made $1.3 billion from merging, floating and spinning off businesses. Then I looked to do it all again. I was always happiest when deals, ideally

4

more than one at a time, were in view. I liked to call what I did visionary and similar in some ways to chess, in that I was always planning the game several moves ahead. I like to think I am good at spotting opportunities and having a sense of how things could turn. If asked about my strengths I'm intuitive – my best results have come when I have followed my intuition, whereas the times I have managed to suppress it have usually ended in disaster. I'm always looking at my portfolio and seeing how I can develop and enhance it, and my time horizon is generally where I want to be in two to five years.

What was it like to add $2 billion to my personal wealth in the space of just two years? It certainly wasn't 'easy come, easy go', although that is how it might look now, but it was definitely rapid. I made my first $100 million in 2002, from the Bravo brewery sale to Heineken. In those years Pharmaco, later Actavis, a generic pharmaceutical business where I was the largest shareholder, had become a public company with a stock market capitalisation of about $50 million – so small that London investment bankers would barely give me the time of day. But Actavis grew phenomenally both organically and through mergers and acquisitions, and by 2008 it was valued at €5.3 billion ($7.3 billion dollars at the exchange rate of the time) and was Iceland's biggest industrial company, second in size only to the banks on the nation's stock exchange. Actavis, in all its guises, was my biggest, most profitable and most complicated investment. It sums up the way I like to do business. In its early days, it involved putting together an equity consortium in a privatisation in eastern Europe. Then there was a reverse takeover of a listed company, the spin-off of its core business, a hostile cross-border takeover of another listed company, a public-to-private leveraged buy-out, financial restructuring and finally a sale to a listed company.

As well as being financially rewarding, I hugely enjoyed the creative energy I was able to exert in devising new strategies and fresh ways of extracting value. I rarely make an investment and say: 'This is the business plan. I'll hold it for five years.' Usually, there is a lot of dealing involved. I'm constantly thinking about how I can evolve and tweak it with another deal. It is like managing a Formula One racing team: you are constantly making adjustments to the car to improve performance and also adapting your race strategy to get ahead of the competition.

How big does a bubble have to be before it pops? The question would not matter so much in relation to capitalism's perpetual crises were it not that every puff of breath into such a metaphorical sphere can be worth millions of dollars. Each inhalation represents an escalating risk but still we gather the air. We all know that bubbles burst, but what an opportunity glistens before that inevitably happens. Iceland was in such a bubble in 2007. It had been building up for some time and, much as I would like to say that I was aware of its impermanence and wiser than others who were profiting from it, I remained seduced. Everyone in Iceland's financial circles was. The siren song was simply too beguiling.

In the Actavis takeover, I made a public offer for the company worth €5.3 billion, putting up 20 per cent of the equity and borrowing the rest. This was the largest European private equity deal in 2007. I still find it incredible when I think about it, but I was hardly alone in my hunger for top-of-the-market profit dollars. Indeed, I was inundated with bankers who wanted desperately to be in on the deal. Some were hammering at the door to get in but it was being kept firmly shut by those on the inside. 'No. We're not letting any other bank in,' they told me. 'Guys,' I said. 'You're lending €4 billion here. Don't you want to diversify your risk?' But the guys who had originated the deal were protective of it and didn't want to do that. I saw their eyes gleam and I took their money.

I think you see those times only once in your life. Of course, there had been earlier bubbles, including the 1998 Russian crisis. There are some similarities. In both, the state became the speculator. There was a casino atmosphere and the biggest gambler of all was the state, which was issuing debt. The events of 2007 and 2008 were global, however. This time, it was as if virtually everyone in western markets was smoking crack cocaine and did not notice when the whole system, the equity markets and indeed nations were about to fall.

I remember in Russia, when we were making beer, our management accountants were asking about our margins and we were telling them that they were about 25 per cent before overheads. Then my deputy came in and said: 'Thor. We're buying all these raw materials. Why are we doing that when we can get 25 per cent on Russian state bonds right now? Why don't we lower production and just buy three-month short-term bonds at a guaranteed 25 per cent? We'll get a much better return on it.' This was from a regular employee with no background in financial speculation. Even he was being seduced by the fantastic returns being offered by the state. Russia needed to fund itself so it was just supporting its debts at higher and higher rates and everyone was buying them. It was unsustainable but a decade later the same thing was happening in Iceland, where the Icelandic Central Bank was offering state paper at 15–16 per cent in an AAA-rated economy with a strong local currency.

What happened is that money got diverted out of the economy into the capital markets. It is like when people stop buying houses and cars and instead mortgage their apartments and start speculating in the equity and government bond markets. Companies can do that too. Directors say to each other: 'Let's not focus so much on fishing or making more food here. Let's just buy this debt.' This is one similarity between what happened in Russia and Iceland before their respective crashes. In Iceland, the situation was stoked up by an unrealistically strong krona and the state issuing paper. Of course, the banks had their problems too, but the biggest problem was the unsustainable strength of the currency. That is what caused the most collateral damage when the bubble was finally pricked.

Another similarity is the oligarchies that had emerged in pre-crash Russia and in Iceland. I would estimate that in 2008 about 30 people controlled Iceland's economy, out of a total population of 300,000. That is one in 10,000: not an excessive concentration of power compared with, say, the US or the UK, but the extent of what Iceland's political and financial oligarchs controlled was, as with their counterparts in Russia, disproportionate, which in such a small country created a huge imbalance.

In Russia I was just a marginal character outside the system, whereas at the time of the crash in Iceland I was close to the centre. I had the biggest balance sheet and the biggest exposure to the economy, but I did not realise how weak the state was. I was also fooled by the ratings. An Icelandic economist has pointed out, and rightfully so, that the Icelandic banks are the only financial institutions in the world that have gone bankrupt with an A rating. With Russia, I was always aware of the fragile state of the economy. My assumption was that it could blow up tomorrow and everything would be gone.

By 2008, Iceland's bubble had been building steadily, with an administration on a gargantuan spending spree. The state ballooned, splashing out on infrastructure, and the mentality was that everyone should join in. Although I take serious issue with its analysis of the economics and cause and effect, Iceland's parliamentary report into the crash is spot on when it refers to the University of Iceland's Psychiatry and Sociology Department description of the country's herd mentality. Icelanders are very much herd animals. No one can stick out. There is no 'you' or 'me'. Everything is 'we'. This makes for a cosy and tight-knit environment most of the time, but it's also very restrictive.

In 2008, people in Iceland believed they were destined for something, that it was time for 'God's frozen people', as a former Icelandic prime minister, David Oddsson, had once referred to them, to take their place. But Iceland was trying to punch way above its weight without regard to the fundamentals. It was like when Iceland's national handball team won silver in the Beijing Olympics in 2008. 'Iceland is not a small country. It's the "biggestest" country in the world,' exclaimed the president's wife at that time. I shared in that moment, having arranged at the last minute to go to Beijing for the game with my wife Kristin. We were on holiday in St Tropez when we heard that Iceland had got into the final. I rang my secretary and asked her to get us to China. I wanted to be there at the moment when Iceland had a chance of winning gold in something. Within 24 hours, we were in Beijing. It was a symbol of how at that time almost anything seemed possible for Iceland.

Everyone buying into a bubble thinks that this time is different. It never is, of course.

As if that wasn't enough, I had a large amount of personal debt and seven banks, an army of lawyers and a nation looking for culprits all breathing down my neck. This is where I found myself at the end of 2008.

Let's do the math, as Americans say. In 2005, *Forbes* calculated I was worth $1.4 billion, making me Iceland's first billionaire. By the peak of the boom, midway through 2007, this had increased to $4 billion, with roughly one third of my wealth in Actavis, another third in Landsbanki, Iceland's second-biggest bank which was privatised in 2002, and the remainder in other ventures. But by the end of 2009, following the government's seizure of Landsbanki and the fall in Actavis's valuation, this had fallen to about $40 million. So if people asked how I was doing, I replied that I still had 1 per cent of my net worth.

Of course, $40 million is more than enough for anyone to live on without working for the rest of their life, but things were more complicated than that. Although my balance sheet at the peak said $4 billion, the question I always kept in mind in the debt bubble was: how much am I personally guaranteeing? That was a checkpoint for me. The answer, when the markets crashed, was that I had personal guarantees of €400 million. One of my advisers, a restructuring specialist, told me that this was the largest personal guarantee he had ever seen in a restructuring. After my father went bankrupt and his €250 million share of our joint guarantees was added to mine, the total rose to €650 million and the proportion of the balance sheet I was guaranteeing rose from 12 per cent to 20 per cent.

As a result, I had a great deal to lose. However, when Iceland was plummeting in the last four weeks of the boom, my actions were the opposite of those of most Icelandic businessmen and players. In Iceland it was always the clan, the insiders on the market, who were the movers and shakers. I was an outsider and remained so, even on my return to Iceland and my emergence as the nation's biggest inward investor. You might expect insiders to take more personal responsibility than outsiders for national crises, but the reality in Iceland in 2008 was the opposite. I was taking on more personal responsibility, whereas most of the insiders were trying to escape personal liability with diverse transactions, many of which I believe will not stand up to the scrutiny of Iceland's courts.

I do not mean to paint me white and them black; I am just looking at it from a different perspective. My actions were not dictated by any great altruism; I simply thought Iceland would weather the financial storm and we would get to the other side. Most of the other guys just said: 'There's not a chance in hell.' But they were pessimists, something I can never be accused of being. Innate optimism is at the heart of everything I have ever done. I believe that to succeed you have to be an optimist and then you build everything from that. In the years after the 2008 crash, the biggest danger was that I would lose my optimism. I came close to doing so but thank God it didn't happen.

I was one year into my 40s when the credit crisis struck the world – an active participant as an international investor and the largest single shareholder in the Icelandic banking system that exploded so spectacularly.

The carousel stopped with a jolt and I got thrown off, losing 99 per cent of my accumulated paper wealth. It did not stop for my sake and I would like to think that something less than a global financial crisis and a total collapse in Iceland would have sufficed as a rousing kick. This book represents my attempt to use those crises, as well as my personal meltdown, to re-evaluate myself in the light of what happened, how I dealt with it and what I did next. But let's go back to the beginning.

Everything is temporary.

2

A TALE OF TWO THORS
1967-1986

> A family is like a forest: when you are outside, it is dense;
> when you are inside, you see that each tree has its place.
>
> African proverb

My father was a workaholic and also a highly functional alcoholic. Actually, he hasn't touched a drink since he went into rehab in 1978 when I was 11. Today I still have a hard time seeing whether his drinking had an influence on me. I guess it must have. Since he considered the drinking so damaging to himself that it had to stop, it must have had some impact at home and therefore on me. The soft science concurs: alcoholism is a family disease. But I cannot locate this influence to evaluate or examine it. I am who I am and I cannot tell you why. To dissect myself, to find the root of every emotion, belief, hidden quality and conspicuous flaw, I would need a brain 40 times more able than the one I was given. And if I had such a brain, I would put it to some better use. Though our experiences and past certainly shape who we are, we are also to no lesser degree who we want to be. I do not just mean what we want to be when we grow up or what we want our epitaph to say, but simply who we want to be today. And a day that I have wanted to set aside to search for emotional scars from my Dad's boozing has yet to dawn.

It is not as if I have buried the pain. I remember my Dad drunk. He was bad at it. I do not remember him being at home a lot then; indeed, he was conspicuously absent. Most of the time it could certainly be explained by his working very hard to provide for his large family. He was a young man with heavy responsibility. But every so often he would disappear for a while and my mother would be anxious and irritated. The drinking was undoubtedly a source of tension in the family. I was too young to give it much cogent thought, but I could feel the strain between my parents. When I was five, my mother and I went to pick my father up at Keflavik, Iceland's international airport. It was less than an hour's drive but my mother wasn't feeling talkative. I stood beside her and watched her staring at the arriving passengers as they entered the terminal. I saw her see Dad. He walked towards us and had I been older, I would have realised that he was more than a little bit tipsy. Before a single word was uttered, Mum slapped him and stormed off. Dad took me by the hand and followed. I do not recall anything being said once we got home, maybe not even until the following morning.

Of course that slap was a shock. I can still hear her hand landing on his cheek. In a sense, that moment in the terminal marked the end of an era for me. Up to that point, my life was an uninterrupted unity. I was I and I was Mum and Mum was Dad and Dad was me. It was unthinkable that one part of this trinity would turn on another. But now there was a rift. The Thor in the backseat driving back into Reykjavik was different from the Thor in the same seat on the outbound journey. I had become my own person.

Mum and Dad had probably displayed their discontent in front of me before, but I did not have the maturity to draw the right conclusions until then. And even though such a moment is important, necessary and a precondition for future growth, we need a good shove to accept what it signifies. Just about everyone can recall a similar breach of the trust they place in their parents. Some children were in for a much harsher awakening than I, and some had to face this breach way before they had the maturity to deal with it. My awakening was probably enhanced by the fact that my mother was a warm and soft-spoken person, and so that slap was out of character and utterly unexpected.

On a fateful day in 1978, a knock came at the door. Dad was in his study and a few men went in to sit with him. One of them was in the kitchen speaking to my mother. The atmosphere was sombre, but I found it hard to understand just how serious things were because I knew all the men from happy social occasions in our home. They were cool guys, with long sideburns. One of them came into my room and removed his glasses. The rims were so thick and heavy that they left a wide red line across the bridge of his nose. He looked me in the eye and asked if my Dad had ever been bad to me. 'No,' I replied. When Dad was drunk, he fell asleep. The man asked me if I was sad when Dad went drinking. I hesitated and said 'yes'. He took me into the living room to sit down with my father and mother and the other men and explained that they were discussing whether Dad should go to a nice hospital for a few weeks to stop him drinking again. He then asked me: 'What do you think Thor? Would you like Daddy to stop drinking?' All eyes fell on me and I was surprised that they were asking me and that everyone was listening carefully for my answer. I said: 'Yes, I would,' and the room went quiet as my words sank in.

A short time later my Dad went to rehab in Hazelton, Minnesota. He was 37; I, his youngest child, was 11, and my oldest brother Orn was 27. While he was there my mother and I went on the family holiday we had long planned to California without him. I went to San Francisco where my second brother Halli and oldest sister Magga, then aged 24 and 23 respectively, were living – I had been waiting, excited, for weeks to see their world. It was a revelation. Iceland had been by and large a closed country. It was only the well-off who had any experience of the rest of the world. Ordinary people started going on holiday to Spain in the 1970s but saw little more than beaches, bars and stalagmite caves. The first generation to study abroad in large numbers had yet to return. Iceland was a country where taxes were high and local industry was tightly protected, with a restricted range of products barely connected to consumer demand. Many things were forbidden: TV on Thursdays, beer and pop music on the radio (save for a 50-minute programme, *Songs of the Young*, once a week). On top of this we endured runaway inflation, strikes, government crises and endless bickering.

Of course, an 11-year-old does not see his home country on such terms. Put an 11-year-old in Moscow under Brezhnev or in Tehran today and he will sculpt a world that suits his interests and enthusiasms. But this particular 11-year-old who was taken from Reykjavik to San Francisco in 1978 made a discovery and a long-term decision.

I still think San Francisco is a wonderful city – the sea breeze coming in as if someone has just turned on the air conditioning and streets tumbling up and down like a rollercoaster. I did not put a flower in my hair, but I did feel as if someone had drawn the curtains wide open. Life was not as it was in Iceland. It was more welcoming, more colourful and happier. The shop assistants were nicer, the food tasted better, and people looked me in the eye and seemed to care about what I wanted and thought. If life really was more like this, I figured,

Iceland was confused, lost in the woods and running in the wrong direction.

Of course, this experience was heightened by the fact that my father was not with us and everything felt as if it was changing in some fundamental way. In a way I was the man of the house now, discovering the big world as I tagged along to work with my brother and sister and saw how they each blossomed in their own way in this fantastic environment. Time and that place were now somehow mine and I had also left some unusually heavy baggage at home. The days and weeks before the paterfamilias decides to confront his alcoholism are not happy times for any family. It was therefore a double relief for me, getting out from under the weight of both my father and Iceland, and that feeling of liberation has stayed with me since. I made a decision in San Francisco that Iceland was one big, broken mess. It was not the place for me and I was not going to live and work in Iceland. I would live my life out in the big world of opportunities.

*

Born in Reykjavik, I am the youngest of five in a colourful family. My father, Bjorgolfur Gudmundsson, was the third husband of my mother, Thora Hallgrimsson, and I am the only child from that marriage. She had one child from her first marriage and three children from her second.

Events later on in my life have given me a strong sense of betrayal, and it starts at home, I guess. Some psychologists will tell you it always does. My parents were both betrayed and stigmatised, so this kind of thinking is probably in my blood. My father went against the mainstream and later didn't want to be frowned upon: he was very conscious of his image. And my mother was the same.

My grandmother on my mother's side was the daughter of Thor Jensen, a Danish-born entrepreneur whose Wikipedia entry states that he 'moved to Iceland at an early age and ... all but introduced big business, and even modern capitalism, to the country'. My mother's father, Hallgrimur Hallgrimsson, was born to Icelandic parents in Canada and raised there until he was 21, when his father became a priest at the cathedral in Reykjavik. With a priest for a father and a bishop for a grandfather, he took a different path and went into business. He got a job at Shell Oil Company in Iceland and worked his way up to chief executive and then chairman. He had an employment contract that would raise many corporate governance eyebrows these days, and when he retired he received the same salary as the chief executive until he died. After that, the salary was paid monthly to his widow.

My grandfather was very old school. He came home for lunch every day, went dutifully to his Rotary Club and lived his life like clockwork. He visited the UK frequently, having clothes made by his tailor in Savile Row and his shoes by a nearby bootmaker. He was cosmopolitan but conservative. He was well paid and had a high standard of living. He had shares in Shell but no other investments and he showed no entrepreneurial flair. As he grew older, dementia set in, and that was very frustrating, certainly for him, but also for his family, as those who have cared for such patients know all too well. I liked my grandfather and wore his old suits when I was at university. I found him inspirational in some ways. He was his own man, very attached to the UK, where he was awarded an honorary CBE in 1956 for his cooperation with the British forces in the Second World War. My father said that I take after my grandfather in some respects, being sometimes both short-tempered and having a short attention span.

My mother was the elder of two daughters and was very

close to her father. She went to a boarding school in the UK at 14, developed into a beautiful young woman and by 18 was hanging out with an acting crowd in London, with friends who included Trevor Howard and Jean Simmons. When she received a proposal of marriage from an actor called David Tomlinson, who later starred in films including *Mary Poppins, Bedknobs and Broomsticks* and *The Love Bug*, my grandfather decided she was getting too much into the London social scene and made her return to Iceland, with a stopover in college in the US. There she met Iceland's biggest sporting star at the time, Haukur Clausen, an Olympic runner and Nordic champion, marrying him when she was 20 and having a son a year later. Soon afterwards, however, she found that he was having an affair with her best friend, and being a headstrong and proud woman she immediately left and divorced him.

Not long after divorcing Clausen, at the age of 23, she met George Lincoln Rockwell, an officer at the US Air Force base in Iceland, at a dinner party at the Norwegian embassy in Reykjavik. Rockwell had served as a commander in the USAF and fought in Korea before coming to Reykjavik and quickly learning Icelandic. He was divorced and had three daughters from an earlier marriage. He and my mother married in 1953 and went to live in the US, where he founded a magazine publishing business, but it was not a commercial success. They travelled around, living in various parts of the US, and had three children together. So by the time she was 27, my mother had four children. All was not well, however: the business failures had caused financial problems and Rockwell became increasingly involved in far-right politics, founding the American Nazi Party in 1959 and writing and publishing controversial pamphlets. (He later published his autobiography, *This Time the World*, in 1961, and the inflammatory *White Power* in 1967.) This was the time of the US civil rights movement, Malcolm X's Black Power movement and Martin Luther King Jr, and their house was firebombed once when my mother was inside with the children. They escaped unharmed but later sold the house and ended up living in a trailer park. Increasingly unhappy and embarrassed about her fall from grace and being dragged into the politics of hate, my mother took the advice of her uncle, Thor Thors, the Icelandic ambassador to Washington, and returned to Iceland and divorced Rockwell.

None of this was discussed when I was growing up, but in 1961 my mother was a twice-divorced mother of four with an ex-husband who was a political extremist, which was not a good position to find oneself in in a small city in Iceland. Then, at a Christmas party in Iceland, she met my father, who was 20 and had just started university. They fell in love and married soon afterwards. The wedding took place at home, officiated by the family priest who had baptised her; it was a very simple occasion. My mother had travelled the world, lived in the US and the UK and gone to the 1948 London Olympics, whereas my father was an Icelander whose only sojourn abroad had been when he was in a football team as a teenager. They were happily married for 58 years until she suddenly passed away during the Covid-19 pandemic after a very eventful 90-year life.

I was born in 1967, four years after they married, and in the same year that Rockwell was assassinated by a former party member in the parking lot of a laundromat in Virginia. Rockwell has become something of a cult figure on the extreme right in the US. Over the years, a lot of Americans have come to Iceland wanting to talk to my mother and her children by Rockwell; they have always been turned away.

My father's background is very different. He grew up in a working-class family, one of five children. His mother was a housewife. His father had a stroke when he was quite young and when my father was only four or five. My father's childhood was gravely affected by the insecurity and anxiety that accompanied his father's bad health. But they were good, solid people who helped each other through the hard times. My father married a two-times divorcee 11 years his senior with four children when he was 22, adopting Rockwell's three children and also bringing up my eldest half-brother, Orn Clausen. It was a pretty unusual situation in the 1960s in Iceland and raised more than a few eyebrows. He was a bright young boy marrying a woman far older than him with four young children from two broken marriages. What was he thinking? No wonder they both seem to have yearned for recognition and appreciation and feared being frowned upon. And those fears were compounded when events turned against them later in life, as they did when my father was arrested.

I am named after my mother's grandfather, Thor Jensen, an immigrant who became the richest man in Iceland. I am 16 years younger than my eldest brother and ten years younger than my youngest sister, but until I was about seven, we all lived at home. My brothers Orn and Halli and sisters Magga and Bentina would take me to movies that I was not allowed to go to and they were cool to hang out with, as they were an eclectic bunch. Halli was a long-haired roadie for some local rock 'n' roll bands, and even made a record of his own. Orn was a long-haired, bearded scholar who was heavily into paganism and the resurgence of the old Viking religion. He and his friends would make offerings to the heathen gods and even built a temple and a 2.5-metre statue of the hammer-wielding Thor that still stands today. He sadly passed away in 2020 after being diagnosed with multiple sclerosis. He was given a Norse pagan funeral, unusual, lovely and very much in his individual style. My sisters were equally independent and unconventional. Magga was a hippie, heavily into Eastern philosophy and karma, and a strict vegetarian who sometimes lived in communes after she left home. Bentina fell in love with a handsome Japanese karate instructor in the middle of the Bruce Lee martial arts craze of the time, much to my parents' dismay, as they thought she was too young at only 19 to marry. But she was going to marry him no matter what anyone thought or said, and she did so. It was fantastic to have all these colourful characters as my family and it was certainly an unconventional one compared with others in the neighbourhood.

Until I was five, we lived in a multi-storey block of apartments where there were many families. There were a lot of half-built houses close by in this newly developing neighbourhood, which we used as our playgrounds. We moved a couple of times but always within the same locality. It was a very loving atmosphere at home, despite the age gaps and the eclectic mix of the household. I could always count on support and advice from an elder in whatever adventure or mischief I got up to. Each of us, grownups as well as children, had many friends, and the home was sometimes like a busy train station, with non-stop arrivals and departures. It was always open to all who came, and my mother reigned there with unparalleled generosity, warmth and grace.

My mother had one sister. Her husband worked for the United Nations in Paris. She would come with her two children to spend summers in Iceland and we would sometimes go and visit them in Paris – my first experience of a different city. My awareness of cosmopolitan life increased through contact with a friend of my mother called Sonja Zorilla, an Icelandic woman married to a rich Argentinian man, Alberto Zorilla, a former Olympic gold swimmer and a hero in his homeland. They did well on Wall Street and lived on New York's Park Avenue, had Picassos on the walls, and would come to Iceland by private plane and throw big lunches. This opened my eyes to another world. Sonja was always very fond of me and later helped me get into New York University and move to New York.

Maybe it was her life that I looked at and wanted. I was certainly always entrepreneurial and looking for ways to earn money. At 11, I ran errands for the university physics lab in the summer and for Iceland's biggest newspaper the next year. I was just a small kid on a bicycle but I got a pay cheque. Even my hobbies, like my comic book collection, paid for themselves. Comic books were an underground culture in Iceland. They were sold not in convenience stores or regular bookstores but in second-hand bookstores, where they were regarded in a similar way to pornography: an undignified but profitable sideline that shopkeepers detested. The hunched old guys in these bookstores saw me enter and then acted as if I had not. These stores were havens for eccentric, tobacco-snuffing know-it-alls. They were not happy or cheery men. They did not think much of comics or children. What would they want with children? You cannot debate or show off your knowledge of literature with a child. When I had found what I was looking for in a stack of comics I had to wait at the counter for the old men to finish whatever it was they were doing. That could take a while. They must have felt it was beneath them to assist a kid. But I had set my mind on buying the comics. This is probably where I got my first lesson in stubbornness!

This cold indifference towards children in Iceland was not exclusive to second-hand bookstores. One of the things that struck me in San Francisco when I was 11 was that strangers were polite to me. Of course there were people in Iceland who talked to children and treated them like individuals, but it was not common. The world of children was far removed from that of adults and few tried to cross the chasm. It's a shame. The old farts at the bookstore and I could have chatted about our interests and projects, which were not all that different. Having initially got hooked on comics because I was in awe of the superheroes, I then developed the same bibliomania that affected the old men. They dreamt of pristine copies of the sagas for their collections, while I scoured the stacks for a copy of an early issue of *Fantastic Four* for mine. I was not searching for the content of the issue but the value created by its scarcity. And I was pretty good at this game, too – no worse than my senior colleagues, I bet. I don't think many of them managed to establish as valuable a collection with as little expense as mine. And their collections were tied to a market that extended just five city blocks in Reykjavik, while I could have sold mine pretty much anywhere in the world. I still own the first edition of *X-Men*; it can only appreciate in value.

I received an allowance from my father but I was always trying to complement it. When I was about ten, I and some other kids were given a patch of land and taught to grow our own vegetables. At harvest time, we were allowed to keep some of what we had grown. Most of the kids just took them home, but I said to my mother: 'I'm going to the market and I'm going to sell them. Do you want to buy them?' She said she had already paid for the gardening course and was certainly not going to pay again for the vegetables, so I went from door to door, asking people if they wanted to buy fresh potatoes. Not many did, so I sold them to the grocer on the corner in exchange for some sweets. I remember thinking that I could trade these things. I knew I wanted to have money in my life and now I knew how to get it.

*

In 1986, seven years after my Dad's friends with the sideburns came knocking, another group of men in trench coats came, took my Dad and put him in custody. This time, the visit was not hushed as before, but tense, rude and mean. I don't know if anyone has done a study on which is worse to go through: forced entry by police or by burglars. People are probably more likely to defend themselves against criminals but the police wield such absolute power that you don't think to challenge it. Two policemen showed up at 7 am to search the house. They took documents and asked my father to come with them for questioning. My mother asked when he was coming back. The men said it wouldn't take long. Dad said: 'Never mind, never mind, I'll be back later.' We knew nothing more until the evening, when we were watching TV with my father's older brother. The first news item showed pictures of my father being led from a police car into a court and said six executives had been arrested on suspicion of perjury and other charges. We had had no inkling. We did not know what to expect. This was such a blow, one of the biggest ever to hit our family. My mother and my sister were crying uncontrollably. None of us knew what was happening and we looked on as the footage was repeated again and again.

The newsreader spoke of major embezzlement and fraud, and by the end it seemed as though he had recited half of the penal law. The report said they had been arrested and would be kept in isolation for six weeks. Six weeks in solitary confinement? That day was a slap in the face, just as shocking to me as the one my mother had given my father 13 years before. Again it signalled a breach of trust, this time between the Icelandic establishment, me and my family. I knew I didn't want to be part of the system in this country. But another thing struck me as I sat there in front of the TV. I felt I was now responsible for the family and realised I had to grow up overnight.

The magnitude of this realisation was extraordinary. As I walked down the big wooden staircase from the TV room, I just thought to myself: 'He's gone. I have to try to take control of this situation.'

The six weeks in solitary were in the end reduced to four. It was three long years before he was charged and two more before he was convicted, and it has taken me much longer to express my view of the affair. I still believe that isolating my father in a small cell for so long was an extreme measure that went way beyond what was called for. As an article in *Scientific American* (17 July 2013) stated: 'Extreme isolation and sensory deprivation can take a severe, sometimes permanent, toll on emotional and mental health.' It was not necessary and should not have happened. We were not allowed to visit and could not get any messages to him. He wasn't allowed to write or receive letters. My Dad says that nothing in life has ever had such difficult psychological consequences for him as that time in solitary confinement. He was devastated. The entrenched system in Iceland was too much for him to stomach and he planned to move as far away as possible, to South Africa. He went as far as gathering all the information on how to start a new life there, but before he took the leap he was offered a job in Iceland. At the same time, social unrest was gaining momentum in South Africa and it didn't look as appealing for a family of immigrants as before.

When I was growing up my father worked as a managing director at a factory making aluminium cans for the food industry. I would go with him at weekends when it was closed and play on the trolleys and forklifts while he was working. We got along well and I looked up to him and saw myself following in his footsteps one day. Then he became chief executive of the shipping company Hafskip, so I worked there in my summer holidays running errands and then as a dock-worker, unloading ships and containers, eventually moving on to be a deckhand on cargo ships sailing into the Baltic.

During those school breaks I would go where the pay was highest and there was the most overtime. And, although I led a pretty sheltered life, it was always getting better. Every house we moved into was bigger than the last and we had better cars too. My father was becoming more affluent. He owned a chain of one-hour photo-processing shops in Denmark and some shares in an insurance company, but almost all his energy and focus were on Hafskip.

It was a great company in many respects. It had a particular vibe to it and looked every bit the young new challenger. The huge cargo ships were painted a solid red and emblazoned with the Hafskip logo, and the corporate look and feel was carried through everything from newspaper adverts to the company's huge cargo terminals by the harbour. In its time it was a bit like Sir Richard Branson's Virgin brand in Iceland, exuding a similar vibrancy compared with the other boring old conservative shipping corporations. When you live on an island, the shipping companies are always going to be the main businesses. My father was just like any other energetic and charismatic young executive with a 'screw it, let's do it' attitude to the system in Iceland at the time. This influenced me greatly and I saw how Dad and these guys were always trying to do something new. Staff morale was fantastic even after the company ceased to be; ex-employees kept on holding the annual Christmas party for years and years. I have never heard of anything like that and it speaks volumes for the camaraderie and uniqueness of the organisation.

Hafskip was neither under the wing of the Independence Party and the power blocks operating in its shadow nor supported by the Progressive Party and its business arm, the Association of Co-operatives (SIS). Instead, it had the support of an uneasy minority within the Independence Party: manufacturers and retailers in Reykjavik who had long been used to living with the fact that their interests were viewed as subservient to those of the fishing industry around which the whole economy was focused. When the fishing industry was doing well the krona strengthened and made imports cheaper, which helped retailers but made it harder for manufacturers, especially if they were seeking to export their output. And when the fishing industry was doing poorly, the reverse was true. The swings in the exchange rate made it difficult for businesses that were not fishing-related to thrive. Furthermore, there was unequal access to loans, unfair allocation of land and other goods controlled by the government, and so on. Running a business in Iceland was simply a hopeless enterprise for ordinary people. If you did not pledge allegiance to one gang or another, sooner or later, like a prison inmate, you would be ambushed in the shower stalls.

Few exporters and importers dared trade with Hafskip. Most were caught in complex webs of interests, favours and protection that forbade dealings with anyone but Eimskip, Iceland's oldest and largest shipping group, or the Association's shipping arm. In effect, Hafskip was cut off from too large a portion of the market to become a competitive player. The solution pursued by my father and other Hafskip managers was to seek business abroad in order to gain a foothold. When push came to shove, Hafskip's foundations were too lean to support rapid growth, and when shipping conditions in the North Atlantic deteriorated the company crumbled beneath excessive leverage.

This is a tale both new and old. Hafskip would probably have died in peace were it not for the fact that Albert Gudmundsson, the financial minister at the time and unofficial spokesman for that uneasy minority within the Independence Party, had previously been Hafskip chairman and on the board of state-owned Utvegsbanki, the company's bank.

So the bankruptcy was not only an opportunity for political squabbling, as when one of the Independence or Progressive Party's pet companies went bust, but also a chance for the Independence Party leadership to clean up its backyard and root out internal opposition. And as always when families fight, it got messy.

Politicians like Gudmundsson exist everywhere. They gather support by helping others, using whatever powers they have. After Gudmundsson beat the party chairman in a primary, winning the first seat on the ballot in the capital and party stronghold, Reykjavik, he became a force to be reckoned with and was made minister of finance.

In office Gudmundsson faced two main sources of opposition: from the public officials who wanted things done by the book and from those in the party who considered his political methods a disgrace. They were men of large interests. Gudmundsson called himself the friend of the little guy, and that is where his votes came from. He pushed his little guys to the front of the line, snuck them a grant or gave them tax exemption, whereas these men were more grandiose. They made sure their friends got the contracting work for the US army base or all fishing rights in Icelandic waters. To them, Gudmundsson was a street hustler.

This was the political background of the Hafskip bankruptcy. Gudmundsson was fired from government, formed his own party and did well in the elections. This weakened the Independence Party enough to pave the way for a new party leadership, one that could reconcile itself with Gudmundsson, eventually giving him a smooth landing as Icelandic ambassador in the Paris embassy; he was a fluent French speaker, having played football for Marseille in France and AC Milan in Italy, the first Icelandic footballer to play abroad professionally. Gudmundsson was no ordinary footballer, earning the nickname 'White Pearl' – Eusébio of course being the Black Pearl. Inevitably people had, and have, different opinions about the Hafskip case, but I cannot believe anyone would deny that the initial hullabaloo made by police, prosecutors, liquidators and other officials, not to mention the comments made by politicians and the press, was out of all proportion to the eventual outcome – probation sentences for the minor charges.

My father was charged on something like 240 counts, but in the end convicted of few. One was that he had paid a restaurant bill through the company's account instead of his own, but the restaurant in question was Kentucky Fried Chicken and he had simply taken the wrong chequebook with him that day. Another was a technical accounting error. In the criminal court in 1990, 14 of the 17 men charged were acquitted. Of the remaining three, my father got a five-month suspended sentence, one man got a two-month suspended sentence and one was fined. In the end, the sentence imposed on my father by the Supreme Court in 1991 was 12 months suspended. When the case started, the managers of Hafskip together were initially charged on more than 400 counts. The criminal court convicted on five counts and the Supreme Court on 20. This truly had been a witch hunt that most people now accept was excessive given the verdicts and the fact that Hafskip was not necessarily bankrupt at the time. The recovery of the estate was about 70 per cent.

If you were to go over any company with a fine-tooth comb, you could probably come up with charges of the sort the Hafskip management eventually got sentences for. I am certain it is true of any company that goes bankrupt. It is irrational to demand that the managers of a failing company, one that is fighting for its life, both give it all they have got and transcend the struggle at the same time. Of course their decisions will be based on a future where the company still exists. Then in the bitterness of a collapse it will be obvious that they had a tendency to play down the problems in order to sustain their faith in the future. Pride plays its part too – as does a sense of loyalty to employees, associates and creditors who have put their trust in the business and those running it. Thus it was with my father and his partners. They had not acted strictly by the book, but nor had they taken money out of the company or abused their powers in their or anyone else's interest. His ordeal was a disgrace to the system in Iceland, that threatens and belittles the nation and people I love.

*

Much the same happened to my great-grandfather, Thor Jensen, who ventured from his native Denmark to Iceland in 1878 at the age of 15. He had lost his father young and been raised in an orphanage. He accepted an unpaid apprenticeship with a merchant in Bordeyri, a remote trading post in Iceland. There he became part of the generation that founded trade co-operatives and youth associations, brought policy and decision-making back home from the colonial power of Denmark, belatedly embraced the industrial revolution with the mechanisation of fishing, changed labour practices and created a new type of society in Iceland.

My great-grandfather became the most influential leader of this new society over the following decades. Many were more prominent in politics, but none had the impact that he did in Iceland. Like me, his great-grandson, more than a century later, he built a fortune and lost it. He was also able to build subsequent fortunes, so he will continue to be my guiding light. And his story illustrates much about my family and Iceland and my role in both.

He managed to make some money in Bordeyri by learning to bind notebooks and selling them. He then used his earnings to buy sheep, paying farmers to keep and feed them. In turn, he sold lambs to those involved in the booming export trade to the UK's fast-growing cities and bought more sheep with the proceeds. After five years he had cash in hand and a good-sized herd.

After his stay in Bordeyri, Thor was hired by a merchant in Borgarnes on a decent wage. But he still kept his sheep and expanded further, buying land in Borgarfjordur and hiring a keeper. Within a short time, he became the town's leading sheep farmer, again making his money from the export trade. After a dispute with the merchant who employed him, Thor borrowed money from Scottish traders he had got to know in Borgarnes and opened his own store in nearby Akranes, and at the same time continued to expand his sheep business. By not only investing his own funds but also taking loans to expand even further, he was as it turned out buying into a bubble.

Perhaps 'bubble' is an exaggeration, but within a very short period in the 19th century the number of sheep in Iceland doubled from 400,000 to 800,000. Everyone in Iceland was affected. It changed the nature of farming, making ever-increasing production its goal. It brought substantial amounts of money into the country and changed the nature of finance. By paying farmers to keep his sheep, Thor was in a sense like the derivatives traders of today, as he was really betting on the selling price come autumn. If high, he turned a profit. If low, he was protecting the farmers from losses.

Ever-increasing production led to a slump in prices in some years. To strengthen their position, farmers created associations that dealt with sheep merchants, sometimes even bypassing them entirely and selling directly to Scotland. These associations were early manifestations of what would later become the trade co-operatives, which were to have a marked influence on Icelandic society and my great-grandfather's life in particular, much to his displeasure.

The bubble did not burst because of overproduction, but simply because a new technology could meet the demand more efficiently. Large-scale refrigeration of meat became feasible, so it could come to market frozen. With that, the British consumer market opened up to the whole world. Those who could produce the most at the lowest price won and Iceland lost its only asset: proximity to the market. So the upswing emigrated from Iceland to Argentina, where it spawned a class of wealthy cattle ranchers.

The shift was gradual rather than sudden, but when there was a lack of demand farmers had no option but to slaughter their stock or feed the animals for another year. For those who had borrowed in anticipation of selling at a decent price that year it became impossible, and my great-grandfather was one of the first to go down with the collapse in the market.

Although it is clear from what he wrote at the time that he attributed his bankruptcy in large part to a number of factors, such as storms, fires and the loss of ships at sea, I think he realised that he went down with a dying market. Despite being the son of a building contractor and being raised in Copenhagen, he was always fascinated with farming, and later in life he would undertake immense agricultural projects. But he never got commercially involved with sheep again. Following his bankruptcy in Akranes he saw no future in sheep, but he was one of the only people at the time to see a bright future for farmers in the servicing of the domestic market.

After getting his fingers burnt so badly, Thor came to the conclusion that the only way for Icelanders to create any real wealth was in the fishing industry. In pursuance of that belief, he went on to become the leading figure in building up the fishing trade in Iceland after centuries in which the focus had been on farming. It took him and his associates only two decades to transform both Iceland's economy and its society. Living standards rose significantly and a more accomplished and robust culture was established.

The achievement of independence from Denmark was not a revolution in this sense. It was merely the gradual segueing of power from the colonial commissioners to their domestic colleagues. It did not result in any profound shift in government policy and was in no way a watershed in the broader context of Icelandic history.

Once he had become wealthy from fishing, Thor started preparing for the founding of Eimskip, a publicly traded Icelandic shipping company, which was to operate between Iceland and neighbouring trading partners, particularly Scotland and Denmark. He hosted the preparatory meetings at his home and was the biggest individual shareholder, and he probably thought he would be chairman of the board. But when push came to shove, his colleagues did not think it proper for a Dane to be chairman of a company that had become emblematic of Iceland's renaissance and was referred to as the nation's 'dream child' during its initial stock offering. He was appalled and never had anything to do with the running of Eimskip again. It must have hurt him badly – that he, the driving force behind the bright new economy of Iceland, was kept off the bridge of its flagship enterprise. When many years later I took over as chairman of Eimskip – a role in which I oversaw its breaking up and reorganisation into a business that was fit for the 21st century – it gave me some sense that the wrong done to him had been righted.

*

After my father was released from solitary confinement in 1986, we went to Denmark for the summer and then I started my final year at commercial college in Iceland, the same one that my father had attended. It had just moved to a brand-new and very modern building. In order to finance it, all the classrooms had been donated by companies. The one I was assigned to had been donated by Hafskip, the company my father had run. So every day I had to walk into a classroom with a large 'Hafskip' sign on the door. This was the height of irony. It was a weird time to be a teenager with all this going on. It took five years for the case to be dealt with, and by then I had graduated from college and left for university in the US.

I felt that Iceland was a dangerous place – picture-perfect on the surface but with cronyism driving the currents just beneath the surface. To me, Iceland was all about conformity and I didn't want to join in – better to be a tiddler in a large pool than a big fish in a small one. I took half a year off and read some philosophy and literature because I was disillusioned with the business world that had let down my father. Remembering the freedom I had felt in California, I picked a campus at the University of California in San Diego. I didn't know anyone there. It was just as far away as I could get from Iceland and the closest I could get to San Francisco. As I have always been able to do, I made it up as I went along, though eventually I transferred to the School of Business at New York University.

In the meantime my whole family was in crisis, fearful of what was going to happen to my father. I have never been able to get the TV and newspaper pictures of my father in handcuffs being led into court out of my mind. A lot of hate letters came through the door and our cars were vandalised, but there were other people who came and said: 'Listen, we don't believe this. Drop by our house for coffee any time.' It was polarised.

My father was a broken man during the years this was going on and I was always trying to find a way to help. I remember going to the gym and pumping it up and saying to myself: 'My father is in prison and there's nothing I can do.' At the same time a voice was saying 'Come on, do something, do something, do something', yet I couldn't do anything. My father said to me: 'Get an education abroad. Try to free yourself of all this. Don't be plugged into the old Icelandic system. Try to find your fortune in a bigger thing.' It was the greatest advice he ever gave me.

In hindsight the events that brought a sudden end to my childhood at the age of 18 were the making of me. From the day my father was arrested the direction of my life changed for ever as I felt the responsibility for the family shift to me. I was full of teenage rage at the state machine, at the injustice in the system. It gave me a jumbo-sized chip on my shoulder and something to prove. That's all gone now. I'm coming from a different place. Too much has happened for me to be that angry ever again.

Life's not fair. Accept it and move on.

3

ADVENTURE CAPITALISM IN RUSSIA 1986-2002

Out along the edge
Is always where I burn to be
The further on the edge
The hotter the intensity

Kenny Loggins, 'Danger Zone'

My youth had been spent in sheltered Iceland and my coming of age in the US, but my development as a young man and the building of the cornerstone of my fortune took place in Russia at a remarkable time in the nation's history. As Paul Klebnikov contends in his book *Godfather of the Kremlin: Boris Berezovsky and the Looting of Russia*:

> Russia's decline from a global superpower to an impoverished country is one of the most curious events in history. The collapse occurred during a period of peace and took only a few years. In its rapidity and magnitude, the collapse is unprecedented in world history.

Klebnikov is talking about Boris Yeltsin's period as Russian president from 1991 to 1999, which closely mirrors my own time as a young businessman making my first fortune in the grim industrial estates and urine-stenched project housing blocks of St Petersburg.

It is not putting too fine a point on it to declare that during my ten years in Russia I witnessed one of the fastest and most significant transfers of wealth in human history. What was it like? Well, my own existence in the early years was hardly glamorous. I lived in a monolithic Khrushchev-era apartment block and worked amid the stray dogs in the decaying industrial wasteland on the outskirts of Russia's former capital. By contrast, when I ventured into town or made trips to Moscow I entered the world of Russia's new wealthy elite that Klebnikov depicts startlingly accurately in his tale of how the nation went from communism to unbridled capitalism in that heady decade. He writes:

> Hundreds of western-style cafés, overpriced restaurants and glittering nightclubs had opened throughout Moscow. Members of the new ruling class with their Rolex watches, Italian shoes, gold bracelets, cellular phones and wives or girlfriends draped in Versace sulked over their drinks. The most beautiful girls of provincial Russia were available for a relatively low price – the best of them became Mafiya molls.

How did I end up working in this whirlpool of societal change? Well, the story started during and immediately after university when I realised that I could no longer rely on my father for work opportunities. I was entering society with a broken image of my father, who had always been entrepreneurial but got eaten up by the Icelandic system. I took a conscious decision that rather than become a company man, working for a salary, I wasn't going to work for anyone. I would work for myself and directly benefit from my labours and dealmaking, assuming all risks of failure and having no guarantee of a fixed salary.

I looked for jobs that had no fixed pay but were success-based. I had picked this up mainly from my older sister Magga, who was my closest friend in the family. She had become an entrepreneur on her return from San Francisco, starting a few small vegetarian restaurants and then making her own granola. She started that business like a typical entrepreneur, ordering big sacks of organic oats, nuts and other products directly from the UK, although she had no production facility. She rented a small bakery in the evenings, when it was closed, and started production there, hand-packing the ingredients and going directly to the supermarkets and convincing them to stock her products. She then did her own brand of marketing through word of mouth and in-store tastings. It worked, and she made up the company as she went along. I worked with her sometimes and got my first taste of a start-up business. She was good at selling and had immense confidence in herself and her idea.

Magga was a mentor to me, teaching me how to build up my self-confidence and engage with people, selling ideas and products. She introduced me to friends of hers who were travelling salesmen and making a lucrative living. I saw that if you were convincing and not afraid of getting doors slammed in your face, this could be a prosperous line of work. In Iceland I sold large books, such as medical dictionaries and an Icelandic travel atlas, and remote-controlled garage-door openers door-to-door in the evenings and holidays while I was at college and university. I figured that door-to-door salesmanship and developing the art of convincing a person to buy a product from a stranger would be advantageous in my professional life, and that's pretty much how it turned out. I often think that the best lessons I learned in business were outside business school, which cannot teach you how to pitch or close a deal – these are things you have to learn in the field.

When I was selling books door-to-door, I came across a house in west Iceland and was invited into the front room, where I found to my great surprise several sheep. The man living there acted as if everything was completely normal, so I proceeded to sell him encyclopedias as the sheep watched, giving no hint that I thought this arrangement was at all unusual. In hindsight, that was also a valuable lesson on how to keep your pokerface in the middle of a deal!

When I moved to the US, there were only a few weeks in the summer between terms when I could go back to Iceland and earn some money. I had to come up with a good idea. I decided to go to the biggest nightclubs in Iceland with some friends and offer to fill them with people in return for the door revenue. They would keep the bar takings and we would split the advertising budget 50–50. I would talk to women who ran modelling agencies and offer their girls free champagne if they came to the club. Then I would go to a sports club and tell the guys that we had some models coming in that night. I found I could stoke that flame for a couple of months and then people would find the next good thing. It worked for me. There was no legacy as I was just a contractor with no infrastructure or overheads. I said to my father as I flew back to the US with the cash I had earned during the break: 'See? I'm doing something different and it's working out fine.'

I met my wife Kristin at one of these Reykjavik clubs. I was training a DJ there, she had been doing some modelling shots and the photographer was the younger brother of a friend of mine. I asked him to introduce me. I was 24; she was 18. We met and fell in love. We went out for a while and broke up, repeating this pattern over many years. But the love was always there.

*

I had a lot of trouble finding a job in New York. It was a bleak time economically, and I remember that when I graduated in May 1991 a headline in the *New York Times* said: 'Job Prospects Bleakest since the Depression'. I managed to get an internship on the trading floor in Wall Street, which would have offered some security, but I wasn't interested in trading. I wanted to do my own deals and build a business, so I helped another entrepreneur start a nightclub in Iceland. Then my father was hired to run a soft drinks and brewery company which had a Pepsi franchise. It had just won a contract to give a massive push to Lowenbrau, whose market share in Iceland had dropped from 40 per cent to 10 per cent. I took a four-month job there and got to know Magnus Thorsteinsson, the head of the brewery, who was from the north of Iceland. An odd couple with a complementary skill set, we went on to work together closely over the following ten years.

The advertising law in Iceland was very strict and you could not advertise alcohol. We needed something innovative, so I created a travelling beer festival. We did a lot of camouflaged advertising, obtained a lot of media coverage and sold a lot of beer. Then my father told me he was thinking of doing something really off the wall. He had sold the Pepsi franchise and was left with just the brewery, an old soft drinks factory and a non-compete clause that prohibited it from making soft drinks for sale in Iceland. He had met up with an old friend, Ingimar Haukur Ingimarsson, and they decided to set up a joint venture in Russia, which was just opening up to external capital. They would ship to Russia bottling equipment

Þorið þið?...Við þorum!

This Reykjavik newspaper ad from 1991 shows Kristin and me near the beginning of our relationship daring readers to visit the nightclub Ingólfscafe, which I ran for a time after graduating from NYU.

formerly owned by Pharmaco, a listed Icelandic pharmaceutical company, and make soft drinks for sale locally. The two old friends would eventually fall out spectacularly over this venture.

The Russian joint venture went ahead in 1993 under the name Baltic Bottling Plant. Magnus was in charge of setting up the factory and I was in charge of marketing. We made two reconnaissance trips. We took a look, came back and said: 'It's a bizarre place but let's see what we can do.' We had heard that Russians wanted something colourful so we produced a batch of pink lemonade and shipped a couple of containers to Russia. I toured the shops, carrying out market research and trying to gauge the demand for soft drinks. But Russia was pretty chaotic at that time. I came across empty supermarket shelves and long lines of people queuing for food; the shops smelled and the service was dreadful. But I realised that we could make something there. Even though we had old products, they could still work. That is what Russia became in those years: a dumping ground for old stock.

I met our Russian partners, led by Gennady Homski, a card-carrying member of the Communist Party who had spent his life operating inside the Soviet system, working his way up from scratch. This new, free-market economy was alien to him and he was looking for guidance in the chaotic environment that Russia had become. Homski and his associates acquired from the state a business that involved the maintenance of catering and kitchen equipment in restaurants in St Petersburg. As a privatised business these guys no longer had a monopoly, but they had a huge purpose-built factory and some land, which they put into the joint venture. The factory had just concrete slabs for walls and mud for floors, so we gave them four months to convert it, drawing up plans for the infrastructure we would need. When we arrived with the containers holding all the old equipment from the Icelandic factory nothing had been done, so the first thing we had to do was construct the floors.

At first, I lived with Magnus in a dilapidated 75 sq m run-down apartment. I was a vegetarian at the time, which was quite difficult in St Petersburg in those days if you didn't want to survive on only potatoes and turnips. In fact, for the first year my diet was mainly Snickers, Mars bars and Pepsi, the products of the two foreign companies that had started production in St Petersburg early on. The chocolates and the soft drink were sold all over the city – and there was no danger of food poisoning.

Coming from the US, where everyone greeted me sweetly and asked how I was, it was a shock to arrive in Russia. If you asked a Russian how he was, you were likely to get the answer: 'Better today than tomorrow.' The Russians were a pessimistic bunch, used to hearing about grand three- or five-year plans without ever seeing anything getting better. So maybe it's harsh to say that they were pessimists; perhaps they were just well-informed optimists.

We rebuilt the factory so we could make soft drinks, and I was told that I would be there for six months with an option to extend to a year. My job was to create a brand, set up the marketing operation and train a Russian to take over, but I ended up staying in Russia for ten years. I had planned to build the factory and go back to New York, but in Russia, as in life, things often do not go to plan.

The other parties in the venture were Ingimar Haukur Ingimarsson and his associate Bernard Lardner, an analyst in London. I called them 'the BVI guys' because they worked through a company registered in the British Virgin Islands. Ingimar was supposed to know everything about Russia, although he had never lived there. He had worked for a well-known entrepreneur called Tony Georgiou, who founded a telecoms business in Russia with other seasoned London investors. Ingimar tried to replicate this with very little capital. A complex character, he could be charming when wooing people, and in meetings with the Russians projected an image of a well-connected investor with a long track record, but as he failed to deliver on most of what he was meant to, more and more doubts arose.

Three factors were working against the venture: our Russian partners were not as strong as we thought or able to deliver as much as we had envisaged; the system in Russia was much more volatile, with a lot more currency risk and chaos than we had envisaged; and Ingimar and Bernard failed. They misrepresented their capital structure, having hardly any capital or connections in Russia, and their knowledge of the operating environment was not what we thought.

A lot of corners were cut and the chaotic nature of the joint venture meant that it was effectively stillborn. The Russians, who owned 35 per cent of the venture, contributed the land and buildings, and Ingimar and Bernard (who had a 65 per cent stake) were supposed to contribute the old Icelandic bottling machinery and some start-up funds. Magnus, my father and I were supposed to be running the venture for the stakeholders who had contributed the machinery and the factory. We had no stake in the venture, but the hope – and promise – of earning equity if the business prospered. However, after the equipment arrived and was commissioned, we discovered that the BVI guys had tricked our Russian partners and Russian customs. Instead of contributing the machinery in return for share capital and thereby avoiding customs duties and taxes as start-ups could legally do, the manifest listed just some items of furniture and supplies. The BVI guys set up another offshore company that 'owned' the machinery to take leasing payments from the Russian factory's monthly cash flow. They had tried to get UK investors for the joint venture and failed. They did put in a small amount of money but then tried to extract funds, as they did not believe the venture would ever become profitable – obviously influenced by their failure to get any investors, which was probably because they had no track record as principals in any deals, let alone risky emerging-market deals.

The company had negative equity and the cash flow was being diverted to offshore entities. The project was unsustainable. We tried to get Britvic to invest, but there was a falling out with Ingimar and Bernard. Ingimar sacked Magnus as managing director, and my father and Ingimar later parted company, with my father buying out Ingimar in 1995. The BVI guys had one employee, Viktor Anitsev, who was their Russian fixer. He was a charming man who had arranged the Russian side of the joint venture and was setting up contacts for them. However, he became disillusioned after the customs affair and their treatment of the Russian joint venture partners. He left abruptly at about the same time as Magnus was fired and I was elevated to CEO.

I had to sort out the mess, but there was little to be salvaged. I got two law firms and a well-known law professor called Valery Musin to do a legal analysis. They advised that the joint venture had been set up so badly that we should forget about it and start up again on our own. Musin went with me to talk to the authorities. That was when we met the deputy mayor of St Petersburg who was in charge of foreign investment in the city. His name was Vladimir Putin and he had been a student of Musin. During an hour-long meeting, Musin explained the findings of the law firms and said that the joint venture was invalid. I was impressed at how quickly Putin grasped the issues. He concurred with Musin's conclusion that we needed to start from scratch and build a new factory with no legacy problems. I would not meet Putin again for almost ten years. When I shook his hand on that occasion in the Kremlin, I had sold the business to Heineken and he was president of Russia.

It has been amazing to watch how this man has shaped Russia over the last quarter of a century. When he first appeared in the Kremlin with real power as prime minister in 1999, while I was living in Russia, he was just what the country needed. A disciplined leader with ambitions to turn Russia around from the downward economic and social spiral that his weak predecessor Boris Yeltsin had presided over while he was in power. Yeltsin was simply a raging alcoholic with a kleptocratic circle of oligarch advisers who were not working in either his or Russia's best interests by any measure.

In Putin's first eight years, he stabilised the economy, curbed the oligarchs' influence and their looting and strengthened the state immensely. He was an absolute hero to the vast majority of Russians who craved a strong leader to ensure a strong Russia that would project its power internationally. People in the West forget this today and don't really appreciate the horrible state of Russia for its inhabitants when Putin took over, or the Herculean task of turning it around when he took the reins of state control.

However, as with countless other historical leaders, the power and glory that Putin manifested in those years corrupted him and he has turned out over the last decade and a half to be the opposite of how he began. He has led the country into a mad war with Ukraine and has wrecked all that he had started building for future generations of Russians. His story of a saviour turning bad and dragging the country to near ruin is unfortunately a classic Russian drama with the usual tragic ending. I feel immensely sad for the people of Russia to see so much of the progress they had made and their future hopes now lying in ruins simply because of one power-mad man and the usual circle of corrupt cronies abusing their positions and wrecking the country. It did not have to be this way. If Russia had only followed the stipulations of its constitution, Putin would have been limited to eight years in power, just like every US president is. Putin cunningly circumvented this very well defined and tested safeguard and eventually erased it from the constitution for his own personal gain. This man has since become a Shakespearean tragedy for the people of Russia.

We wound down Baltic Bottling Plant, while Homski annulled the joint venture contract and got back the building and the machinery. In a deal that I facilitated, the building was sold to Pepsi, which kept some of the equipment and threw out the rest. We then set up Bravo International in another part of St Petersburg, bringing back Magnus alongside me and my father. The Russian managers were made partners. It was a clean break from the past, giving us a new company free from legacy issues of the Soviet era, which would prove important when we later exited from the investment.

In the end we more or less broke even on the first factory, but it caused a great deal of anxiety as the problems increased and we came to realise that the company was terminally ill. There was immense friction between the BVI guys and my father and Magnus, who had done the original deal to get the machinery shipped out to Russia. On top of that there were the Russian joint venture partners, who had been duped. They thought that the BVI guys were contributing an operational factory and working capital in return for a 75 per cent stake, but instead they had contributed 12 chairs and some office supplies. The three parties involved in the venture were not aligned and I was the only one on the ground sorting it out.

There was also a personal issue with Homski, which I would get dragged into solving. He had wanted to help in creating a new business in the drinks industry with me and other management, but the Tambov gang, the largest in St Petersburg, had some sort of hold on him and was demanding money with menaces.

In those chaotic days I became familiar with the Russian term *krysha*, meaning roof, which was important to understand. This was summed up well by David Hoffman in an article published in the *Washington Post* in May 1997:

> Almost every business in Russia – from kerbside vendors to huge oil and gas companies, American and foreign firms, even mayors and regional bosses – pays for the protection service of some kind of *krysha*, according to security experts here.

It meant a roof for a rainy day, security for when you need it. But in reality, it referred to a protection racket where unofficial organisations provided protection to people and property, settled disputes and enforced contracts in areas where the police and the judicial system could not be relied upon. *Krysha* did not imply that the services would be criminal or illegal, although the line was often hazy. I had to deal with our security issues in this environment. When I took charge of the company I inherited a contract with a local security organisation, Zashita, which provided uniformed security guards on our premises and a hotline we could call in case of problems. It was highly professional and above board, although I knew nothing about its backers and consequently its strength in times of trouble. I did not want to know then, because as Roman Abramovich said in a London court hearing in 2013 about his dealings with his *krysha*: 'There was a lot of *krysha* activity in Russia at that time which was well outside the law and was little more than criminal extortion.'

It became apparent to me that whatever the reason for the Tambov gang leaning on Homski, he had no one to help him and it was turning its attention towards his joint venture interest. I would have to confront this issue, though I avoided it for as long as I could. Our security firm was no match for this gang. I needed to change 'roofs'. It is tricky to fire your security firm because you are vulnerable while a new one takes over. In essence, you have to hire a stronger organisation that commands the respect of the one being fired. I switched to a firm called FAP, which had been set up by former senior police officers along with former security personnel from GRU, the Russian army intelligence service. They were older, seasoned men and their chairman was a former GRU general who was responsible for the big Kronstadt naval base in the Gulf of Finland. He told me that he had been involved in security at the Reykjavik summit meeting of Mikhail Gorbachev and Ronald Reagan, and showed me a framed picture of himself and Gorbachev standing on top of a large submarine with its captain.

I considered myself lucky with the ease of the transfer and was impressed by their analysis of the general security situation in St Petersburg and their confidence. They arranged a factory visit by a group of men from OMON, the police force's elite team, at our busiest time on a Friday afternoon. About 30 large, imposing men arrived to take a guided tour of our facilities, much to the bemusement of our customers and staff. It was meant as a signal to anyone following us that we had close ties to the police force. I wondered then if these men in civilian clothes were really OMON or whether this was just some trick. A few months later I was jogging through the town and passed the OMON headquarters, where a lot of uniformed men carrying firearms were entering trucks looking as though they were on their way to a war zone. I recognised half the faces and got a nod from a couple of them.

After that I became extremely wary, almost paranoid, in dealing with anyone from Russia. I would head-butt my way through every problem. My one advantage was that I was a young man with no family. I could not be bought or threatened and I found that, as with most bullies, if I didn't give in to the Tambovs, they would move away and look for weaker prey. I also thought that if I did crash and burn I had plenty of time to start another career. So I worked hard and partied even harder, drinking lots of vodka with other expats. It was like being in an American frontier town. It was a steep learning curve and it changed me. I was responsible for everything, and it was all so badly set up that I never knew if I would have enough money to pay my workers every month. I was suddenly in charge, having to prove myself to an older crowd, so the first thing I did was grow a beard to try to look older than I really was. The Russians found it hard to take orders from someone much younger than them; it's simply not in their culture. I also felt under enormous pressure to help my father. He had sold the original machinery to the joint venture on delayed payment terms, making promises to various people that everything would work out. 'I am counting on you, son,' he told me. 'We can't let this fail.' How was I supposed to react? I could not let my father down or everything would blow up for him in Iceland, where he was already on his second chance after losing everything. I could not let his Russian idea become a disaster. No matter how difficult it all was, it had also set up an opportunity for me which would play out over a decade. His crazy idea in Russia would essentially be my launchpad into the career I made for myself and the key to my fame and fortune down the road.

The Russians did not do what they were supposed to do, and the BVI guys did not put in what they had agreed to invest. It festered into a full-blown dispute that got out of control. We were almost bankrupt at the end of the first year. Magnus ended up being fired basically because, although he had done as good a job as he could, he had been set unattainable targets by the BVI guys.

*

At the age of 27, with only rudimentary conversational Russian, I was asked by the BVI guys to take over as managing director. For me there was only one way to make the venture work. Selling soft drinks was a low-margin and in the end unprofitable activity. No one was prepared to pay much for soft drinks but alcohol consumption was going crazy. It was clear to me that this was the way to go. There was far too much cheap alcohol on the market; the big foreign brewers were yet to risk their capital on setting up production in Russia and there were hardly any imports either. The market was flooded with poor-quality, low-priced and mostly unbranded alcohol. If we were going to make money from selling drinks in Russia, they would need to be premium, branded alcohol.

Alcopops – fruit-based long drinks infused with a shot of liquor – had been sold for some time in Finland and had recently taken off in London. A small quantity of Finnish gin and grapefruit was even being imported into Russia. I could see that alcopops would be a winner in the Russian market because there was no culture of mixing drinks; it was just shots of vodka for men and champagne for women. It was as simple and basic as that. I decided to create a specialist alcopops manufacturing factory. No one else in Russia was doing this.

Alcopops received tax breaks in Russia because the government was trying to steer people away from vodka. Vodka claimed many lives, and even though things have changed for the better in the last twenty years, the *Guardian* pointed out in January 2014 that one quarter of Russian men died before reaching 55, and their average life expectancy was only 64 years, placing Russia among the lowest 50 countries in the world in that category.

Alcohol had long been a major cause of early deaths in Russia, so the government knew there was a lot to gain by trying to change people's drinking habits. There was also a lot of fake vodka for sale, made from petrochemicals and very often deadly. One manager at the plant was hospitalised for five weeks after drinking such store-bought fake vodka. This was the situation when Bravo was started and it was probably one of the reasons that the World Bank gave a $100 million loan facility to the brewery. It was there to support the government, and this was one way of doing so.

Within a year of selling to Pepsi and setting up Bravo, we controlled half of the Russian market for alcopops and the venture was profitable. However, the volumes were small, there was a lot of competition on the way and our market share was only going to shrink.

This venture transformed the business but was not without its problems. Although the Baltic Bottling Plant had nothing to do with the new company, the fact that it was doing well and had the right formula for success enraged the BVI guys, Ingimar and Bernard, who started challenging us in court and asking for settlements. We therefore had both mobsters and ex-partners looking for a cut in the business in exchange for doing nothing, but having a nuisance value to be bought off. I have since come up against this kind of thing on many occasions.

I had found a way to recreate a product that had a history in Russia because it had been imported from Finland. It was not registered in Russia so we could copy it. And there was no copyright in Finland because of a strange arrangement whereby the archaic Finnish state monopoly had an alcopop formula which it gave to one of three breweries every other year. This arrangement, where each brewery could produce for two years before handing on the rights, had been going for decades.

We moved to a new factory, negotiated loans from Russian and foreign banks and suppliers, bought machinery for a small down payment from a new producer in Italy and found an Icelandic contractor who was working in Russia to do some conversion work. It was all done on credit. We had little start-up capital. We pooled our savings and started production at the end of 1996. We were playing catch-up, paying people we owed money to, but then Viktor Piatko, the deputy chief executive, found a tax loophole that changed everything.

We were selling alcohol but we did not have to pay alcohol stamp duty, because the regulations stated that if you brewed at below 5.5 per cent strength, the resulting beverage was taxed as beer rather than spirits, even though we were using grain alcohol. The loophole was closed after about two years, and the Russian government eventually put a tax on alcopops. Competition emerged, but at the beginning no one else was making alcopops in Russia and the tax loophole meant that our profit margin jumped from 40 per cent to something like 80 per cent.

I still had to resolve things with the Russian partners in the original joint venture. They had been kept out of the loop in the operations of the company and attended only one annual general meeting. The company was heavily lossmaking. There were various rental agreements and a lot of cash had been siphoned off to the British Virgin Islands company. The Russians suspected that they had been kept in the dark, and when they found out that Ingimar's side of the bargain had not been what they thought they were furious. Ingimar, who had been the original venture's chairman, was no longer with the company, but when he saw that the new company was making money he wanted to continue this three-way fight, which dragged on for a long time. He went to court saying that the registration of the share transfer between my father and him was done incorrectly. Then he sued, saying that he had never signed the documents. And in a third case he argued that although he had signed the documents, he had not had power of attorney. He threw in one technicality after another, often bizarrely contradicting each other. The legal wrangling went on and on and took an enormous amount of energy to resolve; 1995 and 1996 were pivotal years and the pressure was intense. We had a good year in 1997, but it was only when we started our third Russian business, with the idea that we needed to be making beer in Russia to be sustainable, that things stabilised.

The Russian beer market was really taking off. For every can of 'long' drinks sold in Russia, 40 times as much beer was being consumed, and the market was growing at 20 per cent a year. If we could win just a 5 per cent share, that business would be much larger than anything we were doing in alcopops. Beer was a complementary product, distributed by the same dealers and sold in the same bars. We had the connections. We just needed the capital and the sheer nerve to do it. We focused on long drinks from 1996 to 1998 and started our brewery project the following year. Free cash flow from the long drinks business went into securing the land and some of the equipment, but we needed another $25 million. Russia was booming, so we decided to tap external investment for the first time, going to the London capital markets. We thought we would have to syndicate the $25 million, but a Californian funds group, Capital Research, attracted by the idea of private equity in an emerging market, said that it wanted to fund the entire project. We spent some time negotiating the valuation, estimating future earnings and coming up with a formula that gave Capital 33 per cent of the company. The shareholders all agreed, and we set up a tax-efficient Cyprus-based company to own all the Russian assets.

After a long negotiation that ended on a Saturday afternoon in Copenhagen, the deal was signed with Capital Research. I flew back to St Petersburg the next day and woke up to the news that Russia had defaulted on its debt. The phone rang, and it was a lawyer from Capital Research. 'I'd like to draw your attention to Article 14, which concerns *force majeure*,' he said. 'What's that?' I replied. 'We have a signed deal,' I told him. I had never even heard of the term *force majeure*, but quickly came to realise that this little clause was of paramount importance. It basically means that, even though you have a signed contract, you can get away from your obligation when an extraordinary event occurs, beyond the control of the contracting partners. War is one example, rioting another. And Russia's economy crumbling was certainly an extraordinary event, beyond our control.

As a result of the Russian economic crisis our investors were exercising their right to renegotiate the deal. I flew to London and spent about a week negotiating day and night from a small room at the Metropolitan Hotel, where I and my lawyer lived on room service. Capital Research no longer wanted to equity-fund the project, so we decided to change all the equity in the financing to debt. And, with valuations so uncertain, we agreed to disagree on the value of the company at that time. Capital Research would provide the capital as debt – but it was expensive debt. There was a 30 per cent interest rate and the right to convert into ordinary shares at a 20 per cent discount; effectively it meant that we were borrowing money at 40 per cent per year. Furthermore, if the company was not sold in four years' time, Capital had the right to appoint an investment bank to sell the business. I had taken on a lot and now found myself in a race. Within three or four years, we had to build up and sell the business. There was a very real chance that I would end up with nothing. After all, it was a loan at 40 per cent interest!

I was seven months into the construction of the new Bravo brewery in St Petersburg when the currency crisis hit, having ploughed everything that I owned into this hole in the ground of a brewery. 'What's our position without this investment?' I asked Bravo's finance director. He explained: 'We owe millions to our suppliers, and our customers, particularly the 3,000 shops in St Petersburg and 4,000 in Moscow that we distribute to directly, owe us millions too. The problem is that we owe in dollars and they owe in roubles and this is where we are screwed.' All of a sudden, instead of those assets and liabilities matching, they were massively apart. It was a hugely volatile time: South Korea was also in crisis, the Long-Term Capital Management (LTCM) hedge fund had imploded and there was a lot of talk about financial meltdown. South Korea and Russia, to an extent, were both rescued by the International Monetary Fund; Wall Street was forced by the US Federal Reserve to bail out LTCM.

I was under a lot of pressure as I had virtually all my personal capital tied up in the project, but it focused my mind on making sure that everything in our plan worked perfectly this time. We negotiated hard prices with suppliers and builders. We looked into buying a brewery in Novgorod, the old capital of Russia, and renovating it, but seeing all the Soviet legacy problems, we said: 'Let's start afresh with a blank sheet of paper.' This was precisely the right idea. Go big – plan for the big time. The site we found in St Petersburg had been used as a window-manufacturing plant but was derelict. We found the owners of that business; we bought the land and the building and gutted it. It took about three months to tear everything to pieces so there was nothing left, not even the windows.

The first bottle of beer came down the line in 1999, a year after the work began. We developed a premium beer called Botch-karev, the Russian word for barrel, and drew up a business plan to take on the market leader, Baltika, owned at the time by Carlsberg and Hartwall, a Finnish beverage company. Our plan was to sell at a 5 per cent discount to the market-leading local brand, but I had a change of plan the night before we started selling and decided instead to charge a 5 per cent premium. So we were the new kid on the block and we had the most expensive beer in an extremely price-conscious country

– but it worked. Our advertising campaign was basically to proclaim our beer as the best and most expensive available in Russia. It took off. Botchkarev became a 'must-have' in the Russian beer market and we immediately set about cranking up supply and expanding.

We had our share of problems with the beer factory in the beginning. It took some time to adjust the machinery, and at one stage the bottle-cap machine was giving us trouble. It didn't tighten the bottle caps enough, and the pressure of the beer in the bottles proved to be too much, so the caps came flying off the bottles with a bang. We had American investors from Capital Research visiting during this period and were busy telling them how smoothly everything was running. Then we sat down with them for a cold beer. In the corner of the room there was a big beer cooler. Every now and then we could hear loud bangs from the cooler as the bottle caps blew off. The Capital guys asked what the noise was, but we told them not to worry, everything was just fine. And we gave them more beer, and then some, while I made sure they didn't see the pool of beer that had started to form under the beer cooler. They were very happy with the factory – and more than a little tipsy – when they left later that day.

We designed the Bravo brewery in a modular way that allowed us to quickly scale up production. I took advice from brewery experts in Denmark who told me that the typical mistake people make in designing breweries is that they do not allow themselves room to grow. So we started at a capacity of 1 million hectolitres, with a three-stage plan to take it to 2.5 million hectolitres and then 4.5 million hectolitres.

We had just started on the first module when we realised that we would have to go immediately to stage two, so we started building that. All at once we were producing, marketing and selling a new beer, while constructing a new brewery and doubling and tripling production. We reinvested old capital into the business again and again. When we launched in St Petersburg in 1999, we were still a secret. Nobody knew what we were doing. We never spoke about our plans. In those internet-boom days everyone, it seemed, was making bold claims about changing the world. We were exactly the opposite. We didn't want to attract attention. We just started selling our beer the same day we started production. It was real and out in the market. We called it the 'submarine strategy' and deliberately planned it that way to surprise our rivals.

When we launched, St Petersburg was trying to build its reputation as a 'beer capital' and had a 'beer day', with the three main breweries selling their wares in Hermitage Square in front of the Winter Palace. We saw this event as an opportunity for our own kind of beer revolution. We went to the mayor's department, told them that we now had a brewery and said we'd like a stand. They gave us some space but said no advertisements or bottles were allowed. There were rock bands and close to a million people turned up for a kind of one-day Oktoberfest, and we took the event by storm. We had just started rolling out our TV campaign and billboards but we didn't have a marquee or anything like that. We just had 40-foot container lorries decked out with brilliant logos of our design, acting effectively as mobile billboards.

We parked two of them in the middle of the square and started selling cans of beer. We had the first canning line in Russia, so while competitors were making people queue to get foaming plastic glasses of beer, we could just pass out cool-looking cans. It was a hot summer's day and we had our beer revolution. All the cans were bedecked in our logo. You couldn't go 10 metres in St Petersburg without seeing our name. It was ambush marketing and it worked brilliantly. I still regard it as one of the best days of my life. I thought: 'We are just small guys ... just look at this ... we've got to utilise our momentum to the max.' At that stage only the first third of the factory was complete, but we pushed the other stages through quickly. Our products were everywhere in Russia. We were players in St Petersburg – a city of 5 million people. I bought my own apartment. It was great. When we got to 4.5 million hectolitres, we had the sixth-largest brewery in Europe.

It was a crazy time in all respects to be living in Russia as a young man. Expatriates from all sorts of countries were working for multinationals in Russia and living and partying hard. A lot of people burnt out really badly. Russia in those days was often referred to as the Wild East and indeed I felt a bit like one of those old Wild West prospectors. There was a sense of anarchy, but there was certainly money to be made by the brave and stubborn, and there were few family people in this wild community. I was 33 when Botchkarev hit its European stride in its first operational year in 2000. Work and making money were all I focused on.

This was adventure capitalism in Russia, and what I saw in both East and West in those turbulent ten years shaped my attitude towards both dealmaking and banks, bankers and risk.

*

A great deal of nonsense has been written or blogged about my so-called Russian mafia connections, the vast majority of which is untrue. I say vast majority because it is virtually impossible not to come across what Russians call 'bandits' when operating in the country. The media like to pretend that there is a well-functioning Russian society, which then has to deal with a well-functioning foe, the Russian mafia. My experience is that this is a myth. Society in Russia is just as multi-layered as it is everywhere else, with countless sub-groups, from petty criminals to con artists and corrupt autocrats. When I arrived in Russia, its economy and society was mostly characterised by chaos, accompanied by a good deal of chaotic crime. As for the Russian mafia, I remember an article in *The Economist* in 1994 that said it consists of three layers. At level one are the big, brawny guys in sports tracksuits who used to hang around the now-outlawed kiosks selling cheap alcohol. At level two are the guys driving around in blacked-out Mercedes doing shady deals on mobile phones. Level three is in the government, and is by far the most serious level. I had a little run-in with level one in 1993–94, and then with level two in 1995–97 and 2000–01. But I only twice brushed with level three.

I saw level one early on when I arrived in Russia in 1993 to attempt to revitalise an old, dilapidated factory on the outskirts of St Petersburg that we wanted to use to make soft drinks. That wasn't particularly glamorous for anyone. It didn't involve trading cars, cigarettes or alcohol. So we crept in under the radar. But when we started rebuilding the factory, level one guys were cruising around. 'You're going to need some protection around here because somebody might come and steal your equipment,' they said. We said okay and signed up with an organisation that had dogs and security guys patrolling. But they also said that if anyone bothered us, made a threat or wanted to know who we were, we should just give them their number. And we did have a few incidents. Sometimes, some guys would roll up in a four-wheel-drive vehicle and say: 'Hey, what are you up to? You've got to pay us a percentage.' We said: 'Guys, just call this number here.' And we didn't hear back from them. They were mostly trying it on.

We had dealings with level two when we moved to another

organisation, made up of ex-militia, former police and Ministry of the Interior types. We had a pretty hair-raising experience after switching to them. In 2000, we had a dispute with an Italian manufacturer who had sold us equipment. We paid for it but it was underperforming massively, so we brought in technical people from Pepsi to validate what was happening and they confirmed our fears. We had been sold a truck instead of a racing car and the lower productivity was eating into our budget. We wanted a discount but the supplier disagreed, so we entered arbitration. Then the Italians sold their claim, which was for $1 million, to some Chechens, who said that they had a legal contract and they wouldn't negotiate. We sent the top security guy from our brewery to meet them and he came back with two black eyes. I'd never seen that before. Then the car of one of my business partners was stolen during the night from a secure garage. Kristin was living with me in Russia at the time, but after that I told her she was moving back to London.

We moved on to yet another security organisation where my contact was former high-ranking KGB man Nikolai Rusinov. He ended up solving most of my security problems over the years. Rusinov patiently researched the Chechen gang and found that the main protagonist had a nephew or brother in prison in Siberia. He found him and told him that he could basically choose whether to have an easy or a hard time in prison. All of a sudden the gang backed off, but I didn't know why at the time. That was the last trouble of this kind that I had in Russia. Rusinov gave me advice on how to deal with threats, both real and implied. 'What's in here?' people would ask. 'Are you a tough guy or not?' If you held your nerve and didn't answer, they mostly just walked away. 'There's nothing here,' they would say to each other, or: 'We've got somebody here we can miss.'

Essentially, I was a young, headstrong man with no family, living alone. It was difficult to get to me except by beating me up or killing me. I did get some threats of that happening, but they came about in the usual Russian way after people had downed a few vodkas. You could always ask yourself: 'How real was that? Was it the alcohol or was that real?' The main thing was to keep a low profile. We were as unflashy in Russia as we could be in the early years. I did know personally two people who were murdered. One was Lucky, a Nigerian, who started and owned a local nightclub; the other was Galina Starovoytova, a Russian MP for our area who came to Iceland with me once. There we were given a guided tour through the Icelandic parliament by Geir Haarde, who later became prime minister. Galina helped me greatly with Russian tax lobbying in the Duma. Both she and Lucky were gunned down in the corridors outside their apartments. Galina was highly thought of and, according to an article in *The Economist*, had been offered the top job of running Russia's defence ministry by Boris Yeltsin. Lucky's murder was never solved; and, although two hit men were convicted of Galina's murder, the people who ordered and paid for it have never been found.

At level three, I had a couple of brushes with the government. I didn't want to meet any shady government characters, so I got security firms to deal with them. But once in a while, it escalated to the point where the security firm advised me to meet someone. I was once summoned to meet a member of the Russian parliament. He was obviously corrupt and wanted some sort of payment to 'help' me and make my life 'easier'. It was all vague and I ignored it. Another time a few men showed up, carrying cards that identified them as being from President Yeltsin's office. They told me they wanted exclusive rights to produce long drinks. That was one time I saw my security officer seriously worried. But they didn't follow up.

These guys counted on the people they were threatening to panic and pay them off. I didn't, and so they moved on. Being stubborn served me better than panicking.

In the early days there were also a lot of so-called 'fixers' who took advantage of the chaos and helped normal business people cut corners. This kind of activity was always basically fraud, not unlike the Nigerian letter scams, and it was rampant in the mass privatisations taking place in Russia during the 1990s. It was also an easy way for criminal elements, often referred to at the time as the 'Russian mafia', to use deception in order to get a foothold in enterprises, which they could later use for blackmail or coercion. The fixer might seem like a helpful adviser at first, but would usually turn out to be a very big, very bad wolf in sheep's clothing.

Fixers like this would turn up and say they could help get things done. If we needed a licence for a new factory that would normally take six months, there would be someone offering to sort it out in a day in return for $10,000. Some people fell for it, paid the money, were told they had got the permit and started building, only for the fixer to return and say what had been procured was not quite right. They would have to speak to someone higher up who would need $100,000. This kind of thing happened a lot, and of course it was often fraud. People would sign agreements with one person and then someone else would turn up and say the arrangement had actually been made with them.

Once I was introduced to Baltic Financial Industrial Group, a large industrial consumer group. We met for lunch in their plush offices, drank lots of vodka and they said they wanted to take all our production in return for a 5 per cent discount. I said the deal sounded great for us if they could sell it all, but what insurance did I have if they could not? 'You know who we are. We can do this,' they replied. But I was still concerned that I would be too beholden to the group. 'That's not the issue,' they said. 'If you don't do this, something very bad will happen to you. We're just going to have to kill you to get this done.'

That's how the conversation escalated, so I went to ask for advice from a police colonel called Andriy, who I had met through our mutual love of motorbikes when I sponsored a motorcycle race in Russia, and who had introduced me to Rusinov. But Andriy did not give me the advice I was expecting. 'I'll try to post some security guys around you subtly so you won't see them,' he said, 'but you're never going to fight fire with fire. If you get big, visible bodyguards, you'll be gunned down in your car. If you start driving a bullet-proof car, you'll get bombed. It will escalate and escalate. You've got to go in the opposite direction, play it dumb and keep a low profile. Just keep your ear to the ground and let this pass over.' It was good advice and became the reason we never had any personal bodyguards in Russia. If somebody threatened me in a bar, I would simply hold out my mobile phone and say: 'Hang on! Want to speak to this guy here?', and the person would speak to Rusinov or one of the other guys. That gave me comfort, and it was the norm.

I called Baltic later and acted as though nothing had happened. Eventually, they lost interest in us. The person we were dealing with, Valentin Tatura, migrated somewhere else. His boss, Pavel Kapysh, the founder of Baltic, was attacked in St Petersburg three years later while driving in a bullet-proof armoured car with another car of bodyguards behind him. A van pulled up next to him and blew off both his legs with a machine-gun and rocket-propelled grenade. He died 90 minutes later in hospital and six other people were hospitalised. Talk about escalation. Was all this the vodka talking or not?

I did not have bodyguards at the time, though I would later use them when moving in top society circles in Bulgaria. Instead, my strategy was to make sure that I had easy access to $50,000 in cash at all times. I kept it at home or in my car or briefcase; five little stacks of $10,000. In those days, that was a huge amount of money and probably ten times the going rate for a contract hit, but my thinking was that if I was ever kidnapped, I would be able to negotiate my way out of it. If anyone was being paid to do me harm, I would offer them more than they were being paid to not harm me. It was a deal I made with myself.

There were other incidents. I walked into the men's room at a Russian nightclub in 1994 and found blood splattered everywhere. Somebody quickly appeared and told everyone to leave. Somebody had been shot. On another occasion, Kristin came to visit and we went out with a Russian couple to a restaurant. A large group of men were sitting next to us; a couple of them had guns on the table and started singing songs about their time in prison. And the eight-year-old daughter of an acquaintance of a partner of Bravo disappeared one day for six hours. She turned up unharmed and happily regaled her stunned mother with details of how she had been picked up by a group of men, driven around St Petersburg and given ice cream and other treats. Her father was a Russian national working as finance director for a Spanish company operating in Russia. The men wanted this company to pay something to someone and the finance director's daughter was the weakest link. The message was chilling. The men would always be able to find her and do her harm if they did not get what they wanted. This is what was happening around me in that crazy decade. Violence or the threat of it, however tacit, was never far beneath the surface of everyday Russian life.

*

All this sounds heavy now, but at the time I was in my 20s and working like a madman, and felt that I was in an unreal situation. If I faced the same risks now that I have a family, it would be different, but at the time I didn't want to be the one to back away. I felt that this was my moment. I was in a tough area but I had to hold on and go with it. There were dangers, but this was my time to make a fortune. I recognised that the era I was operating in presented a unique opportunity and I told myself: 'Nothing that you do after Russia can be harder than this.' I would always try to keep focused. I wanted to build a business and then exit and start all over again. Anything else would be a distraction.

My view was that I had signed up for a tour of duty for up to ten years. I would do it and then go somewhere else and settle down. My friends were all getting married and having children, but that was not an option for me at that time. I was well aware of the 'tender trap', which was basically hooking up with a Russian woman who then became pregnant. I didn't want to end up being somehow a part of Russia. It was always a case of going in, making money and coming out again. Of course, I still have an emotional tie to Russia because of my time there. But my motto was: 'Never have anything in your life that you're not ready to walk out on at five minutes' notice. Be totally flexible, because the world can change in a minute.' It sounds harsh, but it is how I operated.

As it turned out, the financial risks were greater than the physical and legal risks, and in the crash of 1998 we came close to losing all that we had worked for. We had a robust balance sheet that just crumbled overnight. When the currency you operate in crashes to the extent that the rouble did in August 1998, it is hard to comprehend the risks that you face. With hindsight I can say that they were much greater than all the other risks that people associate with me. Maybe I was lucky or simply blind to the physical dangers, which now seem more real than they did at the time. After all, the murder rate in Russia was much higher than that in the US in the early and mid-1990s. As Klebnikov writes:

> While official statistics put Russia's murder rate at 20 per 100,000, or twice the level of the United States, the real rate was three or four times higher than in the United States. Well-known and important people were being assassinated in Russia and law enforcement authorities apparently found it impossible to catch the killers.

Like all gold rushes, it wasn't long before the market became crowded. We could see it happening in 2001 with the multinational brewers stepping up their efforts to enter Russia. SAB Miller had bought a brewery, and Carlsberg was making plans to go into the market. Only Heineken was not. The market was on fire, with sales increasing by 20 per cent a year. We were strong in the most lucrative part of that market and started getting a lot of offers. People wanted to buy a 10 per cent stake but we said no. We were adamant: we did not want any minority participation.

Capital Research, our US investor, said: 'When the time comes, we'll sell everything.' And so we did. We had been growing quickly but the compounding nature of our 40 per cent interest rate was hard to live with, so we started discussions with potential suitors in 2000. We met Heineken, Interbrew, SAB and Lowenbrau, which had already given us the right to produce its beer under licence in Russia, enabling us to be the first Russian brewery to get a premium product produced on site in Russia. In 2001 we had a board meeting in Cyprus and agreed to put the company up for sale.

We held a beauty contest with a few investment banks, hired Merrill Lynch and sent out a prospectus to interested buyers in autumn 2001. SAB, Interbrew and Heineken all submitted final bids, but all were lower than what I had been hoping for. I had set the bar high. I didn't want to sell – but I was having mixed feelings. Heineken was the strongest contender, so we flew to London on 2 January 2002 to meet them and see if they wanted to do a deal. We were told that Freddy Heineken, the legendary former chairman and chief executive and owner of a controlling 50 per cent interest in the family beer company, was very much behind getting involved in Russia but had demanding criteria. We arrived in London and checked into a hotel. On our way to meet Heineken the following day, I spied a *Financial Times* front page reporting that Freddy had died the previous night. I took the lead in the meeting and I guess I put on a good show, as we still did the deal, selling to Heineken for $400 million, including a $50 million earn-out if we met certain targets. The date was 20 February 2002. As part of the deal, Heineken asked me to stay on as chairman for two years. A lot of capacity came on stream in the Russian beer market in 2002 and we did not hit the target. I still made $100 million from the Heineken deal, more than I had ever made or even had before. And Capital, which had been so close to backing out, tripled its investment.

We made Lowenbrau under licence from the German company. We were the first plant to get such a licence to produce foreign quality beer. The royalties we generated for Lowenbrau in Russia had a side effect in that Heineken also showed an interest and ended up buying Lowenbrau in Germany as well.

The transaction with Heineken also included 49 per cent of the long drinks company, but we kept the remainder and managed the business. Heineken did not have much interest in that business so a year later I went to see Jean-François van Boxmeer, who was later to become Heineken's chief executive, and offered to buy the Dutch brewer out of the venture. 'Interesting,' he said. 'You actually want to buy the business from us?' I replied: 'Yes. I can pay cash for it now,' and he laughed. 'That's great news,' he said. 'If you want to buy it, basically it means it's worth a lot. If you want to buy it, I don't want to sell.' He tapped his nose. 'You have a nose for business,' he said, 'I want to sit next to you as a seller!' We ended up selling the long drinks company to a listed Russian company and, yes, we both made money on the deal.

It was a time of rough and tumble. When I went back to Iceland people believed all sorts of things about my time in Russia and some still do. They said: 'This guy has made an awful lot of money in a short amount of time and he hasn't been in the newspapers a lot. There's something fishy about that.' My time in Russia comes up whenever I'm in a competitive situation. People keep stressing where I made my money with negative connotations. There is no substance to this and never has been. But that doesn't stop the whispers. There was even an article in the *Guardian* in 2005 noting that in the 1990s, I was 'not only ploughing money into the country but doing it in the city regarded as the Russian mafia capital'. It added that the investment was 'being made in the drinks sector, seen by the mafia as the industry of choice'.

So my Russian years have created a tough legacy. It is hard to fight it, but it has created an air of mystery and I have had to prepare for all kinds of reactions.

This became more difficult when I made the move from business operator to investor. I started this diversification before selling my Russian operations, and in 2000 an investor road show was held for a deal that I was doing in Iceland.

There was a morning meeting with Icelandic bankers and analysts and all the relevant business executives. We asked if there were any questions and after two minutes of silence, one of the analysts said: 'Thor, how was the mafia in Russia?' I had to spend time telling him that I really didn't come into contact with it much. During my ten years in Russia, I reckon that the proportion of my time spent having to deal with mafia-related issues was less than 2 per cent. Nevertheless, it is not the sort of thing that twitchy lawyers, accountants, bankers and regulators want to have to think about when dealing with investments.

Ten years after I first ventured into Russia I came out with $100 million personal profit, having had yet another lesson in how those you trust and count on can betray you. My experience in those initial years of my great Russian adventure was the craziest about-face I had ever encountered, with people who I thought were partners and friends turning out to be totally unscrupulous. However, I never imagined that down the road lay not only much greater wealth but also a betrayal in Iceland that would put anything I experienced in Russia well and truly into the shade.

Crisis and opportunity are two sides of the same coin.

4

EXCEPTIONAL RETURNS IN EMERGING EUROPE 1999-2008

I don't know what they want from me
It's like the more money we come across
The more problems we see

Notorious B.I.G., 'Mo' Money, Mo' Problems'

Within a single decade in post-communist Russia, I had gone from having practically nothing to having millions of dollars in my bank account. However, if anyone had told me that I would be able to multiply this 40 times over the next six years, I would not only have asked what they were smoking, I would have wanted to know what planet they were living on.

Russia had been a hard slog, working my way up from the ground in the concrete suburbs of St Petersburg, having to avoid the stray dogs on the way to the factory and navigate around their human feral equivalents in the nation's harsh new economic environment. The next stage of my eastern European adventure capitalism could not have been more different, however. It would involve consorting with prime ministers in the corridors of power and it would lead to riches that even I, with my limitless ambition and hunger to make my way in the world, could never have dreamt of.

My Bulgarian experience began in 1999 when I was still in Russia, in the process of starting the brewery. Some investment bankers I'd met through fundraising for the Bravo venture came to me and said they knew two entrepreneurs of my age in Bulgaria who were having a hard time finding somebody to invest in their company. 'It's a privatisation,' they said, and my ears pricked up. For me, eastern European privatisations meant the opportunity to make a substantial amount of money, and that is how it turned out.

The two entrepreneurs, Peter Terziev and Georg Tzvetansky, had a pharmaceutical distribution business in Bulgaria, which had been the main pharmaceutical hub for the Eastern bloc in Soviet days. They had markets in eastern Europe, especially Russia, and had put bids in for the privatisation of three of the four state-owned pharmaceutical companies in Bulgaria, advised by Deutsche Bank. While they were raising the funds, the NATO bombing of Serbia began. Every night, the news was full of 'war in the Balkans' headlines and these guys were raising money for a company they named Balkanpharma, so they were being rejected by a lot of investment committees at western institutional investors. I was asked to come and take a look at it to stoke up more interest to rival the Israeli and the Greek consortia that were also looking at it. I think they saw me as a kind of 'dark horse' investor, someone nobody knew much about.

It appealed to me partly because the bankers and the entrepreneurs were all itching to put their own money into this project. I immediately formed the view that this opportunity was one that came around not once in a generation, but once in a lifetime. I went back to Pharmaco, the listed

Icelandic pharmaceutical company that originally sold us the machinery for the Russian bottling venture. I had my father talk to the boss as I thought I might have found something for us to take a look at together. Pharmaco had become an investment vehicle and was behaving like a conglomerate. It was cash-rich and making a lot of investments in Iceland, buying insurance companies, breweries and properties. It needed places to invest its cash. My idea was simple. I knew eastern Europe and Russia on the ground and could negotiate through the minefields. But I knew nothing about pharmaceuticals. Pharmaco knew everything about pharmaceuticals from the distribution end so I thought we should team up. And that's what happened.

Simultaneously, Deutsche Bank, which was advising the entrepreneurs, wanted to invest its own capital through its special situations fund. The bank rules forbade it taking a majority stake, so I set up a consortium of myself, Pharmaco and Deutsche Bank and bought 90 per cent of Balkan-pharma, leaving the company 46 per cent owned by me and Pharmaco, 44 per cent by Deutsche Bank and 10 per cent by the Bulgarian entrepreneurs who had brought us the deal. It was difficult building a consortium to put around all this while bidding on the three state-owned pharmaceutical companies and merging them into the fourth, but that is what we did.

Doing business in Bulgaria is complicated, and what you see is not necessarily what you get – like when people nod vigorously when you are explaining something and you think they agree, only to find they are in fierce disagreement. I still remember my first Bulgarian trip. It was a cold, dark Monday in February and I had had some of my oldest friends over in Russia for a three-day weekend, so I was massively hung over when I arrived in a snow-covered Sofia. It was a miserable day trooping from one decrepit pharmaceutical factory to another, but it was clear that the opportunity was there. The Israeli and Greek bidders had accountancy and venture capital rather than entrepreneurial mindsets. They kept asking the managers they were meeting: 'How are you going to make this work? Have you got any clue how to run a company?' I had much in common with those managers as I was already running my own business. 'I know exactly what you're going through,' I said. 'Here's what I want to know.' I asked them kindly and calmly what the main issues were and we hit it off. It was clear that if the Deutsche Bank people could make the transition from the advisory to the asset-management side, this would be a fantastic deal for the bank.

We closed the deal in the middle of 1999 and the whole business became Balkanpharma. Our biggest market by far was exports to Russia, but Bulgaria was also strong. Annual revenues were about $100 million when I became chairman, and by 2000 Deutsche Bank was already looking for an exit. 'We've got a three-year plan but we'd like to see if we can accelerate our exit,' one of the bankers told me. I was in no hurry. In the year since doing the Bulgarian deal, my father and I had invested in Pharmaco, becoming the largest shareholders. So I thought: 'Let's find a way to use the bank to get some cash on the table.' I came up with the idea of reversing Balkanpharma into Pharmaco, simultaneously buying out the bank. To do that we arranged an issue of new shares. At the same time, Deutsche Bank sold more than half of its shares in a deal giving 60 per cent of the combined business to Balkanpharma's investors. I ended up with just under 40 per cent of the new group and the bank had less than 20 per cent. When it made this partial exit, Deutsche Bank had been in the investment for 18 months and made a fivefold return. Pharmaco staged a road show for Icelandic investors and pension funds, taking about 30 of them to see the assets in Bulgaria. They were as happy as calves let out to pasture in the spring. No one in Iceland had done anything like this before. It went fantastically well and the fundraising and relisting were highly successful.

As 2001 dawned, I was chairman of the combined listed company in Iceland, the first time I had been in a position heading a listed company. I was 34 and eager to use the financial firepower of the public markets to go even bolder and bigger in emerging Europe. My partners at Deutsche Bank had more than quadrupled their money in a short time and sold out to the market while I set my sights on making more acquisitions and growing the company into a global generic pharma powerhouse. My first choice was Delta, an Icelandic developer of new generic drugs that had originally been formed by Pharmaco in 1981. So we talked to the shareholders there.

We met with a lot of resistance from Delta's chief executive who basically killed off the deal for shareholders in order to keep control himself. A couple of years later, I did a hostile takeover of that company by buying 51 per cent of it overnight from large shareholders and outmanoeuvring the CEO who then had to concede control and simply join our bigger group management. We had a lot of cash and started looking for an acquisition in the Czech Republic and Slovakia.

The following year, 2002, was magical – my most successful year in mergers and acquisitions, with the European deal I had been looking for being the third deal I did that year. Delta's business had been doing well and its shares had risen accordingly. It had just merged with Omega Pharma, a company with a great product pipeline that we had unsuccessfully tried to buy. We decided to be bold and mount a hostile takeover of the newly merged business. We hired

Delta's advisers to advise us – once they had resolved any issue of conflict of interest – and set about calling all the shareholders, securing commitments for 51 per cent of the stock over a single day. When stock markets closed one Monday, Delta's chief executive was on a plane, going somewhere to look for a company to acquire in eastern Europe. When he landed, he learned that the tables had been turned: it was his company that had been acquired and he was now working for the people he had opposed.

We used our majority stake and the support of other shareholders to merge Delta and Pharmaco in 2002; in 2004 the merged company changed its name to Actavis. I felt a great sense of achievement in having created one of the largest companies in Iceland, with a research and development arm that complemented its manufacturing operations in, and cash flow from, eastern Europe. Actavis continued to grow but went through a lot of change. One of the Bulgarian entrepreneurs left and sold his stake in 2002 and the other departed a year later. But the Pharmaco deals established me in Bulgaria and in the wider banking markets too. In 2001 and 2002, when I was pitching to investment banks in London, we had turnover of just $150 million and they would hardly give us the time of day. But our growth, both by acquisition and organic, increased that figure fivefold.

In the meantime, I had become involved in other privatisations. Almost by accident in 2003, shortly after I moved to London, I received a call from Advent International, a private equity group. 'Thor,' they said. 'We know you from the brewery financing talks in Russia. We've watched what you did there and are kicking ourselves for not having invested but here's another opportunity. We're bidding on a privatisation of the major Bulgarian telecoms company BTC. We remember you were in a privatisation in the pharmaceutical industry in 1999 in Bulgaria. We've got another investment. Would you like to co-invest with us?'

Advent had competed in the privatisation of Bulgaria's national telecommunications carrier, Bulgarian Telecommunications Company (BTC), and won in an open auction conducted by ING Barings. The bid it lodged through a consortium was the highest but the deal had got stuck and the firm was looking for someone who knew the Bulgarian system to come into the consortium and get things moving. I had not been in telecoms before but I knew Bulgaria.

'Fine,' I said, 'but I want to invest as much as you.' We structured it so that Advent and the investment consortium Carrera, which I led, both took 25 per cent stakes, with seven other investors making up the remaining 50 per cent. It took two years for us to finalise the acquisition and we had to do some last-minute renegotiating in the prime minister's office where I was instrumental in coming up with a solution.

On the ground there was a lot of wrangling with Bulgaria's influential Turkish lobby, which is well represented in parliament. The privatisation was coming undone as the only other bidder was a Turkish/US consortium and the Turkish side was lobbying hard. We spent a lot of time in discussions with people about what was happening and getting to know the company. I remember being in the prime minister's office one night when the deal was back on, and we were discussing the ways in which the government could justify a deal with our consortium, given the past 18 months of wrangling. BTC was a brilliant asset for which we paid a relatively low price of €280 million, though we had to invest another €1 billion or so over four years to rebuild Bulgaria's telecoms infrastructure, enabling internet connections, fibre optics, and so on. The company was predictably inefficient and had almost 24,000 employees when telecoms experts were saying it could be run with no more than 3,000. Bound by a strict programme of who we could fire and not fire, we achieved most of the reduction through a voluntary redundancy programme.

As usual, however, I was not content just to own BTC. Its limitation was that it was a fixed-line only business. 'We've got to have our own mobile phone business,' I said. 'We've got to be mobile operators as well.' There were only two mobile phone operators in Bulgaria at the time so we did a deal to pay €90 million for a mobile phone licence, thereby allowing the Bulgarian government to save face by coming back with a higher price for the company. This meant we got a ticket to the future, and the government got its price. We then immediately started building a mobile phone network, which changed the business case, making it more attractive in the long term but more difficult in the short term. Inevitably, the other two operators sued the government for issuing the licence without opening it to tender, but that was the government's concern, not ours.

After we had owned BTC for ten or eleven months, I started to notice the old private equity mentality creeping in. Just like our first partner in a Bulgarian privatisation, the Deutsche Bank private equity group, they became fixated on exiting with a profit as fast as they could. In both cases, no sooner had we taken over the companies than their possible sales were up for discussion. This is all well and good as far as I am concerned, but it is quite different from my philosophy of wanting to grow and shape the business for a few years to maximise the value, rather than flipping an asset in a quick trade.

Our consortium owned 65 per cent of the company, with the government owning the remainder, but I persuaded Citibank to back me and, after a board meeting, went to all the other international consortium members, offering them the chance to double their money on their investment. They agreed and I was left with the entire non-government stake. It meant more risk but much more potential gain. But it was brilliant: I didn't have to put in a penny myself. I bought out everyone else using the company's increased debt that Citibank had provided, and everyone was happy.

Almost as soon as we had done that deal, a new government came to power and decided to sell its 35 per cent stake publicly, so all of a sudden we were becoming a listed company without even being consulted. This created a lot of problems, not least because I didn't know who would end up buying the minority stake. True to Bulgarian form, the finance ministry decided not to sell the shares for cash but to exchange them for compensatory or restitution bonds issued to people whose properties had been nationalised by previous communist regimes. The government thought it would work well to accept payment at the face value of these bonds, which were trading at a discount. My priority was ensuring we did not get an unfriendly or hostile shareholder, and I also had to be careful that I didn't end up owning any more shares, because that would have triggered a mandatory takeover for the whole company, which was something I did not want to happen.

Our creative solution was to figure out who would be coming into our company and what their agenda was. Could we team up with them? We had staked a lot of our money and our reputation on this deal and I wasn't interested in getting into a fight with anyone. I was told that Bulgaria's Economic and Investment Bank was playing a key role, so I went to meet the team. There were two men and a petite woman with a nice smile and an iron will, who turned out to be the bank's chairman, Tzvetelina Borislavova. 'These people are not going to be easy to deal with,' I thought. It was clear they were no pushover: they knew what they were talking about and had an agenda of their own. I thought I'd rather have them on my side of the table. I liked their way of thinking and their business. They executed the trade flawlessly. They went into the markets and they gathered the compensatory bonds. Both were complex operations but they carried them off skilfully, investing in the issue themselves, as well as buying some for clients. They ended up taking about two thirds of the 35 per cent stake, with the rest going into the market. I got to know them and they said: 'Actually, we would like a strategic investor.' The bank had grown and they wanted to take it to the next level. I liked this privately owned bank so much that I bought a 50 per cent stake in it in 2006, and that was the third investment I made in Bulgaria.

We helped the bank to expand its operations and prepare for a strategic sale, which we organised as a straight auction with three firm bids. It was sold to a Belgian bank, KBC, in 2007 for more than three times book value. That was a fantastic sale. It helped us with BTC as well, and the feisty chairwoman turned out to be a great partner in business. Her boyfriend, Boyco Borisov, head of the interior ministry, was the most popular politician in Bulgaria, and she did a lot to advance his political career. He had the popular touch, and on finding a crew asphalting the roads in the capital on the day he was elected mayor of Sofia, he grabbed a shovel and helped them out. Big, brawny Boyco ultimately became Bulgaria's prime minister.

My investments in both Russia and Bulgaria supported jobs and investment in different ways. In Russia, it was certainly a question of making great profits, but the happy side effect was that there were thousands of jobs created. It was a great feeling to be able to employ people, knowing that the lives of their families were so much better as a result. Those jobs are still there.

In Bulgaria, it was a different story. Jobs needed to be cut, as the company was a mulish giant, unable to take the next step towards the future. But BTC survived, which it wouldn't have done otherwise, and it was a catalyst in modernising the telecoms infrastructure in Bulgaria, installing fibre-optic cables throughout cities and creating a basis for other companies to thrive. The internet revolution took place in Bulgaria, to the benefit of all, even though jobs at this one particular company were fewer than before.

*

In parallel with my involvement in Bulgaria, I invested in the 2003 privatisation of Ceske Radiokomunikace (CRa), a telecoms company in the Czech Republic. Ironically, I had bought the shares, which I sold in November 2006 after the company had tripled in value, from Deutsche Bank.

If this all sounds breathless and conducted at breakneck speed, that's exactly how it was. A few years after first getting involved in Bulgaria, I employed 12,000 staff in telecoms and 4,000 in pharmaceuticals. I used the nation's top investment bankers and owned some of its best real estate. But in Bulgaria I had a very different role from the one I had in Russia.

In post-communist Russia I was on a wild adventure, learning on the job as I went along, making mistakes and fixing them, operating, certainly at the beginning, more or less on my own. I was the entrepreneur building factories, checking costs, watching margins and running around the factories. I wanted to know whether everything was working properly and had to figure out what to do if it was not. Why was that car over there? Why was this tank not full? I was hands-on. And I had anonymity.

In Bulgaria, it was very different. I was highly visible and was viewed as a financier rather than an operational manager. My role was also ambassadorial and political. I knew all the main political players, drank tea with them and worked with them to let them know what was coming up. I felt like an investment king, doing everything from privatisations to leveraged buy-outs, and each success took that feeling to another level.

When I was on the cover of *Forbes* magazine in 2005 Bulgaria's media lapped it up. 'Our Thor is On The List,' ran the headlines. Their Thor? They had nobody of their own on the list, so they adopted me. I was an honorary Bulgarian. I was an outsider, but when it was positive news I was theirs. It felt good to be cherished. I felt that my time had come. However, high on the success of my pharma investments, I decided to copy the model in telecoms and try to repeat the Pharmaco story. I had bought a huge cash cow in the form of Bulgaria's state telecom company, although it needed massive modernisation which we committed to by introducing fibre and mobile phone service. Now all I needed to do was reverse that company into a Scandinavian listed company with access to listed capital markets and use them to buy more telecom companies in the region (the East-to-West arbitrage). I wanted to do a copy-and-paste of what I had already done in Iceland, and I got the chance to try it in Finland. I managed to acquire the biggest single shareholding of the listed Finnish telecom Elisa, a conservative company more than 100 years old and the only Scandinavian telecom operator with no international assets. This was a no-brainer to me, and I thought the investors would welcome someone with a new vision of modernising their company and fully using its potential for scale with merger ideas and ready-made connections in eastern Europe. But that's when I hit a wall.

My reception in Finland was totally different to that in

Iceland, and I found myself unexpectedly in a big fight at this old company which had as many shareholders as the whole population of Iceland – nearly a quarter of a million individual and company investors. I really hadn't thought about this strange historical anomaly, but it had big implications. The media in Finland portrayed me as Viking raider and rallied behind a nationalistic cause to resist any attempt to globalise this long-established traditional company. I had to call an extraordinary shareholders' meeting to vote on my board seats and change the constitution of the company, enabling it to take on more debt for foreign expansion. I was very surprised by how much public drama this generated. More than 16,000 people attended the meeting and the company had to hire the national hockey stadium as it was the only place in Helsinki that could fit everyone in. The meeting was quite a spectacle, with me debating with the old board and countless small investors taking to the stage to say all kinds of things about Finland. One scholar read out parts of the epic poem *Kalevala* about the 'soul of the Finnish people'. Someone else turned up with a wheelbarrow full of paper votes against my motions, a visual showpiece that the TV cameras loved. I found myself in a sort of theatrical event, onstage and in a literal spotlight with little room to manoeuvre.

Nevertheless, there seemed to be thousands of people who liked my vision and were ready to back a new, bolder future. We gradually became more respected in Finnish business circles, but I was unable to achieve my dream of creating a western-listed telecom powerhouse to take advantage of the eastern European mergers that were about to happen over the next year. You can't win them all and this was an experience that I cherish looking back on. Politics has always been my weak point, throughout my career and to this day, but this episode taught me some good lessons about both company and nationalistic politics.

My vision was not coming together on the banking side, with analysts saying there wasn't as much synergy in international telecoms as in pharmaceuticals, where you get real economies of scale. So I sold my Bulgarian and Czech telecoms investments within about ten months of each other. BTC was sold to the private equity arm of AIG, a US insurer, which popped out of the woodwork when I was expecting Greece Telecom, Deutsche Telekom or Turkish Telecom to buy it. Lehman Brothers advised us and AIG bought our 65 per cent stake for $855 million – far more than we were expecting. This sale wasn't without complications either. Towards the end of the auction, I had lunch in London with Saad Hariri, the son of the late prime minister of Lebanon, and prime minister himself in 2009–11. He was the head of Oger Telecom, a Saudi/Lebanese company that owned Turkish Telecom, and he signalled that he was interested in buying BTC. I was keen and thought it would fit well with the group's Turkish operations. Then AIG made a late bid and I was summoned to Bulgaria to see the prime minister. 'We don't want to sell to the Turks,' he told me. 'We want the Americans.' I told him it was basically down to price, but the prime minister made it clear that I should bear in mind the time that might be needed to clear the deal, depending on who I chose. 'Fine,' I replied. And of course we sold to AIG. I have no regrets about that. We made almost €400 million profit on that deal.

At the time, I didn't know if the prime minister was anti-Turk or if the Americans had lobbied him, but later I found out this was a classic example of the US flexing its muscles.

Another time, I was planning on buying a 51 per cent stake in Mobtel, one of two telecommunications companies operating in Serbia. Mobtel was 51 per cent owned by a very colourful character called Karic, with the Serbian state holding the remaining 49 per cent. Karic wanted to sell his share, but his plan was to then turn around and buy the 49 per cent share from the Serbian government. I remember entering his huge office in Belgrade and being instructed to sit down in front of his large desk. Then a woman came in with a large, impressive book and opened it on the desk. Karic picked up a nice gold pen and looked at us with a peculiar expression on his face, not smiling or grinning, but obviously very proud of what was going on. Then he wrote something in the book and closed it, and the lady took it back. He looked us in the eye and said this was the last signature needed for him to run for president of Serbia (which indeed he did a few months later). During our meeting, he also took a phone call and talked for some time. After he had hung up, he told us that this had been the prime minister congratulating him on running for president. Obviously all of this was meant to impress us, and it did. I was close to doing this deal. Then I got Iceland's president, Olafur Grimsson, to visit Serbia with me. We talked to many different officials, and the message from all of them was that I shouldn't have anything to do with Karic. Nobody said it out loud, but the clear inference was that the state might take some action against Karic.

Strangely, while doing this deal, we found that phrases that I and members of my bid team had used between ourselves were repeated back to us during negotiations. We had obviously been bugged in the 'Business Club', the glitzy club in Belgrade where we held many of the negotiations.

Also, during due diligence, we discovered that Karic owned not only Mobtel but also the company providing security to all of its offices. On further examination, we found that the security company was also being paid to provide security to many other offices which apparently did not exist. None of this felt good, so I decided to walk away. Shortly afterwards, the Serbian state nationalised Mobtel and later sold it to TeleNor. This is definitely the greatest deal I never did.

One of the best deals that I *did* do in this period, however, was to set up Play, a mobile telecoms start-up in Poland that is now one of the nation's big four companies in this sector.

My attempts to parachute into a special situation in listed equities were not always welcomed. In the UK, I tried to take Cable & Wireless private, meeting a couple of times with its then chairman, Richard Lapthorne, who listened to my idea to break the group in two, told me the company wasn't interested and then proceeded to do pretty much what I had suggested. Some deals also went spectacularly wrong. One was a former Finnish co-operative, Amer Group, which owns some of the world's largest sports brands and equipment-makers, including Wilson, Salomon and others. It had a large private golf club in Helsinki and a big chalet in Courchevel, which to us looked like corporate excess. The idea was to sell off the Wilson and Salomon brands, but we faced opposition from the board and, as happened with Elisa, we ran out of time when the markets crashed and we had to retreat from aggressive positions, focusing instead on fire-fighting in our bigger investments. I wanted to merge Amer into something bigger, and Novator, the investment company I had set up in 2004, had a meeting with the chief executive, Roger Talermo, and his Finnish institutional shareholders. I could see so much potential to shake up the company. There were 83 staff in the Helsinki headquarters, which could easily have been run by five because there were no operations in Finland. Salomon was run from France, Wilson from Chicago and other operations from Seattle. I wanted to fire Talermo and call a shareholder vote. We couldn't convince the other shareholders, but shortly after we exited – I had lost about €60 million on my investment – it was announced that Talermo was leaving the company.

Just after I sold BTC, I bought close to 5 per cent of German insurance giant Allianz, which proved to be a disastrous mistake. I had started pursuing an activist strategy in Finland, taking relatively small investments in companies and lobbying for change to unlock value for shareholders. Now I wanted to try it on a grander scale and break up Allianz into its banking and insurance arms, but I found it impossible to rally support for a perceived attack on 'fortress Germany'. I learned through these two deals that politics often overrides good business ideas. This was a prime example showing that the agency theory I had learned in school did indeed have a lot of truth in it. People often have very different interests in the same assets. We ended up losing about €350 million in a super-leveraged structure. At the time, it was my biggest single loss, though the events of 2008 would make it pale in comparison.

Those disasters apart, however, my self-made life as a special situations agent moving from country to country in search of financial action was tremendously exciting. Looking back, it is perhaps not surprising that I didn't want to get off the carousel even though I knew intuitively that it wouldn't and couldn't keep going for ever. The signs were there towards the end, but the markets were with us for such an uncommonly long period. There had been plenty of privatisations and I was operating in eastern European and Scandinavian markets that I knew. In Bulgaria, for example, we were operating in a different league compared with the rough and tumble that we had experienced in Russia. We mixed with mayors and prime ministers and always travelled with armed bodyguards. And we always tried to fit in with the local culture – even when we had to eat calf brains.

Bulgaria was the best time. I was an outsider there so I didn't have a peer group. I wasn't part of the system. I was allowed to just be. We were also making a great deal of money and I stayed with the tried and trusted financial partners that I had worked with before. Deutsche Bank and Advent could be relied upon. The deals kept coming. A particularly enjoyable one was in Sweden with the publicly listed and respected investment bank Carnegie, in which Straumur bought a 20 per cent strategic stake and I joined the board before exiting a little under two years later, through a share placing in which I more than doubled my investment. It was fulfilling and highly creative and that's what gets me excited. The phone was always ringing with new opportunities that presented a new challenge and got me fired up with thinking about how to make the most of it. It was addictive and I felt almost invincible. But of course it couldn't last.

There were occasions when my time in Russia was a disadvantage and was used against me. For example, Actavis made a hostile bid for Pliva, a large international pharmaceuticals company based in Croatia, in 2006. The chief executive didn't want our takeover and got a US drugs group, Barr Pharmaceuticals, to counter-bid for it as a 'white knight'. Soon it became clear that the public relations strategy was to focus on my time in Russia, with Barr hiring Kroll, an investigations agency, to help it in a PR battle.

Barr ended up buying Pliva, but I became friends with the US company and liked its deputy chief executive, Paul Bisaro. Ironically, he later became chief executive of Watson Pharmaceuticals, which bought Actavis in 2012, and in May 2014 he became chairman of the merged company, in which I retain a stake and which retained the name Actavis.

*

As the money flooded in and I made that *Forbes* front cover, doors kept opening for me and I gained access to a new stratum of people and power. The World Economic Forum in Davos is one example. People talk about it being a networking magnet for the kings of capitalism, but that's only half the story. I always came back pumped up, energised and with a notebook full of ideas and potential deals. The annual Davos meeting inspires people to make a change; it challenges you on a personal level to have a higher purpose, and gives you a deeper recognition of the challenges of the world. In one way it is like being back at school, and the closeting effect of so much wealth and power being concentrated in one small Swiss village is electrifying.

Of course, some of this is plain ego-tickling. I met icons such as Sir Richard Branson, Google founders Sergey Brin and Larry Page, and an interesting up-and-coming internet executive called Jack Ma. Ma's company Alibaba was the largest and best-known publicly quoted Chinese company. Ma, however, would fly too close to the sun and in 2022 the Chinese government decided he had become too powerful. He disappeared for many months and the government announced that it would be breaking up the company into smaller units. Ma later reappeared in Japan, where he is now teaching at a university.

I also remember one summit where I had just got my first iPhone and was speaking on it when I felt a tap on my shoulder and turned to face Jorma Ollila, the Royal Dutch Shell chairman who at the time was chief executive of Nokia and probably the most respected businessman of the era. 'Thor?' he asked. 'Yes. Sorry, I just got a call,' I replied, turning off my mobile. 'I've seen your pictures in the Finnish business papers where you're making waves,' said Ollila, who I had never met before. Then, pointing to my iPhone and smiling, he quipped: 'Just one piece of advice. Get a real phone.' It was a jokey remark but it illustrates the unpredictable nature of modern business. Nokia was at its peak and was about to suffer a sharp fall in fortunes. And now the Finnish company no longer makes mobile phones, having sold that business to Microsoft.

At another Davos meeting, I was helping to launch a climate change mitigation initiative and we threw a party, inviting celebrities and chief executives galore. As we were entering, a colleague on the organising group asked if I could stand in for him in greeting and looking after supermodel Claudia Schiffer, our guest of honour. 'Claudia Schiffer?' I replied. 'More than happy. With great, great regret, I'll do it!'

I went down to wait for her and then the mobile rang. It was Blackstone Group's chairman Steve Schwarzman wanting to meet me in five minutes. But I was in the lobby with Claudia Schiffer about to arrive, so I grabbed another bystander whom I knew and said: 'I've got the dream job here for you. Will you take over?' He took over and I went to meet Steve. 'I hope you realise what I'm doing for you here today because meeting you I'm giving up meeting Claudia Schiffer,' I told him. 'Really? Is she here?' he asked. 'Yes. She's here. She just walked into a party down the corridor.' After hearing this, he was, of course, much more interested in going to the party and meeting her.

After our meeting, we met Claudia and chatted to her. I discovered that we lived close to each other. But our conversation was cut short when my assistant arrived with Rupert Murdoch's assistant in tow. 'We need to borrow your car,' he said. 'Take the car,' I replied. 'Take it. Leave me alone.' Then a very relaxed and jovial Rupert Murdoch appeared, having had a bit more than his fair share of the champagne at the Google party in the next hall to ours. 'We really should get him back to the hotel,' said his aide, 'But, Thor, you're the only one the driver recognises. You've got to go with him.' So again I said sorry to Claudia as I escorted a happy Murdoch to the car. Of course, she was gone when I got back. That's 15 minutes of Davos in a nutshell.

It was also during this period that I was asked to give a lift to Iceland in my private jet to former Soviet Union president Mikhail Gorbachev. My first encounter with Gorbachev had been in 1986, as a 19-year-old student, when I answered the doorbell at our house in Reykjavik, which was not far from the Russian embassy. Outside was a police officer who told me that a motorcade would be passing soon and our parked car had to be moved. I duly did as I was told and stood on the pavement to witness something quite extraordinary in little Reykjavik: a big convoy of cars escorted by motorcycle police, and in the middle a huge black Russian ZIL limousine. I knew that President Gorbachev was inside and that he had been at a meeting with the US president, Ronald Reagan, in Höfdi.

Little did I know that this event in Iceland would lead in less than a year to the signing of the INF (Intermediate-range Nuclear Forces) treaty that all but ended the Cold War and in the longer term would lead to the dismantling of the iron curtain between eastern and western Europe – and the opening up of incredible opportunities for me.

Twenty years later, I received a call from someone at the foreign ministry in Iceland asking if it would be possible to borrow my private jet to fly Gorbachev from Germany to Iceland, where he was going to give a lecture to mark the anniversary of that momentous meeting. It was an irresistible opportunity to meet the man, so I immediately said: 'No problem. It will be my pleasure to pick him up and take him to Reykjavik.' While he has always been admired in the West,

Gorbachev was deeply disliked in Russia during my time there and was widely blamed for the chaos that accompanied the break-up of the Soviet Union. I had always styled myself as a challenger and a force for new thinking to bring about change. Now I was in the company of the ultimate challenger to a bad system.

Gorbachev had been travelling with Vladimir Putin as an adviser, and when I picked him up, he was accompanied by his usual translator, Pavel – instantly recognisable because of his funny moustache – and the head of the Green Cross humanitarian organisation, who was introduced just as Alexander. All four of us settled in comfortably for the three-hour flight ahead

I was a bit nervous, but there was no need. We talked about Gorbachev's time in Reykjavik and the differences between the Soviet Union and the Russia I had lived in for ten years. He was very surprised that I had lived in Russia for so long and during that crazy period of Russia's history. His entourage all knew my beer brand and were impressed that a young Icelander had been behind the venture. Once Gorbachev had opened up, we chatted for most of the flight. I had greeted them and made opening smalltalk in Russian, but I told them early on that I would prefer to converse through the amiable translator. As Gorbachev was a very energetic speaker, Pavel kept asking him to pause to allow him to translate, but Gorbachev kept saying: 'Thor speaks much more Russian than he admits – don't worry, he understands fine.' So I missed out on quite a lot of what he was saying, but it was enthralling nevertheless. He explained he had been disappointed by the American side in Reykjavik, in that they did not believe he was genuine in his insistence that the arms race had got out of control and that both sides had to not only stop making nuclear weapons but also start destroying the ones they had. He told me: 'I suddenly realised that Reagan was born in the same year as my mother, and that there was a whole generation between us. I was the typical eager young guy whom the older man listens to with reservations. This was going to take longer to get going than I had hoped for, and I had a much steeper hill to climb in gaining their trust than I had envisaged.' It seemed a very familiar theme to me.

As we landed in Reykjavik and disembarked in front of a bank of photographers and journalists, it was strange to reflect on how much my life had changed from being a young student hoping for a glimpse of this great man in his bullet-proof limousine. Twenty years on I was an international globetrotter who gave lifts to world statesmen. It felt good.

When I look back, it is interesting to remember that Gorbachev later went from being the second most powerful man in the world to a man with no role or office whatsoever in a matter of a few days. But then I know how quickly the fortunes of men can change.

I would be lying if I said that all this was not intoxicating. I like my trade, I like making deals, and I enjoy the rough and tumble of working with the larger-than-life characters at the top level of the business world. Kristin tells me that I have a passion for colourful characters from the highest to the lowest levels of society and I guess she's right. I like eccentrics and the highly individual. Dealing with them is a way of breaking through the monotony of life. I've always been that way. Most people would consider these guys too weird to be around, but I find them interesting.

We are all on the same gravy train though and I remember being acutely aware of that from the start. For ten years, I decided, life was going to be hard work, but then I was going to be extremely rich and have a life of luxury. I would live overseas, own my own plane and buy a yacht. I lived out that dream but it lost its appeal. When I spend more than a few days on a yacht, I quickly become bored. There's great truth in the old saying in the yacht world that a boat owner has only two pure moments of happiness from it: on the day he buys the boat, and the day he sells it. The plane was great. I could go anywhere I wanted, but most of the time it took me to the next business meeting. Sitting on a yacht and lying on a beach are not really for me. I don't see how a person with the ambition and drive to get there can ever switch off. I think of my brother-in-law, an artist who just grabs his guitar and writes a song when he feels like it. It's all about doing what you want to do. I have always been a serial dealmaker, but it is not so easy to plan your next deal when the credit markets freeze and the heady tap of leverage is suddenly turned off.

In 2005 my three main business interests – pharma, telecoms and banking – were roughly equal in size, each valued at about $5 billion. Of course I did not own all the equity, but I congratulated myself on my balanced business strategy. That was my business model: to keep a balance of diversified interests that wouldn't all crash at once. Through Novator, I saw myself pursuing a number of strategies. I could be an activist in a public company or a caretaker or midwife in a private equity situation, taking assets, cleaning them up and getting to a position from which I could exit.

My mistake with the so-called balanced strategy, of course, was that when a nation's banking system goes down, everything is affected. With hindsight, I should have spotted this in 2008 because the similarities with 1998 and the end of the first Russian financial boom were striking. The Klondike feeling was back. People were rushing in and because the returns were diminishing, they were venturing further upstream in search of gold.

In Russia, I was able to get out in time. This time, I was too deeply entrenched. As an investor, I was being chased by banks every day. 'What do you want to do next?' they would ask. 'Want to deal in real estate? We'd love to help you. Can we lend you some money?' The banks were hugely overborrowed themselves and yet chasing new opportunities to lend. We should have spotted the dangers of the situation a mile off.

In some ways we did. I remember that Davos conversation with Steve Schwarzman at the beginning of 2007. I said: 'Aren't the markets unusual right now? There's too much lending. It doesn't feel right. I feel like everyone is chasing the same assets but prices are still going up so I've started selling assets in Bulgaria and the Czech Republic. I'm a little bit of a seller and a bit sceptical about buying, but I'm still looking at doing a deal.'

'You're absolutely right,' he replied. 'When this much money is being offered, as a general rule of thumb, take as much as possible, as it is being offered and won't last.'

Later that year, in August, I met Steve again. I had just taken Actavis private in a €5.3 billion deal that Deutsche Bank was rolling €4 billion into. This deal could so easily have plunged Germany's biggest bank into serious financial difficulties. I had built Actavis into one of the world's biggest generic pharmaceutical companies in a competitive and consolidating industry. As industry consolidation quickened after 2006, I felt we had to decide quickly whether we were going to become predator or prey. Both could have worked, but we decided that because of the state of the lending markets we were going to become predators, leveraging up Actavis and buying other companies. We bid for a Croatian generics company, Pliva, which ended up being bought by a US company, Barr Pharmaceuticals, and went a long way down the line to try to buy the generics division of Germany's Merck. Bankers fell over themselves to provide debt and convince us to bid and, although we ended up backing away from the price being asked, we had credit lines of €3.4 billion–€4 billion committed on a potential deal. This opened my eyes to the amounts that banks were willing to lend on such deals, so I decided to use that arsenal of debt to buy the 60 per cent of Actavis that I did not already own.

It was a pure leveraged buy-out struck at €5.3 billion – 17.5 times earnings before interest, taxes, depreciation and amortisation (EBITDA) – and of this 12.5 times was leverage, making it by far the largest transaction on the Icelandic stock market. I rolled in my equity which was worth roughly €1 billion and borrowed the rest, so basically I put in 20 per cent equity and 80 per cent loans, which is very high risk. I was buying the company at a high price and I put my hand up now and admit that I made mistakes. I didn't do all the due diligence I would have done on any other purchase because I felt that I had been with the company for eight years and knew the people running it, who as co-shareholders would have what City bankers refer to as 'skin in the game', and whose rewards would therefore be linked to the business performance. That was a big failure because the Actavis management was too ambitious and stretched the budget too far, probably in the crazy spirit of the times. But Deutsche Bank made far greater mistakes. It would normally have managed the risks of providing €4.3 billion of debt by syndicating the loans upfront, but it decided not to do this so that it could underwrite the whole deal itself and take all the fees before syndicating later.

Just as I was caught out by the Russian currency crisis in 1998, however, Deutsche Bank's plan was scuppered by the tightening of the credit markets shortly after we signed the Actavis deal in August 2007. It was then unable to syndicate the loans on decent terms so held on to its position in the hope that conditions would improve in 2008, which of course did not happen. The bank put all the debt on its own book and got stuck with it in 2008 when the credit markets got much worse. It had taken an enormous bet and now had to live with the consequences.

When we closed the buy-out deal, I flew my team to my yacht in St Tropez and we partied for two days, celebrating the biggest deal we'd ever done.

There in the south of France, I left the boat, went into the famous Nikki Beach bar and ran into Steve Schwarzman again. I told him about the deal. 'Interesting,' he said. 'Deutsche must be in a world of pain right now. You've timed it perfectly.' And this was from a master of timing in the financial markets who had just finished a $4 billion stock market flotation of his own company. I had no idea what he was talking about. But just as Deutsche Bank had wired the money, the market had begun to turn and the syndication markets closed. Later on, our deal was compared with the last helicopter leaving the US Embassy building in Saigon in 1975 before the city fell to the North Vietnamese army. There were certainly no more deals being done. The credit markets crashed in 2008. Deutsche Bank was deep in the mire. And so was I, of course.

Ambition is the toughest boss one can ever have.

5

NEVER GO BACK
2000-2007

Is this the real life?
Is this just fantasy?
Caught in a landslide
No escape from reality

Queen, 'Bohemian Rhapsody'

In 1988 I had left Iceland, promising myself that I would
never return. Fourteen years later I broke this pledge, and
I am not sure I will ever forgive myself. I rationalised it by
telling myself that I wasn't physically relocating. My centre
of gravity was now London. Nevertheless, getting involved
in the Landsbanki privatisation of 2002 definitely represented
a breach of my vow never to be a big fish in a small pond.
With only 320,000 people at the time, Iceland was about as
small a pond as a nation can be, and since my financial return
I have been cast as a giant shark. In returning, I reinforced the
symmetry between my life and that of my great-grandfather,
Thor Jensen. I became a part again of the Icelandic community,
though importantly never part of the nation's political system.
And I set out on a path that would take many years to wind
to its conclusion.

Iceland's three biggest banks, which together handled 75 per cent of all banking in the country, were the private bank Islandsbanki and the two state banks, Landsbanki and Bunadarbanki. Landsbanki was the oldest and most respected. In 1997, the government decided to make both Landsbanki and Bunadarbanki stock companies, but with all the stock still owned by the state.

In 1998, the Swedish Enskilda Bank showed interest in buying a third of Landsbanki, but the talks fell through. Later that year the government decided to publicly sell off a 15 per cent stake in each bank. The demand for shares was enormous and it was clear that the state could have sold its entire stake had it wanted to. In 2001, parliament permitted the sale of the rest of the state's shares in Landsbanki and Bunadarbanki on the basis that the state should not be doing business that the private sector was capable of doing. In its efforts to sell its shares in Landsbanki, the government enlisted HSBC to find buyers abroad. For the time being, no attempt was made to sell Bunadarbanki.

The attempts to sell Landsbanki were futile, despite HSBC contacting almost 30 investors, mainly financial corporations. The government's commission on the privatisation recommended in December 2001 that a further 20 per cent stake be sold to the public, which happened in June 2002. After that, the state was left owning about 48 per cent of the bank.

This was how things stood when my father, Magnus and I, through Samson, the holding company in which we were partners, contacted the government and expressed an interest in buying at least 33 per cent of the bank's shares. I had spotted one more special situation: it was a completely failed privatisation, and I figured the whole bank was for sale. This led to Samson acquiring 45.8 per cent of Landsbanki. In parallel, the S-Group (a hastily assembled collection of politically connected companies led by the industrialist Olafur Olafsson) bought 45.8 per cent of Bunadarbanki, or Kaupthing as it became a few months later. Following privatisation, little changed in the structure of ownership of Landsbanki and Kaupthing prior to the crash, but there were repeated feuds between the owners of Islandsbanki, resulting in Jon Asgeir Johannesson's Baugur getting the upper hand in the bank (renamed Glitnir) in 2007.

My role is to be a catalyst for change and a kind of midwife. Companies are born and I pass them on to their ultimate parents, be they other individual investors or the stock exchange. My plan was to take Landsbanki, make it international and then sell it. We ran out of time.

I still ask myself time and again why I did the Landsbanki deal in 2002, choosing to become the biggest investor in Iceland's banking system. The answer, I suppose, is ambition or weakness in the form of a need for recognition in my home country. Ego certainly played a large part. However, hubris started creeping in, slowly but surely in the following years. What is beyond doubt is that I allowed myself to be seduced. I had $100 million from my first major business success burning a hole in my pocket and bankers ringing every day asking if I would like them to manage my money. I could have just put it all in a bank but I went a step further.

How did I manage to combine two errors in one strategic move, taking a major stake in a bank at the same time as returning in a business sense to Iceland, the little country I thought I had almost left for good? I guess I just fell into a trap that I set myself. The thought process went like this: 'I've got all this cash. Why should I put it in a bank and let bankers manage my money? Why do they think they know best how to manage my money? Why don't I just invest it myself and buy a bank?' So that was what I did. Samson Holdings agreed to pay $140 million for a 45.8 per cent stake in Landsbanki, the old national bank of Iceland, following a lengthy political bidding process. It was an incredibly intricate privatisation, the biggest such deal ever done in Iceland. It provided a tickertape homecoming parade for me – and for my father especially – but it was the biggest mistake of my life. It was a busy time for me: within a month of bidding for Landsbanki, I also engineered the Pharmaco–Delta pharmaceuticals merger, creating the company that would later become Actavis. Now, at the age of 35, I had most of my assets in the country, controlling with my father two of its biggest companies.

This was a new era in Iceland. Things were about to change in a big way. The political power brokers had decided that the country was ready to embrace the free market with fervour. The Iceland that I had grown up in and left as soon as I could was a centralised economy run by a small power clique and dominated by cronyism. In some ways it was the Soviet Union without communism, a closed society cut off from much of the western world. This was the system I hated, even though I loved the people and the country. Icelanders had never had a great deal to call their own. A dirt-poor country up until the Second World War and independence, it had no traditional European cultural foundation or framework. Instead, Icelanders had 19th-century nationalistic romanticism, which was so powerful that it managed to keep the country isolated from most of western civilisation for most of its history.

But the return to the country of my birth, when it was recovering from the bursting of the dotcom bubble, coincided with the massive opening up of Iceland to the global capital markets, a development that would eventually destroy a lot of the country's values and principles. The creation in 1994 of the European Economic Area (EEA), of which Iceland was a member, was the biggest game-changer for the country economically for generations. It created immense opportunities for free trade, benefiting both Iceland and the rest of Europe. But it also played a crucial role in the development of an Icelandic economic bubble. So-called 'carry traders' from Wall Street to Hong Kong would chase the high interest rates the Central Bank of Iceland began to offer after the turn of the century. They would borrow money at low interest rates in one country and invest it at high interest rates in another, seeking to make money in 'something safe'. Iceland had a good reputation in that respect as it had never had the problems of the South American and Asian countries that had played this game before. It was virgin territory with a seemingly attractive profile to anyone willing to take a modest risk.

The privatisation of Iceland's banks, in which I was to play a major part, led to a notable increase in competition, with cheaper and better banking services and a much broader range of financial products, including low-rate, long-term mortgages, a market that had previously been serviced mainly by the public Housing Financing Fund and by pension funds. The greater availability of mortgage financing led to an exceptional increase in house prices, which rose by almost 100 per cent in nominal terms in less than five years. Meanwhile, the privatised banks made good use of Iceland's EEA membership, establishing branches overseas and expanding into other EEA economies. Ample liquidity and low interest rates on international capital markets, mainly caused by the low interest rate policy of central banks in the wake of the 2001 dotcom crash and the economic effects of the 9/11 terrorist attacks, offered Icelanders more than enough foreign credit to finance this expansion.

As a result, the Icelandic banks and investors expanded, snapping up assets in Scandinavia and the UK in particular. Meanwhile, a domestic credit boom, mainly consisting of mortgages and new corporate loans, had begun. The additional spending power, in the form of an inflow of foreign capital and newly created bank credit, had to end somewhere. Consumption and investment ballooned. Imports rocketed. Few nations, if any, have ever managed to run such a spectacular current account deficit as Iceland in 2007, when it represented 25 per cent of the country's GDP.

As money flowed into Iceland like never before, the currency appreciated and inflation came down – a wonderful combination for businesses, politicians and policymakers. This made Iceland even more attractive to the outside world, and the country's self-confidence grew to such levels that it began to control events at the expense of common sense and critical thought. Iceland basked in a new-found international glory and a sense of euphoria spread like wildfire. 'Our time has come' became the mantra that led to the country's painful downfall, with the currency losing more than 50 per cent of its value against the dollar in the year before the 2008 financial crisis. In that global meltdown, the Central Bank of Iceland would become the only central bank in the world to go completely bankrupt. I would both play the game in this new era and be played by the game. My investments in Iceland would rocket in value beyond my wildest projections, and I would also be able to get access to capital by taking loans in the international market that would have been unthinkable before the new millennium.

I was raised in the belief that it is hard to get loans to start risky ventures, and my education would later confirm this. However, this era was something else; loans were being offered before you had even thought of asking for them. We were living in a dream world, but not just in Iceland; this was a global phenomenon, the debt bubble as it was to be referred to. However, nowhere was it as pronounced as in

Iceland, which seemed to be in the perfect sweet spot for a risk-taking entrepreneur. Later, it would become clear that it was actually in the eye of the perfect storm that was brewing. Using the ancient spiritual associations of my first name, my investments in Iceland looked like thunder and lightning, but they turned out to be a blunder that was frightening. The crucial tool that an entrepreneur must have is access to capital. Accessing cash had been a challenge for me with my ventures in Russia and Bulgaria, but as I said in a speech at the New York Stock Exchange in November 2006: 'I usually approach investments from a contrarian standpoint. I want to enter markets where there are not many other participants or capital sources and the risks form a natural barrier to entry.' I added that I was attracted by transitional economies, primarily in emerging Europe and Iceland, that had four characteristics in common: high growth, great margins, limited competition and few international investors or lenders.

I went on to argue that Iceland had been liberalised over the preceding 15 years to such an extent that a highly central-ised and bureaucratic economy had been replaced by an open liberal economy and society. At the time that I returned to the country in 2002, I recalled, Iceland had practically no competi-tion from abroad in its domestic markets, limited capital avail-ability and a sound and sensibly valued currency following a rate adjustment in 2001. Over the next six years these condi-tions totally changed. This was energising as it gave me the opportunity to pursue a lot of new ideas. It was a great time for a deal junkie with imagination and vision, and it felt great. Things started to take off at a remarkable pace and I was having trouble keeping up with my endeavours as they grew quickly in size and scope.

But from the start of 2002 I greatly underestimated the political risk in the Landsbanki privatisation. The ruling party had liberalised and reformed Iceland over more than a decade. Our Landsbanki bid was a huge benefit for the party because it meant it could get the privatisation under way. For me, the Landsbanki deal was supposed to be merely the start. As usual, I was thinking ahead to my next deal. I expected the government to privatise Bunadarbanki, the biggest of the two other main Icelandic banks, within a year or two. Landsbanki would have plenty of cash to make a bid that would be hard to beat. But that deal didn't happen. The minority party in the coalition government put pressure on the ruling party, saying it had chosen us for Landsbanki so there had to be a different buyer for Bunadarbanki, and of course the chosen ones were their political cronies.

It was nonsense, of course. No one else had the $150 million of foreign capital needed for the Bunadarbanki privatisation, and saying that our Landsbanki takeover was connected to support from the Independence Party was ludicrous to me. The party making this claim was the Progressive Party, of which Magnus actually was a member. My father was certainly a follower of the Independence Party, while I had never been a member of any political party, did not vote in Iceland and had no political affiliations. It was never political on our part, albeit the politicians had clearly found something to sink their teeth into. It was ridiculous, but some political deal had been made so that Bunadarbanki would not be auctioned off sensibly. This thwarted my original plan. It didn't make sense to privatise two banks at the same time. It would remove my first-mover advantage, and I thought it would put too much expansionary pressure on the system. The government should have sold Landsbanki, collected the money and waited a year or two before selling the other bank at a much higher price. The privatisation had failed in the previous years, and now the government was botching it again. Once we had made the bid the government used it to manipulate the process. The most outrageous example was when the privatisation of Landsbanki was well under way and the government swiftly sold Landsbanki's shares in a big insurance company to the political cronies who later bought Bunadarbanki. It was unbelievable. The Progressive Party leader's family had an interest worth millions in that deal and, true to Icelandic form, this merely cemented his standing in politics, whereas it would have ensured his downfall in other countries. He was foreign minister at the time, but later took the reins as prime minister.

The Progressive Party put together the S-Group, which had no fresh international capital and was leveraged to the hilt, using borrowed capital and then borrowing again on top of that. When I pointed this out the government said: 'Thor, what does it matter to you?' It did matter to me because this group was so leveraged that, to repay its loans, it had to rapidly increase the value of the underlying stock. So that this could happen, a deal was secretly negotiated with another bank, Kaupthing, which in return for a 51 per cent controlling share helped finance the acquisition of Bunadarbanki. Furthermore, the government promised that young people would be able to get 90–95 per cent loan-to-value mortgages, which soon escalated to 100 per cent. This was pure madness and led to the creation of a property bubble. I believe it was one of the main catalysts for Iceland's financial crash.

I should have walked away once I had figured out what was going on. I should have said: 'I smell a rat and this is dangerous.' That was what my intuition was telling me, but I ignored it because I thought I would be portrayed as a failure or a bad loser if I claimed that the deal was rigged. Instead, I wrote letters to the prime minister, the economics minister and the privatisation committee and did media interviews in which I said that the privatisation process for both banks was opaque and unclear. I told them that even Bulgaria's privatisation rules were more transparent than Iceland's. But my comments were ignored. Later, there was a parliamentary inquiry, which basically brushed over everything. After the crash, it became clear that what I had been saying had been justified.

An example of how unclear and confusing the process was, is when I was called to the prime minister's office on 10 September 2002. The head of the prime minister's office, who was also the chairman of the privatisation committee, handed me a letter stating that the committee had chosen our holding company Samson as the preferred bidder for Landsbanki. But as he handed me the letter, he said that Samson would of course have to pay more than it had offered before. It was confusing to me, as our offer was conditional upon the accounts being right, as we had a well-founded suspicion that there were more bad loans in the loan book than were reflected in the official accounts – a legacy from the old system of loans going out to political cronies. I was not going to get trapped into nailing down a price and ignoring the effects that these bad loans would have on the value should they prove to be there, so I refused to accept the letter. At this he got very nervous, as there were TV cameras and journalists waiting on the front steps of the ministry. They had clearly been tipped off that this was about to happen at the same time as I got the phone call to come there. I did not feel comfortable participating in this, and when I got downstairs I asked the security guy to let me out through the back door, and slipped away into the night without the media catching me. If I had gone through the front door and they had asked me what just happened, my reply would have been: 'I am not quite sure myself.' A member of the privatisation committee later resigned in protest over what he called the bizarre way that the process had been handled.

Another reason I didn't walk away was that I knew I would be criticised for such an action in Iceland and did not want to deal with the consequences of that. I feared the criticism that would ensue and the rumours that would be spread which would hurt me, not only in Iceland but abroad. People would say that we didn't really have the money, that the sale of Bravo to Heineken hadn't been the great deal it truly was, and so on. But my father was confident that it would all end well. I said to him: 'Why are you so confident? I have a very bad feeling about this.' But he just replied, in the most typical Icelandic way: '*Thetta reddast*,' meaning that it would all work out fine somehow in the end. It did not help that the media were concentrating on the personalities rather than the privatisation. The story became about my father redeeming himself by becoming Landsbanki chairman and a major shareholder. It was a great story about a once-famous Icelandic family making a grand return, but the attention that we received made me uneasy. On the day the deal was completed I was weary and apprehensive. 'Be careful with all the publicity,' I said to my father. 'Good publicity is often followed by bad. Something could go spectacularly wrong and this is a small society. People patting you on the back now will be the same ones who spit at your back later.'

After the Landsbanki and Pharmaco deals went through, I was far from comfortable with my new status as Iceland's best-known businessman. I didn't have many mentors or people to bounce things off. My father was my confidant but he had become more like a personal friend, and just like me had no experience at this level. I had no older peer who had done deals of this size and could give me advice. All this made the Landsbanki privatisation feel like the riskiest deal I had ever done. I did not feel safe. I worried that I would not be accepted in Iceland, having dipped in and out of the society

My father and I were regularly featured in the Icelandic media
during the boom years, the targets of both praise and envy. We got
our share of caricatures too. (Cartoon by Halldór Baldursson)

I grew up in. That is something I had never fretted about in
Russia, Bulgaria or anywhere else I had made money, but in
Iceland I felt especially vulnerable.

I still maintain that the Bunadarbanki privatisation put an
enormous strain on Iceland's economy because it meant that
Kaupthing, which was until then Iceland's smallest bank, had
to grow rapidly to boost its share price so that the $150 million

raised to pay for Bunadarbanki could be repaid in three years. We had come up with money to privatise what was one of the largest but most old-fashioned banks at the time and thought we would have one or two years to sort it out and modernise it before the other state bank was privatised. But what happened elsewhere in Iceland as a result of this double privatisation rather blew us away. This ushered in an incredible boom period in the Icelandic economy, never seen before.

The Landsbanki takeover began with spectacular success. I had expected to double or triple my money in four years but it went up tenfold. I viewed it as an investment in Iceland's infrastructure that carried some reputational risk but no financial risk. There would always be someone in Iceland who would want to buy the bank back from me. In 1998, when I was in Russia, I witnessed a crash much like the one in Iceland in 2008. But, of course, I expected things to blow up when I invested in Russia and Bulgaria. Iceland had an AAA credit rating. It was supposed to be safe. Kristin probably had much more of a sense of the danger than I did. She said to me: 'Thor, you're a risky investor. What if everything goes wrong and you lose everything, like both our fathers did? What's going to happen to us then? Do you have some money put aside? Do we have anything for a rainy day?' I said to her: 'Just look at the bank shares. That's an asset that's never going to go away. The Bulgarian investments and the other eastern Europe telecoms investments are subject to huge political instability. But the Icelandic bank will be okay.' I honestly believed Landsbanki was my least risky asset. As I should have realised at the time, Landsbanki's rocketing share-price rise was a symptom of Iceland's tiny financial system becoming overheated and overstretched as the economy boomed, growing by 30 per cent from 2003 to 2006.

The bubble had started following the crash in Iceland that

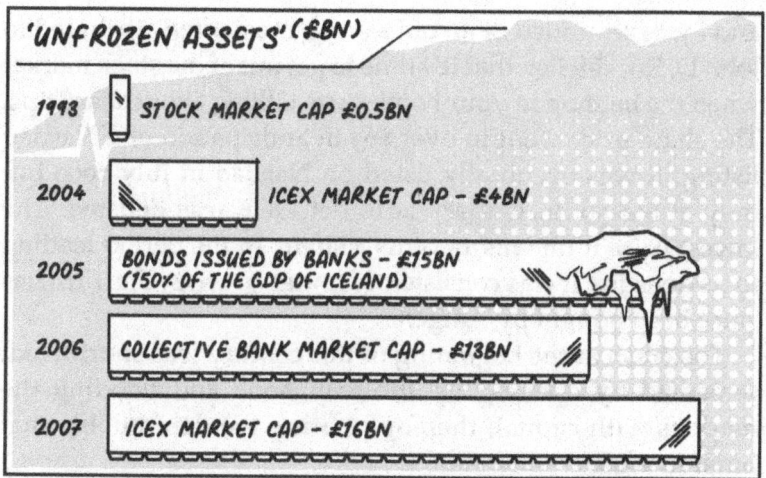

'UNFROZEN ASSETS' (£BN)

1993	STOCK MARKET CAP £0.5BN
2004	ICEX MARKET CAP – £4BN
2005	BONDS ISSUED BY BANKS – £15BN (150% OF THE GDP OF ICELAND)
2006	COLLECTIVE BANK MARKET CAP – £13BN
2007	ICEX MARKET CAP – £16BN

A bubble waiting to burst: Iceland's financial
growth from 1993 to 2005 was exponential.

coincided with the dotcom collapse of 2001. That resulted in
Iceland's biggest-ever collapse of a building contractor and
the bankruptcy of both its largest agricultural producer and
biggest media and newspaper publishing company. A record
number of homes were in negative equity or bankruptcy.
It had all been stoked up by stock market speculation such
as unregulated grey market dealings in shares in deCODE
Genetics, a Reykjavik company founded in 1996 to identify
human genes associated with common diseases using population studies. The firm rapidly went from an unlisted scientific research company to Iceland's fastest-growing business.
I bought shares in it at $7 each in 1997 and sold them in 1999
for $35. Shortly after the sale, I was sitting in a taxi when the
driver told me what a great opportunity was to be found in
deCODE shares, and that everyone who could was getting
in on the action. There was a gold-rush feel to his comment

and I was reminded of an old saying, most often attributed to John D. Rockefeller, that it's time to get out of the stock market when the bellhop in your hotel starts talking about share tips. The share price went to over $65 in anticipation of a Nasdaq listing. It was eventually listed on Nasdaq in July 2000 but only at $28.50. In January 2010 deCODE was delisted. The lowest price it hit was 15 cents a share. In the period leading to its delisting it was consistently under 50 cents. The firm has since been bought by Amgen.

The crash at the beginning of this century was short-lived, remedied by opening up the loan book and flooding the markets with capital, thereby creating the debt bubble that burst in 2008.

The cast of players in Iceland's business scene at the time of my return fell into three camps: the operations of Baugur and its chairman Jon Asgeir Johannesson; the growing empire of Kaupthing; and my own grouping, with its investments in Landsbanki, Actavis and Straumur (see later in this chapter). Baugur had 60 per cent of the retail business in Iceland. It also owned the biggest newspaper, TV channel and most of the magazines. It was a conglomerate with access to cheap capital, amassing assets but never selling and cashing in. I had little to do with Johannesson, who seemed to me to have an insatiable appetite to buy everything but never sell anything. I could not connect with him or understand where he was coming from, and so I was always on guard dealing with him. We had a couple of meetings but I could never find a way to work with him. To me, there always seemed to be a lot of hot air surrounding him and his activities.

I first came across Kaupthing in 2000 when we hired them to advise us on the deal I did with Deutsche Bank to reverse Balkanpharma into Pharmaco. Kaupthing was led by chief executive Sigurdur Einarsson and deputy CEO Hreidar Mar

Sigurdsson in Iceland and by CEO Armann Thorvaldsson in the UK. They did not know anyone in the City of London until I hooked them up with Deutsche Bank, which gave them experience that they lacked and opened a lot of doors. Thorvaldsson admits in his book *Frozen Assets* that after that Kaupthing borrowed ideas and templates from Deutsche Bank, copying them for Kaupthing's own transactions. Thorvaldsson was the person at Kaupthing I had the most respect for; he was smart and had good people and communication skills. I never perceived him to be in the innermost circle of the owner and management group, which was very tight, living and partying together in London. I didn't have much time for the others. In the middle of 2008, in the subprime crisis, Sigurdsson came out of an investor conference and said Kaupthing was very strong and had no subprime exposure. After the crash, it emerged that this was blatantly not true.

*

My return to Iceland was laced with historical irony.

The shipping company Eimskip had a dire influence on my father's life, as well as my great-grandfather's. Eimskip was led by a small group of men who kept control of the company with a minority of shares. Eimskip stock had been inherited through the generations and large amounts had been spread among many. An active stock market did not exist in Iceland until the end of the 20th century. The only place to sell Eimskip stock was at the company's headquarters, where it was bought at nominal value by its managers, enabling them to increase their share little by little. The key to their control was the 12 per cent held by the University of Iceland fund, which had been formed with the Eimskip stock of Icelandic settlers in Canada who wanted to give something back to their homeland. But the university did not benefit from this gift. The fund was run by Eimskip managers, and its vote was the backbone of their control of the company. After my father and I took over the helm of Eimskip in 2003, we made sure that the intentions of the settlers were followed and gave control of the interest to the university. We then helped the university to sell the holding for cash. The fund has since financed new buildings and provided grants for graduate research students.

Let's take a step back in order to understand the importance of Eimskip. In 1985 Eimskip had bought rival shipping company Hafskip, which my father had run and which was ruined by a disastrous foray into the US market – though my father remains convinced that the connection between the Eimskip leadership and politicians, public administrators and financiers helped engineer Hafskip's downfall in Eimskip's best interests. In the end, Eimskip bought the assets of the bankrupt company for pennies in a secret deal one week before Hafskip was put into administration, and used them to take over Hafskip's business connections.

This was at the start of a great upturn in Eimskip's fortunes. Icelandic companies had always had limited access to loan capital. For most of the modern era, companies' loans were rationed according to their goodwill with the political parties, which ran the banks. It was only the state treasury, state power company and the largest state-owned banks that could seek loans abroad. SIS, a coalition of Icelandic trade co-operatives at the core of the Progressive Party's power and by far the country's largest company, was the only privately owned entity that could take a foreign loan without intermediaries. Foreign banks considered the Icelandic market too small to be worth the time and effort to evaluate its potential and risks. Therefore they gave loans only to the state, state-owned companies and SIS, which they considered too big and important to Iceland to be allowed to go bankrupt. SIS, crippled by debt, went all but bankrupt in 1992. Landsbanki, then a state-owned bank, took over all its assets and debt, gradually winding the company down thereafter. SIS's operations had become disparate and its size and power had effectively turned the individual co-operatives, which were supposedly the owners of SIS, into subsidiaries. When SIS finally buckled under the exorbitant debt, many of the co-operatives went down with it.

The consequences of the SIS de facto bankruptcy were not as severe as many anticipated. Nobody missed a business that for years had not made a profit. Better-run, more modestly envisioned companies that served their customers better because of it filled the gap left by SIS. Also instrumental in softening the blow and preserving Iceland's creditworthiness was the fact that Landsbanki took over SIS's most valuable assets, sold them and settled debts with foreign banks.

With SIS out of the way, the biggest remaining companies had an opportunity to seek foreign loans directly. Eimskip was then the biggest publicly traded company and jumped at the chance to become the conglomerate that SIS had been. In the last decade and a half of the 20th century, Eimskip had changed from a shipping to a holding company, owning or running a consortium of transport companies operating on land and sea and in the air. They and their biggest allies were promptly nicknamed the Octopus, as their tentacles seemed to reach every part of the business environment. When Iceland's parliament, the Althing, authorised hypothecation of fishing quotas early in the 1990s, Eimskip's easy access to foreign credit gave it a head start in the race for the fishing quota. Within a short time Eimskip was one of the largest fishing-quota owners in Iceland.

The growth of Eimskip frightened some members of the Independence Party, however. They feared a shift in power, even a re-centring of it away from politics and towards the business sector. They wanted to guard the colonial power structure where the state and politics hold all the aces. This is why *Morgunbladid*, the Independence Party's newspaper and the largest in Iceland at the time, began to harass Eimskip towards the end of the century, particularly on fishing.

The story of Eimskip shows how the establishment wanted to run its companies: the way they had always been run. The CEO of Eimskip had a private elevator up to his office. Eimskip treated its management and biggest customers to lavish salmon-fishing trips, on which white-gloved waiters in tailcoats brought them champagne and canapés by the river. It was degenerate and snobbish. This was the old elite, the men who cared first and foremost about wielding their own personal power.

When my father and I later became influential in Icelandic business, we led a takeover of Eimskip and I took over as chairman, a role my great-grandfather had sought when the company was founded. I immediately set about breaking the company up. The investment arm of the company merged with what later became Straumur Investment Bank, where I was chairman. Eimskip's share of the listed Icelandair was sold. The fishing business was also sold to people with experience in the field. Other assets went elsewhere. Most of these companies did not fare well under new ownership.

The shipping company was sold to an airline and logistics group called Atlanta, in which our old partner Magnus Thorsteinsson was one of the biggest shareholders. It seemed like a new beginning, with more transparency, a greater number of players and a new generation in charge. That sounded good to Iceland's business community and media. However, this was a precursor to the overdrive that Iceland's business culture was entering, with disastrous consequences.

Another caricature of me, here as Samson from the Old
Testament. The tiny politician on the right rages as I tear down
the establishment, brandishing scissors to cut off my hair and
deprive me of my strength. (Cartoon by Halldór Baldursson)

People don't realise how sick and stale Eimskip had become.
But taking part in chopping off the Octopus's tentacles guaranteed me very powerful enemies further down the road.

How do I analyse the way I thought and acted at the time
leading to the crash? I have to admit that I was to a significant
extent driven by personal competitiveness and rivalry. Most

of the key players were born within a few years of each other, in the capital city, and attended the same schools. The CEOs of the three big banks were even old rivals from participating in student politics at the University of Iceland. We were all aware of each other and were being measured side by side. It was bound to get personal and once it does you are always in trouble. I enjoyed seeing myself on the front page of *Forbes* and liked being in its list of billionaires. I had wanted to become wealthy and independent of others and to make a name for myself outside the clannish little world of Icelanders. I wanted to outdo my peers. But from my first appearance in the *Forbes* list, I put pressure on myself to find my next trick, even though I was the only one of my Icelandic peer group to make it on to the list. I got to about 300th richest in the world and said to myself: 'Alright. I'll be higher in next year's list and higher still the year after that.' That's the problem once you have arrived; you carry on competing but you are essentially competing only with yourself. I also started looking in the rear-view mirror and thinking: 'Is any Icelander coming up behind me?' It was a way of motivating myself, of keeping ahead of the pack. They say that the first wave carries you out the farthest. It means that you have to ride the momentum and get as far out as you can on the strength of the waves or trends of the time. I wanted this tide of free-flowing capital to carry me out as far as possible.

I had long had a fascination with these lists. The first one I read was in 1988 when I was going to California and picked up a magazine in the airport lounge with an article that listed Iceland's richest people. No. 1 was a self-made man who, like Sam Walton in the US, had made his money through supermarkets. In second place was a meat-processing baron and third was a wholesaling and credit king who had become an avid art collector.

I think now that I was still trying to prove a point to myself when I got the validation from *Forbes* that I was Iceland's first billionaire. 'That's right,' I said to myself. 'You're an achiever. You've achieved more than anyone in this respect from your country.' Then I began telling myself that I was very different from my Icelandic peer group and the *Forbes* ranking was validation of that. I guess some arrogance was creeping in along the way. Pushing the ranking higher would further distinguish me from the others. I suppose it was a good motivator in a sense, but it also brought out my vanity, which is dangerous. I failed to see that. I started to be noticed after Pharmaco went public, and after I sold the brewery in 2002 I began to get huge press attention. I went on to pick up pretty much every business award in Iceland.

The most dangerous time in business is when you're officially declared a success.

6

THE VERY PUBLIC MELTDOWN OF GOD'S FROZEN PEOPLE 2008-2009

Searching for a destiny that's mine
There's another place another time
Touching many hearts along the way, yeah
Hoping that I'll never have to say
It's just an illusion, illusion, illusion
Follow your emotions anywhere
Is it really magic in the air?

Imagination, 'Just An Illusion'

'There's no one on the island telling them they're not good enough, so they just go ahead and sing and paint and write,' states writer Eric Weiner in his book *The Geography of Bliss: One Grump's Search for the Happiest Places in the World*. It had also been like this in Iceland's financial boom.

In taking advantage of cheap and plentiful money, I and others in Iceland had been asking for trouble, though we had never contemplated the scale of the disaster to come. On 6 October 2008, I could only watch on television as the prime minister, Geir Haarde, announced that, with its three biggest banks collapsing and the krona in freefall, he was placing Iceland in emergency measures. It was a moment of déjà vu – I had heard the same speech by another prime minister on another Monday in another country, Russia, ten years before. Just 24 hours earlier, Landsbanki had put a proposal to the government that would have shored up the bank's finances, with the help of a £200 million government loan. The proposal was rejected and the company was put into receivership. It was too much to take in.

The financial collapse of the country that I was born and brought up in and is still my homeland has troubled me for years, and that fateful weekend of 5–6 October 2008 when the economy imploded remains the most bizarre set of events I have ever encountered. In hindsight, it was a baptism of fire that simply made me grow up faster to become stronger and hopefully wiser. Glitnir, the former Islandsbanki, with Baugur's companies as its largest shareholders, was the first bank to go. In September, its managers had turned to the Central Bank of Iceland for assistance, as Glitnir couldn't meet its obligations. The Central Bank decided to nationalise the bank, however, by acquiring a 75 per cent stake for €600 million rather than assisting it. This badly-thought-out action led to a credit rating downgrade on both sovereign debt and the debt of all Icelandic banks, which led to even more liquidity problems. After this there seemed to be no turning back, and Glitnir dragged the whole system down. The nationalisation actually never went through, as Glitnir was placed in receivership by the FME or Fjarmalaeftirlit, Iceland's financial services authority, a week later.

I have given only one interview with the specific aim of explaining my view of what happened in the crash, and perhaps that was one interview too many. I may regret devoting this chapter to the subject too, because it is in my nature to look forward, not back. I certainly have no wish to enter the blame game that is still being played over who was responsible and who said what, when and why, because in disasters of this magnitude you can't point a finger at one person. And the economic crisis was a global crisis, even though some Icelanders still seem to see it as an Icelandic phenomenon. Though I lived in Iceland until I was 18, I have always seen myself as an outsider; and this deepened and intensified during my ten years in Russia and my later London-based forays into eastern Europe. I never returned physically to Iceland as a permanent base, but I did come back financially, and maybe that was my biggest mistake. I certainly have no plans to re-root myself in my homeland, although I am managing my responsibilities there carefully.

So why revisit the misery of the collapse of all three of Iceland's major commercial banks, brought to their knees by difficulties in financing their short-term debt and a run on deposits in the UK? With the nation's consequential pain all too tangible, why look back when I want only to study the road ahead? And why get involved in Icelandic controversies again when I have already learned – from the one interview I gave in 2008 – that telling my side of the story only invites more questions and heavier criticism?

I sought counsel on this issue at the time and received the wise advice that speaking up would only make matters worse, so I kept quiet for a couple of years. I speak now mainly because I care passionately, not about rescuing my own reputation, which is what it is, but about the truth being told and answers being given. There are uncomfortable facts to be faced, along with damaging false allegations and an untrue narrative that have persisted for more than a decade and need countering. However, this chapter is not so much a delayed attempt at self-justification as a recognition that nobody in

Iceland can avoid this period of history for ever. It's time to do the accounting and reveal the real narrative, based on facts, not speculation.

Relative to the size of its economy, Iceland's banking collapse is the largest suffered by any country in economic history. At the end of the second quarter of 2008, Iceland's external debt was €50 billion; its GDP in 2007 was just €8.5 billion. Clearly the government had borrowed far too much on the international markets. The krona fell precipitously in value, foreign currency transactions were heavily restricted for many years afterwards, and the market capitalisation of the Iceland Stock Exchange tumbled by more than 90 per cent. The full financial cost of the crisis is at least three quarters of the nation's entire GDP at the time, and the economic costs were felt for years, as Iceland struggled with recession and austerity measures relating to the deficit in the immediate period after the crash.

I feel strongly that some myths about Iceland's financial collapse need to be debunked. The first is that it was caused solely by the behaviour of its banks. This was an early reaction fuelled by anger about the scale of the losses but, as tempers have cooled, there has been more rational analysis. In a lecture at the University in Iceland in September 2011, Robert Aliber, a former professor of economics at Chicago University, said that the economic crash in Iceland can largely be traced to fractures in the international financial system, as can the crisis that hit the West at full force in autumn 2008. Aliber does not absolve the banks or their supervisors from responsibility, but his view is that the distorting impact of a relatively sudden, massive flow of capital into such a small economy was a fundamental cause of the crisis. And because Iceland was connected to the international financial system, it could not be stemmed. My belief is that Iceland's meltdown was inevitable given the government's economic policy and the Central Bank's exchange rate policy, though of course I accept that the banks carry some responsibility for it by growing too big too fast.

A second myth is that the collapse of Iceland's banks has had a disproportionately severe effect on the nation's householders. The evidence suggests that instead Iceland's foreign creditors took the heaviest hits when the banks crashed. Iceland's households were certainly hurt – there is no doubt about that. But households were damaged by the devaluation of the currency and by the state of the country's indebtedness, not by the collapse of the banks per se. Iceland's banks have become the fall guys for much greater systemic faults in the national and international system, but this is principally because it suits both those on the left, because it confirms their view of capitalism and opened their way into government, and those on the right, who have wanted to distract attention from their own failed economic policy.

There has also been a failure to grasp the effect of carry trading in the run-up to the crisis. In a free international system, capital moves from countries with low interest rates to those where rates are higher. Loosening restraints on currency trading obviously has the effect of increasing it. After the turn of the century Iceland started to attract serious interest from investment funds specialising in such carry trading. Capital flowed into Iceland, the currency strengthened, inflation decreased, a false picture of well-being emerged, and the government and the business community briefly basked in reflected glory.

However, when capital flows into a country because it pays the highest interest, it has to find people to lend that money to at a higher rate of interest. This need leads to greater risks being taken as to whom and for what money is lent. At first this is not obvious because the flow of capital strengthens

ICELAND'S CURRENCY CRISIS
2008 – ISK PER 1 USD

the currency and the weakness of the system is hidden. The strengthening currency compensates for the low interest margin. In Iceland in the years leading up to the crash, the perceived solution was to chase second-rate business opportunities abroad, financing these with too much credit at high interest rates. The problem is that as the money keeps pouring in the value of the currency increases. If doubts creep in, the carry traders cease their business and the impact is reversed; the currency falls in value and the underlying weakness of businesses propped up by loans is exposed, and eventually the house of cards collapses.

*

The events of the fateful weekend in October 2008 when Iceland imploded were so extraordinary that anyone who now claims to have seen it all coming is either lying or guilty of Schadenfreude. Of course many people, myself included, had been cautious earlier on in the economic cycle about how long the boom could last. But in 2008 in Iceland there was a ridiculous complacency. The administration had been in power for 16 years and had been on an enormous spending spree. The state had ballooned, infrastructure spending had soared and there was a strange, irrational feeling that Iceland's time on the world stage had come. As Philipp Bagus and David Howden comment in *Deep Freeze: Iceland's Economic Collapse*:

> A nation with a population only slightly larger than Pittsburgh and a physical size smaller than Kentucky erected a banking system whose total assets were ten times the size of the country's GDP. The prices of housing and stocks soared and so did Iceland's wealth. The traditional fishing-based economy was altered dramatically. Financial engineering became the preferred career path of ambitious youth, instead of the traditional nature resource management. People from all walks of life wanted to work in the banking industry. Young children, when asked what they wanted to grow up to be, innocently and unhesitatingly answered: 'Bankers'.

Bagus and Howden may be exaggerating when they add that young men on the streets of Reykjavik were as likely to know the Black–Scholes derivative formula as the yields of the day's salmon catch, but they reflect the mood of the boom. Everyone seemed to be buying shares, leveraging up and not giving much thought to the potential consequences. The few prophets of doom who existed were shot down or marginalised. In the post-traumatic shock that followed the crash the focus changed, and there was a witch hunt for crooks and villains. During the boom time, however, people were trading in the markets with their eyes open, so I contend that they should be accountable for their actions and face up to the consequences. As the biggest individual financial loser from Iceland's meltdown I have done so, and I believe that all those who let themselves get carried away must accept responsibility for their actions too. They seemed to think that the boom would last for ever. But who can blame them? There was this enormous bubble based on escalating asset prices and leveraged funding. It was unsustainable and it is about time that Icelanders admitted it, rather than continually looking for others to blame. Of course, I was in that same bubble myself. Hulda Thorisdottir, a psychologist, and Karen Erla Karolinudottir of the University of Iceland published a paper in February 2014 examining the phenomena of motivated reasoning and confirmation bias in the years before the crisis. They explained:

> The Icelandic people [have] had to grapple with *the realisation that in many ways the prosperity of years past had been an illusion* based on the banks' non-viable business model of relying on the continuous flow of inexpensive credit and very risky investments.

A member of the government said that I had a 'social and moral duty' to bring my money back to Iceland, while opposition parties talked excitedly about the possibility of expropriation. I understand the anger. I know what it is like to lose money, but defining moral responsibility is a personal decision and it is always clouded by what is possible. At the time of the crash, my companies were investing billions of krona in a new telephone network that cut bills across Iceland. I was investing in a data centre in Iceland funded by foreign co-investors and had just put 400 billion krona into Iceland's stock market to take Actavis private. Sure, I had assets outside Iceland, but how liquid did anyone expect these to be? People who made such comments had not thought through the issues. At the same time, I was in very delicate discussions with the banks, and comments like these almost blew up the negotiations. The winding-up boards of the Icelandic banks were very sensitive about being possibly seen as lenient toward me.

Part of the reason is that they banded me with the 'Viking raiders' who had invested in foreign assets with cheap credit from Icelandic banks. The term, which was widely used in an amusing way by the media before the crash, became one of denigration after it, a convenient catch-all phrase for targeting everyone's anger.

I refuse to be classed alongside such operators. I have lived abroad for 26 years, more than half my life. I don't have Icelandic funds to invest abroad. I earned my capital abroad and made the mistake of ploughing much of it back into Iceland. Others started businesses in Iceland and leveraged their local assets to acquire businesses abroad. I did things the other way around, bringing money into the country. When I sold my companies in Russia, Bulgaria and the Czech Republic, I was paid in cash, not in paper, and that cash paid for Actavis and was pumped into Iceland's financial system. I did not sell a single share in Landsbanki, Actavis or Straumur, the investment bank of which I was chairman.

I do not deny that many of my companies, along with others in Iceland, were highly leveraged. The 3,300-page Special Investigation Commission (SIC) report into the crash for Iceland's parliament put it on public record that Landsbanki's exposure to companies I invested in increased by 58 per cent to €973 million in the 19 months to October 2008. The commission also raised questions about Actavis and Landsbanki's currency loan exposure to companies I invested in, but these questions were misleading. Some of the harshest criticism was in the UK media. An article in the *Observer* in August 2011, by an Icelandic journalist and a British colleague, made a number of allegations. Before it was printed, the newspaper sent me a list of statements, which I answered in full. Few of my answers made it into the paper.

Although the commission wrote at length about how the rules should have been structured or interpreted, that is not how they were at the time. I broke no rules, even though my worst detractors have certainly accused me of doing so. My activities in Icelandic quoted companies were well documented in company papers. I gave personal guarantees on top of other securities. After the crash, people realised that most of the bigger players had never given any personal guarantees at all. And I don't have any bankrupt companies apart from Samson, which was Landsbanki's holding company. I don't fear any probes because everything is above board and the information is readily available.

Perhaps not surprisingly much was made of my lifestyle: my former 'penthouse' Park Lane office, homes in Notting Hill and Buckinghamshire, and Challenger private jet in Farnborough; a 42-metre yacht called *Element*; my collection of luxury motorbikes; and an Aston Martin bearing my initials on the number plate. At the time of the article's publication I neither used nor operated the private jet or yacht, as they were sold after the crash. I still have the old Aston Martin and six motorbikes. Since the 2008 crisis, I have become accustomed to heavy public scrutiny of my private life.

The claims made in Iceland were much more hurtful, however. I was accused of having willingly and knowingly used Landsbanki to set up some kind of Ponzi scheme to enrich myself, without any concern for the well-being of my fellow countrymen. Then there was the allegation that the Samson holding company, owned by me, my father and Magnus Thor-steinsson, did not pay for our shares in Landsbanki. It seems that no matter how many times I have denied this, showing all the documents that prove me right, people still believe it.

The third accusation was that I had, along with my father and a handful of other businessmen, transferred huge amounts of money from Iceland in the days of the crash. It was a major news story and I was forced to take the TV station Stod 2 to court. When they realised that they could not back up their story, they retracted it, and the news editor resigned. But mud sticks and there may still be people who believe this. Any accusation that paints me as a ruthless and dishonest man hurts, but that is not to say I don't have regrets from the boom era. I have lots. I should have followed my intuition much more. Like everyone else I got sucked into the herd mentality, and I started to believe the boom would last. In 2006 I thought that what was happening was unsustainable. That's why I sold the assets in Bulgaria, EIBank and BTC. But I was proved wrong that year and the next. I started to think that maybe I was just out of touch with the new world. Maybe I didn't under-stand that this was truly an epoch in which different rules applied. My instincts were telling me there was just too much air in the system, too much blown-up equity, too many inter-related transactions and overblown asset values. I thought there would be a correction and I would have a strong enough balance sheet to cope, but I failed to see how international and correlated Iceland's financial transactions had become. I failed to see that everything would go down at the same time.

That is not altogether unreasonable: Landsbanki, Kaupthing and Glitnir rank in the world's top ten biggest banking bank-ruptcies, and when combined as one big Icelandic banking collapse would rank as the third-largest corporate collapse in history. Foreign banking institutions alone were said to have lost €30 billion in the crisis. And, at the time of the 2008 crash, I reckon I was the largest personal investor in Iceland's economy. In hindsight, I should have never put so much money at risk in Iceland.

So why did I do so? Part of it was my ego and need for recognition in an Icelandic comeback, but it was also laziness. It was just easier for me to operate in Iceland and I reckoned that, having built a strong financial base there, I could make my name in London and the international markets. People overseas were asking 'who is this guy?' whereas in Iceland doors opened much more easily and I went with the flow. My father had his dream job back in Iceland, asset prices there were continuing to spiral and my Icelandic assets pushed up my ranking in the billionaires list.

After the crash, the public mood in Iceland turned hostile. My house in Reykjavik was paint-bombed and pictures of me and Prime Minister Haarde with our birth and death dates were spray-painted on a wall outside the house, while my child and pregnant wife were alone inside. We also had a rock thrown through the window for good measure. We, the prime minister and I, were the two people Iceland blamed the most, it seemed. I was philosophical about it and got the damage painted over. But it alarmed Kristin and she didn't feel comfortable being alone in the house with a child. She got very upset when my car was covered in red paint, whereas I got irritated; it was nothing compared to what I had dealt with in Russia, where there was a real danger of physical harm. This was just some paint and cowardly acts carried out in the middle of the night.

The effect of the crash on my personal life was harder to ignore. Kristin had voiced her fears about Iceland, and being more risk-averse than me was shocked that bank shares had turned out to be the riskiest assets of all. She, like everyone else, was blown away by the speed of what happened at first, but then she became angry. 'I knew this would happen,' she would say. 'I knew you were doing everything too fast.' We argued a lot in 2009 when I was trying to deal with the fallout. She was irritated that I hadn't seen the collapse and she found it tough to deal with, especially when she read bad things about me in the media. I have always kept my work and private lives separate. But this was something extraordinary. Because of my work, her world was crumbling, and many of her best friends in the banking sector lost their jobs.

It also didn't help that, as the crash played out, Kristin was pregnant with our second child, who was born in March 2009 on the weekend that Straumur was taken over by the Central Bank of Iceland. I was in the maternity ward as she was giving birth, stepping out into the corridor to receive a call from the Straumur chief executive asking me to call an immediate board meeting. The plan was to ask for a moratorium on the coming Monday. It would have bought us the time to get the bank's affairs in order, as it was clearly not on the brink of bankruptcy but did have temporary problems with liquidity. The bank had already managed to get creditors to hold off while assets were being sold, so all it needed was time. It was in a prime position to lead the reconstruction of the Icelandic financial sector for two important reasons: its diversified income and asset base, with a very small percentage of both being in Iceland; and its experienced international team of bankers, who were on much better speaking terms with the international finance community which had been so badly burnt by the actions of government officials and the Icelandic bankers who had failed to come up with any contingency plans. Bankers from London to Frankfurt, who were essential in any reconstruction effort, were very sceptical of anything coming from the 'Icelanders' (hence a foreigner was put as the head of the central bank at that time as a countermeasure) but were more open to dialogue with seasoned international players.

The Straumur team was handling the situation carefully and confidently during this weekend, only to be taken by surprise when the FME suddenly called a meeting at 4 am on Monday, 9 March 2009. It transpired that the state had decided to use the emergency law passed six months earlier to take over the bank, although the law was designed not for this but to halt a run on banks by customers whose deposits were fully protected. Straumur had no ordinary deposit accounts, just a few with big professional institutions which could have been catered for in a moratorium. The central bank refused to help Straumur and it was obvious that the government – especially with a general election in prospect – was afraid of supporting any actions that could be interpreted as supporting the much-vilified man who had been labelled as one of those responsible for the crash. The government later claimed that this action had been necessary to safeguard the deposits of the Housing Financing Fund and some pension funds with the bank. The decision to take out one of the few remaining functioning banks was a hard blow to the staff and to the 25,000 shareholders who lost all chance of any recovery from a restructuring plan supported by all creditors of the bank.

That the takeover of Straumur enhanced the problems within the Icelandic financial system seemed to be a price the state was willing to pay, though within days it bailed out a handful of local savings and loans institutions in politically important constituencies with three times the amount Straumur had asked for, all of which was lost within a year or two. By the start of business on the Monday, the FME had managed to thwart an attempt to get a judge to grant a moratorium and had taken control of the bank. They then put in a board of Icelanders inexperienced in running a company, let alone a substantial international financial institution, who then set about selling the bank's foreign assets at fire-sale prices, disregarding the fact that signs of recovery were now visible and IMF and other international aid had been secured.

When I wanted to radically change Straumur to de-risk it and bring in professional management from abroad, I got into a major debate with two fellow shareholders and board members who in different ways were products of the kind of false thinking prevalent in Iceland at the time. One of them had an old Icelandic money background and the other had inherited a fishing business. Thordur Mar Johannesson, Straumur's CEO, had advised both of them to leverage up their family companies through the bank. To them, he was incredibly smart but they didn't have a clue about what they were doing. When I said: 'We have got to change management,' they said: 'Why? This guy is brilliant.' I replied: 'He's brilliant now but the amount of risk we have in the company by always betting on local bank shares rising is crazy. We could go pop just like that.' He had built up a large position in Glitnir, managed to sell it profitably and now wanted to do the same again with Kaupthing shares. It was a one trick show and lacked any vision to build a diversified business. They didn't see the danger signs. They had maybe €100 million to their name but it was all done through Johannesson, who had leveraged them up and put them into various businesses and instruments. They were sky high on monopoly money and just wanted to take more and more turns. They had no sense that this was not a game.

I narrowly won the battle at a shareholder meeting and fired Johannesson, and the two other board members quit and sold their shares. Together this trio formed an investment company called Gnupur, which invested in Kaupthing shares. Gnupur was a mini-cosmos of sorts for business life in Iceland at that time. It had old money, fishing-quota money and a young chief executive. It could seemingly do no wrong, but it became the first investment company to go bust at the beginning of Iceland's financial meltdown. It was the collapse of Gnupur after only one year of operations that prompted a London-based Merrill Lynch analyst to forecast that something major was about to go wrong in Iceland. His view was that if a sizeable investment company could not carry on, nor could Iceland carry on in the same way for much longer. I had sensed that, but was in too deep to be able to get out in time. It was a highly stressful time. That Straumur weekend was tough. But that little boy born on that fateful weekend had perfect timing and has been a blessing for us.

Kristin and I, together with our families, were all experiencing the same emotions as everyone else in Iceland. Who was to blame? It is clear to me now that what happened in 2008 was the result of a severe systemic fault, not only in Iceland, but on a global scale. One of the main follies in the aftermath has been trying to pin all the blame on individuals. Great crashes are usually caused by systemic faults. That's the received wisdom on the 1929 crash and subsequent Great Depression, which have been studied more than any other economic anomaly of recent times. There is no mention of a cast of villains being involved in that. Certainly, with a systemic fault, there are people who play bigger or smaller roles, but in Iceland in 2008 there was no great plot. Things just got out of hand.

The Icelandic businessmen were kings, and President Olafur Grimsson was the cheerleader. He went too far, like so many in those crazy years, even hinting at the genetic superiority of the Icelandic nation. It was ludicrous. But for all the ups and downs of his actions, I have to compliment him in that it was his work that saved Iceland from the crazy hangover of that incompetent weekend in October 2008. I believe he was kept out of the loop then, but thank goodness he used his power to step in later and take control of a chaotic situation. In the international feud that arose over Icesave, Landsbanki's online savings accounts, which was turned by public hysteria from a molehill into a mountain, he played it cool, using logic and reasoning to bring it to the right forum: the European Free Trade Association (EFTA) court in Luxembourg. He did this by twice vetoing a parliamentary bill, and in subsequent referenda the nation upheld the veto. His actions saved not only billions for the treasury but also Iceland's national pride and standing in the international community. Of course he took a risk, but he is a man after my own heart – he analysed the risks before he bet, and his bet paid off.

*

I think I will always regard what happened in October 2008 as by far the biggest betrayal of my life. Instead of saving Landsbanki, the government was somehow falsely convinced by Kaupthing that it was the bank most able to weather the storm. The evidence supports my belief that, in time, our position will be vindicated.

In hindsight, the government was duped into supporting the weakest bank, resulting in it having nothing left to support the strongest bank at the critical point in the crisis. It spent €600 million on Glitnir and €500 million on Kaupthing, but zero on Landsbanki, as it had basically run out of cash by then. Looking back now, this seems extraordinary, but then again – would handling it differently have changed the outcome? Was the Icelandic banking experiment, starting with the government's privatisation programme, always doomed to fail, since the Central Bank of Iceland could in reality never support the scale and unbridled international growth that the banks were allowed in the run-up to the crash? The implicit support of the tiny Icelandic central bank was always going to be too flimsy a foundation for the three main commercial banks to rely on.

What infuriates me is not that my investment was wiped out because the government made no effort to save Landsbanki, but that it could have contained the problem that later arose with the bank's Icesave savings account. I would probably still have lost my money if the government had provided the loan, but the fallout for the nation would have been greatly diminished and the prejudice and recriminations that followed would have been much less. Because I was associated with it in people's minds, even though I was never at the helm of Landsbanki and never took any decisions there whatsoever, the fact that all the TV cameras saw me going in and out of government meetings on that crash weekend cements me to its nexus. I could have stayed in London instead of flying to Reykjavik to try to help, after being asked by three prominent bankers and politicians. But it was a desperate call for all hands on deck, for everyone to try their best – regardless of position. I simply had to give it everything I could. Not to do that would have been cowardly.

My initial reaction to my critics was to ignore them and keep a low profile. I had learned in Russia that taking that approach was not only common sense but also essential for survival. Maybe between my Russian exit and the disaster of 2008 I had become overconfident, even arrogant. It was perhaps like someone who hasn't had a drop of alcohol for ten years and then goes on a bender. You go overboard and make a spectacle of yourself. When you become rich, there's an overwhelming feeling that you have to use it somehow. This is why people buy ridiculously expensive watches. There's no reason to do it. Why is it that the same people who look at a balance sheet and quibble over the smallest thing then go out to an expensive restaurant and pay way over the odds? They don't care. But when their world turns topsy-turvy they face the cold reality and there is the shock of having to come to terms with their circumstances. When I became one of the most unpopular men in Iceland, it was a nightmare because I found myself in the very public spotlight that I had never sought. It was overwhelming.

I felt it all the more because in Iceland's false boom years, my father, Magnus and I were the only entrepreneurs who actually brought significant amounts of cash into the country. We were wealthy when we went into business in Iceland. We put our money to work, became wealthier and then got the greatest financial repercussions. I lost almost everything. My father went bankrupt and lost everything for the second time and Magnus also went bankrupt, while other players in Iceland, including shareholders in Kaupthing and Glitnir who had borrowed against stock to become fantastically rich, were richer after the 2008 crash than when they started. I think that is grossly unfair. How is it that out of the three big banking groups, only three people have been declared individually bankrupt and that my father and Magnus were two of them? The reason is that we gave personal guarantees whereas others did not.

Of course, a lot of people in Iceland are still being investigated. Some had their assets frozen and there were a lot of court cases. My father took all this very hard. He was in the same position as a large slice of the Icelandic population, but he had done nothing wrong and was never charged with anything. Believe me, they would have charged him if they could, having established the Office of the Special Prosecutor, with 130 people at work for six years going over every trans-action, deal and decision. He took his chances with the rest and fell with them. He got caught out by the bubble. As for me, I believe I have been vindicated, though the reputational damage is done.

*

What have I learned? That legacy problems always come back to haunt you; to always deal with things systematically; and to always try to tie up loose ends. There is another lesson too, which comes as much from my advancing years as from my financial meltdown. As an instinctive entrepreneur, I am always driving away at things. When they go right, people tell me I'm a visionary, but that doesn't always compensate for the effort, the stress and the times when disaster strikes. As I get older, I'm finding that I'm not always up for it. I had enormous hunger in my youth; I don't need to be so hungry now. And I am changing my attitude to risk. As a young man, I used to fret that people did not see the wood for the trees. I find myself in that position now. When I look at opportunities, I see risks everywhere. Am I wiser or just more risk-averse because I have been burnt? It's a natural reflex. Will it impair my entrepreneurial abilities in the future? I think it probably will. Actually, I would say that this experience will comple-ment my abilities with very valuable experience; the kind that you can only learn the hard way. Misfortune breeds persever-ance, and I have been through a great deal of misfortune, so I would basically say that I am now better off than before. It's a hard fact for me to admit, but it is undeniable reality.

I'm not looking for the next rocket. I'm looking for a much more moderate future. I don't feel the need to prove myself any more and I have a family to think of, so I'm looking to do what a classic family man does: to preserve wealth for me and my family and then work out how to give the rest away because I think excessive inherited wealth can be a curse on future generations. When you're young, you're terrified of life generally, but you still take risks that you wouldn't countenance when you're older because by then you know a lot more about the dangers. Life becomes about limiting the downside, which also hinders the upside.

So what do I do about the knives in the back? Do I just ignore them? Can I extract them? A wiser person would say don't get yourself in a position where people can take a shot at you. Don't get in harm's way. But the only way to ensure that you'll never be hit by a car is never to cross a road. That's not an option, so you have to find a balance, but you can avoid much of the flak by simply not being there. You can't avoid the knives in the back but you can make it further for people to throw them. London was a shelter for me. That's what saved me when I was vilified. My father didn't bear the brunt of the criticism; that was reserved for me. But he was living in Iceland and I wasn't. He told me a story about one of the low points in the aftermath of the crash that illustrated what he was dealing with. He was out walking his dog on a sunny day and as he approached a man with his two small daughters on their bikes they stopped and the father said: 'You see that man, he's one of the men who have destroyed our country.' He spat at my father's feet and continued on his way. That was the sort of thing he had to deal with. I've not been into bars in Iceland much since the crash. I was on my guard for the first few years and still am. It's hard to break the habit once you have been publicly vilified. Sometimes I still have a sense of unease, but it's mostly confusion and old habits. The level of online abuse and prejudice in the years after the crash is hard to ignore. However, things in

Iceland have moved on so much that two generations of Icelanders do not really remember this time at all. It seems like a different country and I feel perfectly at home and at ease there. Iceland is a country of extremes where people are either loved or hated. I don't want to be loved or hated. I just want people to be indifferent.

It took a bit of effort to begin with. The first time I went to the gym in Reykjavik after the crash, Kristin was extremely worried. 'It's the biggest gym in town, a huge social venue. You'll get a lot of bother,' she warned me. 'No,' I replied. 'I'm doing this.' So I went there and was expecting a fist fight. I walked in and stepped on a running machine. It was crowded in there and someone I knew from a long time ago looked me in the eye and walked past. 'Here it is,' I said to myself. 'This is what it's going to be like.' But minutes later I got a tap on the back. 'It's you,' he said. 'I didn't recognise you.' We shook hands and the same thing kept happening. Others came by. 'Thor, where have you been?' they asked. Iceland's foreign minister was there – the political master of the restructuring encountering the outcast, the untouchable, the villain of the piece. But even politicians came over, shook my hand and said: 'How are things?'

Of course, in Iceland no one says much to your face. It is a small community, and rule number one in a small forest is that all the animals have to be friends. There's always the fox that breaks the rules, but most of the sniping and gossip goes on behind your back. Co-dependence is a hard-wired fact of life there.

That's not to say it was bliss before the crash. I was always frustrated that people didn't seem to appreciate how different I was from the other Icelandic entrepreneurs, how diversified my business was and how I injected capital into the economy instead of shipping it out. I felt I was being lumped in with people I shouldn't be. I was irritated that I didn't get recognition in my homeland. Looking back, I suppose all this was just vanity, the trickiest of all sins, so sly and manipulative that you can easily lose sight of your core values.

I may have decided at the age of 18 that I needed to be my own boss, but I have also learned that one's own ambition is the toughest boss of all. Maybe the target for me in the world following the crash is toning that ambition down to something real and manageable – though my sense of adventure and need for disruption will always keep me on my toes.

I have also been thinking more holistically about what has happened to me over this period. The biggest difference between 2006 and 2008 (and the two years that followed) is that, when I woke in the morning, I often asked myself: 'Where am I? In which country?' This says a lot about the pace of things. I was travelling so much. In the immediate aftermath of 2008, in contrast, I was waking up and asking: 'What day is this? Is it still yesterday, or is this a new day?' I felt like the lead character in *Groundhog Day*, waking up again and again on the same day. The main difference is the feeling of momentum. On the way up, I was on a journey. At the bottom, I seemed stuck in another place.

If it looks too good to be true, it ain't true.

7

HOW TO LOSE $4 BILLION IN TEN MONTHS 2008-2009

If you like to gamble, I tell you
I'm your man
You win some, lose some,
All the same to me
The pleasure is to play,
Makes no difference what you say

Motorhead, 'Ace of Spades'

What was different about the crash in 2008 that made it a
storm I couldn't ride? I had weathered the Russian currency
crash of 1998 and the dotcom collapse of 2001. My investments
were diversified, in banking, pharmaceuticals and telecoms,
and I was operating in much the same way as I usually did,
financially engineering ventures on the back of as much
leverage as I could muster with an eye for mergers, spin-offs
and other ways of creating value. After my Russian years, I
had tried in a haphazard way to be a kind of asset gatherer,
collecting interesting businesses while I could finance them
with the debt that banks were all too happy to provide. The

deals came fast and furiously, but as I was looking at assets in central Europe, a lot of new faces started to appear among potential buyers. Instead of other lone capitalist raiders like me and one or two native banks, some of private equity's biggest names, including the likes of KKR and Blackstone, were beginning to crop up. Auctions were getting crowded. Instead of four or five people bidding for an asset, there were now often as many as 14 or 15. It was becoming too competitive. Assets were going for the wrong prices and it was time to sell, rather than buy. So I began offloading businesses, selling the telecoms companies and the Bulgarian bank in 2007 for fantastic prices. We made a profit of €400 million alone on the sale of the Bulgarian telecoms assets to the equity arm of AIG, a US insurance group. And I started to look for a way out of the Icelandic assets.

With Actavis, in which I had close to a 40 per cent stake, I went in entirely the other direction. We had been trying to double its size by bidding for Merck, a German pharmaceuticals manufacturer, and Croatia's Pliva, but both were sold to US rivals. During that exercise I saw the amount of debt you could pile up on these companies and said to myself: 'Why don't I use these debts and increase my stake in what I have?' It was easier and involved less execution risk, so I talked to bankers and ended up doing a deal with Deutsche Bank to take Actavis private through a €5.3 billion buy-out. Looking back, its huge leverage, with debt representing some 80 per cent of the total, was a kind of totem for the times. There was no problem at all in raising the debt; everyone seemed to want to provide it. After all, Deutsche Bank had made a fivefold return the previous time it had helped me finance the company. The most famous investment banks in the world were screaming to be allowed into a deal that one year later would be generally deplored as a clear sign that prices had got way out of control and the bubble was about to burst. Deutsche Bank was the same. It desperately wanted this deal and didn't want anyone else in the picture. Any kind of perspective on money had been totally lost. It was a mad, mad era of financial folly at the very top of the market, but the deal sailed through without any hitches and brought an enormous influx of cash to Iceland.

People have said to me that the deal could have sunk Deutsche Bank. It was my deal – and I put my hand up clearly for it – but the multiples that it was pitched at now look nothing short of staggering. We put in 12 times leverage and 5 times equity, with the result that Europe's second-largest generic drugmaker was valued at 17 times its underlying EBITDA. Why did we value Actavis so highly? Well, it was the height of the stock market bubble and I was full of hubristic ambition. The company was growing strongly and I thought the buy-out was a great deal. Actavis was going from strength to strength so I would take it private, sell it in two to three years' time and make three times my investment. I thought I would end up making more than €2 billion on the deal – my best return ever. It all stacked up and the investment banks agreed. So many of them wanted to throw money at this deal: Citibank, Lehman Brothers and Royal Bank of Scotland were pleading to get in and lend money for it because it seemed such a no-brainer. In the end, we said no to all of them, however, because Deutsche Bank, the adviser on the deal, now wanted to handle the provision of the loan as well. We thought the bank would syndicate the loans, but as that would have meant giving away some of its underwriting fees, it decided to take all the debt onto its balance sheet. 'We'll make more money that way,' one of the bankers told me.

Just one year later, when we had a major quality problem at one of Actavis's factories, the maths did not look anywhere near as pretty. When you are producing beer and have a quality problem you can fix it fairly easily, but when a pharmaceutical company has a quality problem people can end up dying. Thank God that did not happen in our case, but the US Food and Drug Administration still stopped production at the plant. No one saw this coming and it was little short of disastrous, slicing away as much as one quarter of the company's US cash flow. It is rather like a middle-distance race. If you're leading the pack and fall down, by the time you've got up again the other competitors have got so far ahead that you'll never catch them up. And the more highly leveraged you are, the harder it is to get back in the race. However hard we tried we couldn't recover the ground we had lost. And this wasn't our only problem, as it turned out the company was weaker than we had been led to believe.

I needed to put more money into the business, by far one of the biggest companies in Iceland, so that it wouldn't be taken over by Deutsche Bank. We had assets enough, and were working on selling them, but for the time being we had liquidity problems, so I borrowed €150 million from Landsbanki in March 2008 to rescue Actavis and fund salaries. This is what I was most criticised for in Iceland after the crash. 'How could you borrow this in September 2008?' my detractors cried. But I had started the process in March, borrowing in monthly instalments, with the last and largest payment coming in September. I gave a personal guarantee against the borrowings and, most importantly, that guarantee involved me pledging my holdings in Play, the Polish telecoms company, which was my most valuable and debt-free asset. Even so, the loan proved insufficient to get Actavis back on track and we were still busy scuttling around when the financial crash struck.

By 2009, Deutsche Bank was getting seriously concerned.

'Look, we've taken a large risk here and so have you,' they told me. 'The money you've put up is not enough and we need to deal with this.' In the business world, the saying goes that when you owe the bank a million, you have a problem, but when you owe it a billion, the bank has a problem. The €4 billion we had borrowed from Deutsche Bank was still sitting on its balance sheet, topped up by accrued interest to €5.8 billion. If the bank let Actavis go into freefall, some of its operations around the world would have to stop immediately. Actavis had a German company, for example, and under German law, as well as in many other jurisdictions, if there is an indication that a company might be heading towards bankruptcy, the directors are personally liable from that point even to the extent that they might be held criminally liable and go to prison. They have to stop the operation. 'We're reaching that point in Germany, Italy and Austria,' I told the bank.

Analysts came in and ascribed to Actavis a value in a freefall insolvency of just €1.4 billion, leaving a gap of €4.4 billion on what Deutsche Bank was owed. That would have crystallised a loss of more than €4 billion for the bank, so it had a serious problem. We started negotiating and agreed to restructure. Deutsche Bank did not revalue the loan until later, when the dust from the financial storm had settled. The whole thing was somewhat opaque and the numbers were well hidden in the annual report and only seen by those who knew what to look for. As for my own losses, when I took Actavis private my equity in the deal was €1 billion, after which I put in the additional €150 million I borrowed. It all went. My equity in Actavis became worthless. People say: 'Was that real equity?' But the point is that we had interest from other companies that were willing to pay that price at the time of Actavis being taken private. I could have walked away with over €1 billion if I had decided to be a seller, like other Actavis shareholders who sold out for cash at the time. Instead, I stayed in the company, making an earn-out deal with Deutsche Bank under which I was able to earn fresh, new equity.

The 2010 restructuring was extremely painful and embarrassing for Deutsche Bank, so much so that by the end of the negotiations I could hardly get anyone there to pick up the phone. When we signed the restructuring agreement, the only people who came from Deutsche Bank were the two who had been involved with the day-to-day work. When the head of investment banking later lost his job, Actavis was a large part of the reason and it must have caused a massive headache in Frankfurt. In 2009, a hit of more than €4 billion to Deutsche Bank's balance sheet would probably have led to the bank seeking a capital injection and possible state intervention. Some bankers even said to us that this could lead to the then German chancellor, Angela Merkel, taking the keys to Deutsche Bank. Perhaps they were right. What would people have thought of 'fortress Germany' then?

I am not trying to pretend that I am not also highly culpable, but there are some important differences between my actions and those of the bankers. Something all too easily forgotten in Iceland is that when the Actavis buy-out deal was done in 2007, it involved €3 billion of foreign money being paid to Icelandic shareholders and creditors in cash, an event so unprecedented and significant that I believe it lengthened Iceland's financial bubble. It dwarfed the €140 million that we paid to the Icelandic government in the Landsbanki privatisation and was far larger than any amount brought into the country by any other investor. The bubble in Iceland was all about Icelandic companies borrowing from Icelandic banks to buy assets abroad and individual investors flocking to buy the shares in those companies. The Icelandic banks were borrowing money from German, Japanese and US banks and then relending it to Icelanders to do deals such as Baugur's purchase of famous London toyshop Hamleys. But it was all going out. I was the only one bringing money in.

Furthermore, the investors stumping up funds for the equity portion of this deal, including me, put in their own money and bore their own losses. I personally put in €1 billion. Deutsche Bank, by contrast, made close to €200 million in fees on the Actavis buy-out in 2007, and got its loan back. Although it did not get all the interest, this led to handsome bonuses for its bankers, but the deal ended up putting the bank at risk of needing some help. This highlights a failing with the system that is sometimes called an agency problem, whereby bonus-hungry bankers take inordinate risks on behalf of their banks which foot the bill when things go wrong. It also leads to a lack of responsibility and accountability when deals become a problem. No one showed up to sign the contract when we renegotiated the deal in 2010. Why was that? Because no one wanted to stick their neck out. Why should they? If it went bad and they were seen to be responsible, they would be in line to be fired. If it went well, they would just be seen to be doing an average job.

I took my chances and lost. I am not ashamed of that. I am also far from alone in the fallout of 2008. In private equity deals, what often happens is that managers are offered a share of the profits but are required to plough some of their savings into the deal as well. If people are willing to do that, they are genuinely aligned. That works well in the private equity model but somehow it is absent in the way the banks work. There was, however, one exception: a bank where employees were encouraged to put their bonuses into the company's stock. This bank enjoyed the highest employee ownership ratio of any of the investment banks and the fortunes of its staff were directly linked to the risk decisions they took. Unfortunately for those employees, its name was Lehman Brothers.

*

I believe the Actavis deal and the money it brought into the country kept Iceland afloat longer than would otherwise have been the case. I was never a believer in the Icelandic krona. I made and paid my offer in euros, and my advice to selling Actavis shareholders was to keep their gains in the European currency and not to exchange it for krona. The shareholders had done well. When I created the Actavis of today and became the largest shareholder and chairman in 2000, the shares were at 24 krona. I was now taking it back in 2007 at 90 krona, but the stock had actually multiplied in value 22.5 times in the seven years because there was a stock split – the same growth as Apple enjoyed in a seven-year period after introducing the iPhone. I was proud to be able to pay all my fellow investors out in cash, making some of them very well off indeed.

Extracting myself from my misplaced investments in Icelandic banks was much more difficult. I knew that I could not sell the 40 per cent stake in Landsbanki or the 38 per cent holding in Straumur, the Icelandic investment bank of which I was chairman. I held both stakes jointly with my father but realised that they were simply too large a piece of the financial infrastructure for them to be allowed to be sold without a great deal of time-consuming regulatory scrutiny. And I had grave concerns about the strength of the krona, the management of the Central Bank and Iceland's financial system. I kept thinking of what had happened in Russia ten years earlier. The Icelandic krona was being artificially strengthened by the government, which was offering foreign investors krona-denominated bonds at excessive rates of interest. As the coupon on the bonds went from 10 per cent to 12 per cent then 14 per cent and 16 per cent, my forebodings grew. More and more it seemed like Russia all over again, with a government boosting interest rates to get cash so it could fund itself; and the krona exchange rate was just as artificial as that of the rouble in 1998. But this time it was happening in my own country where I was heavily exposed to the economy. I needed an exit plan.

There was no way to sell; everyone in Iceland was leveraged to the hilt and there was no buyer in the system with enough cash. So I planned to merge Landsbanki and Straumur, and reverse them into a much more liquid listed equity overseas. Potential foreign partners could see Iceland's problems just as clearly as I, so the plan had to involve merging the operations slanted to business outside Iceland. Fortunately, Landsbanki was doing most of its business abroad and was 62 per cent funded by international deposits in 2008. Straumur had opened in Denmark, bought franchises in Finland and Sweden, and acquired one of the best central European investment boutiques in the Czech Republic, so 80 per cent of Straumur's revenues were coming from Europe, not Iceland.

I knew that executives within Landsbanki and Straumur would resist becoming part of a bigger organisation. I also knew that I needed fresh blood from outside Iceland because everyone in the country seemed to be thinking the same way. So I fired the chief executive of Straumur in 2007 and looked for an experienced foreigner to take over. Getting that past the board was much tougher than I had expected, but I persuaded them that we couldn't just do business with the usual suspects in Iceland. It was too great a concentration of risk. We had to start finding other people to lend money to; other people to do deals with. There was not enough diversification of risk in the Icelandic system, and the krona and the Central Bank were not strong enough to support the system. We needed to look further afield.

I hired William Fall, an Englishman who had formerly been Bank of America's head of international banking, in charge of 30,000 staff. I told him that I wanted to de-risk the bank, relocate it and make it part of something else. He shrank the balance sheet in a plan called 'Shrink to Safety' and we moved our accounting to euros, against strong opposition from the Central Bank of Iceland, which also fought our plan to list our shares in euros. I also made considerable efforts to bring new foreign shareholders into Straumur and Landsbanki. I wanted William to head the international operations of the merged Straumur and Landsbanki and then spearhead the search for an overseas partner, but I faced a lot of resistance inside Landsbanki. We spoke to Collins Stewart of the UK, to Carnegie of Sweden and to Norwegian, Hungarian and emerging-market banks, but the attitude at Landsbanki was that a foreign merger would be done over its dead body.

There were structural difficulties in that although the two banks had similar net equity of about €1.6 billion, Landsbanki's balance sheet was expanding as Straumur's was contracting, and Landsbanki had an equity to debt ratio of about 8 per cent while Straumur's, at 20 per cent, was more than double the legal requirement. Furthermore, I was trying to swim against the tide. I had been sceptical of Iceland's ability to sustain its economic boom since about 2005, but I kept being proved wrong. I simply ran out of time. I wouldn't be able to execute this merger and make my exit from Iceland's financial markets.

The depth of the impending crisis only really hit me, like everyone else, when Lehman Brothers fell in September 2008. I was in the Czech Republic and went into the office of our investment bank there on the Monday to hear that Lehman had gone down. Everyone was saying: 'What the hell is happening?' I knew that my investments were not in good shape to deal with this blow as all financial institutions were vulnerable under the circumstances. Apart from the problems at Landsbanki and Straumur, I was carrying huge losses from my disastrous investment in Allianz, where I now saw I would not be able to catalyse a split-up of the company. In addition, the quality issue at Actavis had ended up with the company's CEO being fired. It was presented as a technical glitch that we could get over, but for a highly leveraged company to have one third of its EBITDA stripped away was apocalyptic. Thus I had serious problems with major investments, and after Landsbanki crashed in October 2008 and Straumur fell seven months later, all my other assets came under pressure. I owned shares in companies ranging from a Finnish telecoms company to an international sports manufacturer and when I tried to sell them, the prices fell on the belief that I was a forced seller. I was receiving bids at 50 cents in the dollar. It took a long time to get out of those positions.

How much did I have to liquidate? Almost everything. All the assets in publicly quoted shares went, and my investment in Landsbanki went from being worth €1.7 billion at the beginning of the year to €600 million by 4 pm on Friday 3 October before ultimately falling to zero on the Monday, the following business day. Straumur survived but had to write down its assets by 50 per cent; its shares then plummeted, trading at less than a third of book value. It's amazing that so much value could be lost over a single weekend, and now of course the sceptics say: 'Did you ever make all that money? Was it ever there?' or: 'How could you lose it so fast?' But it just went, destroyed by the international financial bomb that had hit Iceland. As with the blast effect of any bomb, the damage spreads ever further from the initial point of impact to reach buildings on the periphery so that they eventually collapse or become so unsafe that they have to be pulled down.

My approach had always been to look at the value of assets and see whether the deals that were possible were good value. Should I be buying these assets? Should I be selling them? Could I do something else with them? It had never involved my having to analyse the risk of something going bust. Even after Lehman fell, I don't think anyone imagined that AIG would be next. But the 12 months after October 2008 were spent liquidating. Prices and values all around seemed to be dropping continuously. The liquidations made everything worse and there was no respite. It was just down, down and down. I thought I was highly diversified, but in this global contagion everything fell in the same way.

What could I have done differently? I have spent thousands of hours thinking about this since the meltdown. It is clear to me now that my time in 2008 was not well spent. I should have been much more forceful in pushing Straumur and Landsbanki together, but besides internal resistance at Landsbanki, something else was making such a deal difficult. I had dealt with the bank politics, but I had opposition closer to home in the shape of my father, the chairman of Landsbanki. Unlike me, he had always courted popularity in Iceland, behaving much like a politician in shying away from conflicts, fights and skirmishes. So he was reluctant to take on Landsbanki's CEO, who was opposed to a merger with Straumur. 'The CEO is delivering record profits,' he argued. 'Even if I wanted to fire him today, how would I explain it?' All this was perfectly valid, but the same could also have been said about the Straumur CEO I had fired. He had made record profits for the bank, but the point was that he had bet the farm. If the biggest trades that produced those record earnings had gone wrong, they would not just have been bad trades, they would have bankrupted the bank.

It is easy to say with hindsight, of course, but to a degree I did see the same thing happening at Landsbanki. I couldn't pinpoint one thing. But I was sceptical of the relationship with Baugur, to which it was lending way too much money. Baugur was effectively bankrupt by the end of 2007 and I had been saying for a long time that it was just taking too much risk. It kept buying up assets on UK high streets for a full price but never sold a single one. It was always buying, and then someone in the group would form a daughter group so that assets were often being passed on within the group for a higher price, creating virtual profit. There were a lot of what I would call 'virtual transactions'. When I made this argument, people inside Landsbanki always said it was just rivalry between me and Baugur's chairman, Jon Asgeir Johannesson. It wasn't, but it took a long time for Baugur to unravel and for others to realise the truth. Johannesson was seen almost as a pied piper to Reykjavik's financial community. Bankers and investors seemed to follow him everywhere and of course the fees were lucrative. I said to one of his bankers: 'He pays you a lot of fees. He's never going to try to push down the fees because he's not interested. He's just trying to borrow to the limit and then he's going to say: "I'm too big to fail."'

I was also wrong to wait so long. With the domestic battles I was fighting, it was too tempting to just wait for Baugur's inevitable implosion and the trouble that would cause for Glitnir, which was now majority controlled by Baugur. Then I could have done a deal with Glitnir's creditors to merge the bank with the Landsbanki/Straumur combination. As always, I was highly motivated by the prospect of a bigger deal at the end of the rainbow. We would merge the whole thing. I would have a reduced stake in a bigger bank and gradually migrate out of Iceland. I even had a backup plan to split the Icelandic, foreign and contingent assets if a wholesale migration was not possible. But events were spinning out of control too quickly.

Baugur and Glitnir imploded, as had been forecast, but at the same time the Central Bank of Iceland ran out of cash and effectively became bankrupt. I didn't see that coming but nor did anyone else. And we had come close to combining Straumur with Collins Stewart. That was the best deal I could see, but Collins Stewart's chief executive, Terry Smith, called in August 2008 and said he was having second thoughts and wanted to wait. A Norwegian bank was also keen but we thought it was on the wrong stock exchange. Failing to follow that one through was a mistake.

At the time it didn't seem too bad to have to wait. I had lots of misgivings about Iceland's boom, but when I criticised it and tried to do something about it in 2006 and 2007, I was proved wrong. I thought the market would crash, but nothing happened. People around me would say: 'Are you the only grumpy old guy here? You're always saying you're concerned. Well, what are you concerned about?' I started to think: 'Am I just grumpy or am I jealous of people who follow in my footsteps? What is it? Maybe it's a personal thing.' But it turned out that my instinct about Iceland was fundamentally correct. Unfortunately, I suppressed it.

By the autumn of 2008 there were people in Iceland who knew that something was seriously wrong and some of the key players began shifting their strategies. But we were a bit different. We said: 'If Iceland falls, we've got assets elsewhere.' But sitting in London in September 2008 I had no idea of how bad it would be. It hadn't crossed my mind that everything was going down. I had met the prime minister at the end of July. 'Is there anything we can do?' he asked. 'Can we combine the banks to make them stronger?' He'd just hired a local economic adviser and was obviously worried. I said: 'I've looked into this and been advised on the matter by Credit Suisse and Deutsche Bank, but if you combine Landsbanki and Glitnir (which was always rumoured) you've also got to include Straumur because it has the management team and excess equity you need in order to get a stronger equity ratio.'

He, like everyone else, thought we had more time. The banks wanted to wait too. Credit Suisse and Deutsche Bank both told me in July 2008: 'Forget about doing anything in August or September. Everyone is on holiday and the window for deals is shut. We'll do it in the autumn.' It would never have been a quick process. The deal would have had to have been structured as one bank taking over the other, which would have triggered change of control provisions in loan agreements and involved reams of documentation and due diligence. We were being advised that the liquidity crunch that was afflicting global capital markets would mean that creditors all over the world would use the opportunity of a bank merger to take about €5 billion off the table here. We would need the government to stand behind that €5 billion. Credit Suisse and Deutsche Bank would bridge it but the government would have had to be part of the transaction.

I said to the prime minister: 'I think we should be looking at doing it this autumn.' He gave a nod and asked: 'Do you think this is possible?' I said I thought there were two key factors. From a shareholder's angle the fact that Glitnir's biggest shareholder was already in massive problems had to be addressed. Baugur had exceeded all credit limits, and it was obvious to all outside the Baugur camp that their days were numbered (a court in Iceland would later determine that they were in fact bankrupt at that moment in time). This would be problematic if there was to be any kind of merger. The second key factor, and the more fundamental one, was the fact that the banks' creditors were now essentially calling the shots. 'It doesn't matter what the key shareholders want to do,' I told him. 'If the creditors don't give you a break in doing this and finance you, it's hopeless. It's all up to them.' I suggested getting two banks – maybe Credit Suisse and Deutsche Bank or UBS – to stand behind us and market this to the creditors. But this is not something that can happen over a weekend. It takes months. We decided to talk again when global markets, which are essentially closed for the summer, were back in gear.

Following the events after the Lehman crash, at first I had the classic feelings of trauma: shock at the realisation of what was going on and adrenalin rushes to sell, meet pressures here and run around putting out fires there. Then there was an enormous amount of anger: with the politicians, with the people who worked with me, with the bankers and most of all with myself. You could call it gutless arrogance and rage. There were external and internal accusations. How the hell did this happen? Why didn't I see the signs and take avoiding action? Why did I hire so and so or fire a particular executive? I asked all these questions and more with increasing bitterness. Then I got to the final phase of sadness. It's just really sad and you start to lack the will to do much about it. I'm a fighter and I went every day to fight during the crisis. But I could feel my energy sapping and a voice in my head asking: 'What's it all for?'

First, my personal financial circumstances had to be dealt with. I was facing personal bankruptcy and had to put out the fire in my own house before attempting to help others do the same. I had two options, both perfectly valid, in the restructuring that followed the crash of 2008. Because of my domestic circumstances, including being unmarried, living in the UK and other personal reasons, some of my assets were in trusts for my children. At the time of the crash those trusts were worth about €200 million, so at any point in the restructuring I could have told the banks where to go, declared myself bankrupt and lived off the assets I had safeguarded. That was the 'quit' option, which would have meant lawsuits, attempts by creditors to break the trusts and effectively living my life in courtrooms for years. Then again, I could have just lived on a beach and hired lawyers to handle that.

I won't pretend that this didn't become appealing at times when I was exhausted after days of negotiating with demanding bankers. What was interesting was how different banks approached it, how some people wanted to work on salvaging value while others were after blood. A lot of the banks and resolution committees were chaotic. I think I could have done the restructuring within a year if I'd been dealing just with commercial banks. It took two years because I had to deal with bankrupt banks and the liquidators. 'Why do I do this?' I would cry, and some friends echoed the sentiment. One told me: 'Thor, this is a unique situation. Just declare yourself bankrupt. Take time out. Recharge yourself. Live off your cash. Nobody will stop anybody from going bankrupt in this crazy time. And you're hardly going to miss many money-making opportunities. Things are going to be dead for a while. Lie low and wait for three years or so. Your time will come again.' I was achingly tired after 18 months of arduous negotiations and I admit that I thought: 'This sounds good.' But it wouldn't have told the whole story and would have meant surrendering to the banks, the creditors and the strategists aiming to bring me down. The second option was to fight, pay my creditors and redeem myself, so I took the option of voluntarily opening up the trusts, giving the banks part of the proceeds from them in exchange for a value-split formula that could return me between nothing and up to €600 million if performance were good over three to five years. I could have been left with absolutely nothing, but I would always be able face myself in the mirror – something I couldn't have done if I had taken the 'easy' way out. The actual financial outcome turned out to be that I became a billionaire in the 2014 *Forbes* and *Sunday Times* 'rich lists' and I have stayed on them ever since.

The personal consequences of all this may sound somewhat surprising, given the financial losses involved and the intense scrutiny that I was experiencing in Iceland, where some polls seemed to rank me as public enemy number one. There was immense pressure and the negotiations with bankers and creditors seemed to take for ever, so it would be easy to paint these two years of my life as unremittingly bad and the boom years of money, personal jets and yachts as nirvana. That is not how it was, however. Some elements of my life actually improved during the two-year financial hell that I and everyone else in Iceland were trying to deal with.

One element was my relationship with Kristin. During the boom years, she mainly stayed in London while I was travelling the world on business. We had our first child in 2005, at the peak of my professional life, and it was a tough time: she wanted to settle down while I was buying a jet and a yacht and buzzing around the world. It was not a good time for our relationship and we separated in 2006 for some months, later getting back together. This doesn't reflect well on me, but I guess I came late to fatherhood and needed time to adjust to the idea.

My relationship with my father had also suffered in the boom times. In August 2003, we had issued a statement saying we would henceforth focus on different things. My father, who had been on the board of Pharmaco, stepped down and decided to focus on Landsbanki, where he was chairman. At the same time I, as chairman of Pharmaco, became more involved in the day-to-day operations of the company. I bought my father's share of Pharmaco. We agreed that Pharmaco carried greater risks as an investment than Landsbanki. In addition, being chairman of Landsbanki needed all my father's concentration.

I owe much to my father's willingness to try new adventures. He had been my business partner in Russia and in pharmaceuticals in Bulgaria, where we had worked closely together and made great returns. When he focused back on Iceland, he found a position he was comfortable to retire into and I thought his adventure-seeking times were in the past. I, however, was a young man and wanted more adventures, forming Novator as my investment company and having lots of ideas about what I wanted to do next. I was going into different, uncharted territory and wanted to do it on my own with my own company. My first opportunities in business were clearly there because of my father's contacts and willingness to try new adventures – but it was a different era now.

My father was in his element at Landsbanki. As chairman of Iceland's major bank, he got the public plaudits he craved and enjoyed being respected and revered at the bank. He could bask in the knowledge that he had redeemed himself in the eyes of his country. Some people even took to nicknaming him the Count of Monte Cristo. But to my surprise, this was not enough for him. He started playing the Monopoly board game that was taking place in Iceland at the time, investing in what I would call trophy assets and leveraging up with companies abroad. His investment in the English football club West Ham United, which I thought questionable, summed it up for me. Coming from a working-class family in a poor Reykjavík area, where he played for his local neighbourhood club as a boy, my father felt an instant connection to West Ham's East End spirit – a club built on working-class pride and grit. Pouring in his own fortune, he chased ambition boldly, bringing in stars like Carlos Tevez, whose relentless brilliance in the Premier League matched the very best, dragging West Ham to survival with goals and fight that captured the club's soul. Though the controversial Tevez deal brought legal turmoil, my father's vision gave West Ham a thrilling chapter of hope, only for the global financial crisis to sweep away his dreams, leaving behind a legacy of daring ambition and fleeting glory. He relished his role as a saviour and benefactor and was eager to take big bets by personally underwriting the club's spending at the time in order to quickly resurrect their true potential. He was in his dream role in his most beloved hobby of football, which he followed religiously to the very end of his life.

This was a young man's game my father was competing in, and he was at a distinct disadvantage in it. He had to rely too much on advisers and was not travelling enough, so wasn't getting the insights and perspective necessary for that kind of venture. He came into everything too late, just in time for the crash, which left him personally bankrupt and ruined emotionally as well as financially. It is sad because he would probably have avoided bankruptcy if he'd been satisfied with his role at Landsbanki. It was his other investments that got him into trouble, and this ultimately caused me even more frustration after he went bankrupt. I had grown up with a man who had been wronged and sought vindication and I too wanted to clear his name.

However, the apple seldom falls far from the tree and, just as I had become drunk with the boundless opportunities in business and exuberance of the times, the chance to own his own Premier League football club as well as the very shipping company that had literally put him out of business was irresistible to him. I see that more clearly now with hindsight than I did during the crash.

It took him a long time to process the scale of his personal rise and fall and to come to terms with it. However, the situation was helped by the fact that although his name was tarnished in the media for a few years after, in the many circles he moved in he was still very popular and hugely respected to his dying day.

I also always had huge respect for my father's willpower over alcohol. It speaks volumes for his perseverance that he never once fell off the wagon through all his ordeals or triumphs, but stuck to the decision he made in 1978 when I was in San Francisco as a boy. That perseverance is something my family came to take for granted from him, but actually should not have done, as we have all gained from his personal determination. Personally, I have always marvelled at the self-discipline he was able to muster for that through incredible adversity and plenty of opportunities to start drinking again. He was fond of saying 'where there is a will there is always a way'. I drew a lot of inspiration from that.

I was unable to help my father after the crash in order to avoid his bankruptcy. I simply had such an enormous and complex problem with creditors myself at that time there was zero capacity to rescue him simultaneously. I have faced criticism over this from sceptics who claim that I could have settled with my father's creditors as well as my own, saving him from going bankrupt. But the task that I faced after the crash was enormous. There was no way that I could have settled with my father's creditors as well, beyond taking on his share of our shared liabilities. I did talk to banks to see if there was any way to reach some sort of settlement. But it just wasn't possible.

So domestically, all was not as well as it might have seemed during the years of my greatest financial successes. It was a difficult time personally. In business, I was enjoying the thrill of the chase and the rewards of success. Domestically, there was conflict and rivalry. Emotionally and spiritually, there was a great imbalance. I would go to the Monaco Grand Prix with my yacht and party and take Kristin to the Oscars, but it all felt a little hollow. I tried to think about hobbies and interests, so I put some money into a film production company in Iceland and ended up as executive producer of a film starring Queen Latifah, an American singer, rapper and actor, among other things. It was an expensive attempt to tie one of my favourite hobbies, movies, to my business life. The same reason made me invest in Indian Motorcycles, the old and respected American brand. Both were in fact vanity investments, where I let my hobbies lead the way, instead of looking at the bottom line. But even though the movie experience was nothing to write home about, Indian Motorcycles took a great turn for the better. We managed to shore the ailing company up and it has now regained its former glory, much to my delight. Since 2011, Polaris Industries has owned the company and is giving Harley-Davidson a real run for its money as the company's first real challenger in decades – just like at the very start of this legendary rivalry when Indian launched in 1901 and Harley followed two years later. I still get a kick out of hardcore bikers approaching me at rallies and shaking my hand respectfully, saying: 'So you're the guy who rescued Indian. Respect, man.' These were the very words that Sonny Barger, the founder and global president of the Hells Angels, said to me in Sturgis, South Dakota, in 2012 when he stopped by the Indian show tent with his crew to look over the latest line-up. It was great praise from a very controversial man and felt pretty surreal and satisfying at the same time.

Strangely, when my financial world disintegrated my domestic life began to improve. Perhaps that isn't so surprising. I still had my house in Notting Hill, enough money to live extremely well and money put away for my children. The humility involved in going through a financial restructuring is also a prerequisite for rebuilding relationships.

I started to see a spiritual mentor every three months or so who gave me advice in a totally different context. 'You're the best at what you do,' she would tell me. 'You know how to invest but you're burning the candle at both ends. Your health is suffering. Why don't you invest in yourself, invest in your health?' I started working out and I got a return on that. She said to Kristin: 'When he doesn't listen, send him an email.' It seemed to work. Becoming a father again helped as well. In the middle of the crash, we were having our second child. We got married at the end of 2010. Family life was getting stronger and one way of building up capital was replaced by another. It was an intensely frustrating period but it also allowed a lot of reflection. I would walk my dog saying to myself: 'What a wonderful neighbourhood I live in. I've got the best dog. I'm walking back to the nicest house that I know. I built this house and I have children and a wife waiting for me. This is just great.' These kinds of things, which I didn't have time for before, were all kicking in. It wasn't so much that it was all I had left, but that I had finally begun to wake up and smell the coffee. I made more friends locally and started doing all the things I had moved to London for in the first place.

One of my major mistakes was that I was in too much of a hurry to try other ventures and didn't pay enough attention to Iceland's problems. I was trying to lay as many bets as I could while the plentiful supply of surplus capital lasted. But I had lost focus and was involved in too many things. I sold Bulgarian telecoms group BTC but then, before I had finished a project with Finnish telecoms firm Elisa, I was engrossed in the Actavis leveraged buy-out. Before completing my ill-fated investment in Amer Sports, I made a derivative bet on Allianz, with an even worse outcome. And I also negotiated a complex deal to come to the rescue of the beleaguered Polish owners of QXL, an early online auction competitor to eBay that had run into trouble. The company then recovered, with its shares rising a staggering 1,260 per cent in 2005, making it the year's best performing stock on the London Stock Exchange. We then sold it to Naspers, a subsidiary of a South African media group. The problem was that I couldn't handle the pitch or the speed because there were so many things going on. My focus was always on doing the next deal, restructuring and rejigging something I already had, and not so much on the oversight, which is an important check and balance. I was not good at that. I'm always more interested in creating something new. I had lost my ability to focus, something that had served me so well in Russia, and which is essential for an investor looking after his money.

My mindset during the storm-riding years had always been: 'I've got clever people around me, so keep going. If the plan isn't good enough, my people and the banks will stop me. My mission is to champion the plan. If it gets shot down, so be it. If it is good enough, it will happen and probably succeed.' This had worked in the past, but with the Allianz deal, for example, people in my organisation started to accuse me of railroading things through.

What was going wrong? I'd had so many successes in making money that I seemed to lose any sense of danger. I had begun to make investments without having a full grasp of them. I knew how to run manufacturing companies making beer and pharmaceuticals and how to build factories. But once I got into financial institutions and started to play around with highly leveraged derivatives, I made many mistakes. I had moved far away from my beginnings in Russia. I had spread my risk by having a diversified portfolio of investments in banking, telecoms and pharmaceuticals, but I had too many projects going on. So when Iceland imploded, my liquid investments were hit because I was a forced seller in a falling market. I organised structured sales processes to recover some capital but it was like trying to ice-skate uphill. It was too late. There was little I could have done differently at that time. I could not have sold the shares in the banks before the crash, though I could have and maybe should have liquidated the other listed businesses and reduced my balance sheet.

So why didn't I get off the carousel before it crashed? It is easy to ask that now, of course, but it is like being at a party that you know has been going on for far too long. You're not the drunkest person there and you're certainly not the instigator, but it is difficult in the middle of the party to be the lone voice saying: 'Hang on; hang on. Let's lower the music, tone it down; have a glass of water.' That is not what happens and it was a bit like that. I got carried away in Iceland. My intuition told me that what was going on there was not sound. But the country was awash with business ideas and loans to fund them, and it was too easy to say 'yes'. Now it is clear that I was in a fool's paradise and I was the biggest fool. I had a ticket to go somewhere else but I didn't use it.

Most of my fellow Icelanders involved in the financial system at the time didn't know any better. One reason why people didn't see that the good times were not sustainable was the phenomenon called suspension of disbelief. It basically means that people willingly dismiss the facts that prove that all is trickery or illusion, in order to enjoy the part they want or need to believe. We know that a magician doesn't really cut a woman in two on the stage, but we accept the trick so as to enjoy his superb showmanship. People sometimes get so caught up in a book that they forget it's all fiction, or they immerse themselves in movies about creatures from outer space or drawn characters in a cartoon, commenting on why the characters make this decision or what it says about their personalities – all the while enjoying the fantastic ride. They know that it's not possible for anyone to conceal their true identity simply by putting on glasses, but it's essential for Superman to get away with it, and therefore the audience chooses to believe it.

Sometimes people want to believe the whole concept, but criticise a minor fault in the reasoning. They might make the observation that no one can walk away unharmed with hair unruffled after many serious blows and kicks to the head. But at the same time, it doesn't seem to bother them that the character was actually fighting robots from outer space. This is how life was in the boom years. We saw some irrational faults, but we swallowed the rest, hook, line and sinker. And most Icelanders had never tried anything else.

I don't have that excuse. There were plenty of other places I could have gone to invest but for a deal junkie, Iceland was such an easy place to score. When I invested in Landsbanki less than 5 per cent of its operations were outside Iceland, so I was very much betting on the nation. This meant that I couldn't try to dismantle the power structures or criticise the lending practices, even though I could see the risks. Between us, my father and I had the biggest stake in Landsbanki, but another 30,000 investors owned slices of it too, and it wouldn't have been right to speak out against the bank's big customers. I was conflicted but now I am free. Now I can speak my mind.

In a fool's paradise, make sure you are not the biggest fool.

My christening party in 1967, at the Reykjavik home of my parents, Bjorgolfur Gudmundsson and Thora Hallgrimsson. I am on my father's lap, with my mother to his left, surrounded by grandparents and other relatives.

As a boy with family friend Sonja Zorilla, whose cosmopolitan life and home on New York's Park Avenue was to influence my view of the world. Sonja later helped me move to New York and get into New York University.

My mother, Thora Hallgrimsson, as a young woman in the late 1940s.

Me at the centre with (left to right) my siblings Orn, Magga (Margret), Halli (Hallgrimur) and Bentina.

Christmas in the early 1970s: I am sitting on the floor with (left to right) my sisters, Bentina and Magga, my father, Bjorgolfur, my mother's parents, Margret and Hallgrimur, and at far right my mother, Thora.

As a teenager in the 1980s with my father, Bjorgolfur Gudmundsson.

Happy heritage: my grandmother Margaret Thors, third from the left, with her mother, brothers and sisters in front of our historic family home at the Frikirkjuvegur mansion in Reykjavik in the early 1920s.

Outside the Church of Our Saviour of Spilt Blood in St Petersburg on my first trip to Russia in March 1993.

A humble start: in the bedoom of my run-down apartment in St Petersburg.

Me (at left) and my partner Magnus Thorsteinsson (third from right) with technical advisers and translators inspecting the first factory site in St Petersburg, May 1993.

Me (kneeling at front) with staff at the surprise launch of Botchkarev beer in St Petersburg in 1999: it was an instant hit.

Celebrating the opening of the Icelandic consulate in St Petersburg in 2000 with Botchkarev beer. Left to right: me (the new consul), Icelandic foreign minister Halldor Asgrimsson, Oscar-winning Russian film director Nikita Mikhalovits and St Petersburg's mayor, Vladimir Jakovlev.

In 2002 the president of Iceland, Olafur Ragnar Grimsson, (second from the right) visited the Kremlin. As the Icelandic consul I shook hands with President Vladimir Putin, with Kristin beside me. His story of a saviour turning bad and dragging the country to near ruin is unfortunately a classic Russian drama, with the usual tragic ending.

When Bravo was sold to Heineken in 2002, I made my first $100 million, and this report of the signing appeared on the back page of the Icelandic newspaper *Morgunblaðið*. In the aftermath of Russia's invasion of the Ukraine in 2022, Heineken, along with hundreds of other Western companies, announced they would quit operations in Russia, and in 2023 the company was sold for €1. The estimated loss for Heineken was reportedly €300 million.

Samson's owners (left to right) Magnus Thorsteinsson, me and my father, Bjorgolfur Gudmundsson, signed the contract for buying 45.8 per cent of the shares in Landsbanki on New Year's Eve 2002. (Photo: Kristinn Ingvarsson)

Sigurdur Oli Olafsson, CEO of Actavis, with me in August 2008, at a press conference after I fired the old CEO and Siggi Oli took over. Siggi would later go on to head Teva, the largest generic pharmaceuticals company in the world. (Photo: G. Rúnar)

Signing the deal with Watson Pharmaceuticals for the purchase of Actavis in 2012: (left to right) Fabrizio Campelli, Head of Group Strategy at Deutsche Bank, Paul Bisaro, CEO of Watson, and me.

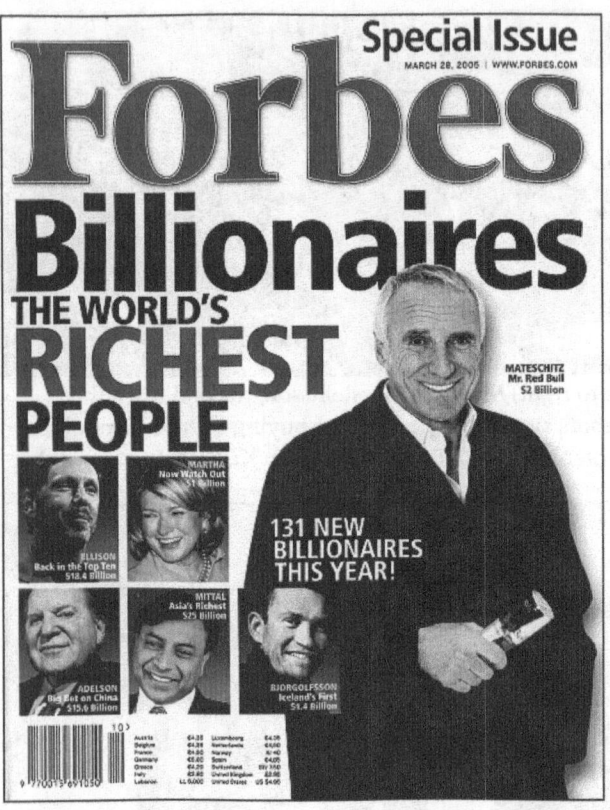

In the *Forbes* rich list, March 2005.

Pall Skulason, Dean of the University of Iceland, making a presentation to me in February 2005, watched by Icelandic minister of culture and education, Thorgerdur Katrin Gunnarsdottir. Under my leadership of Eimskip, grants were made from the company's so-called 'University Fund' to the university for the first time. Previously Eimskip's managers had retained the funds. (Photo: Kristinn Ingvarsson)

Cutting a dash – the photo of Thor that accompanied this tongue-in-cheek accolade of 'sexiest billionaire' in the *Financial Times* magazine, 23/24 September 2006.

Giving the graduation speech at NYU Stern School of Business, May 2009. (Island Photography)

At the Daytona Bike Rally, Florida, US, in 2008 (above left) with my friend Sigurdur Olafsson (at right); (*below left*) heli-skiing in northern Iceland, 2019; (*below right*) hiking in 2019 with Kristin in Hornstrandir, Iceland's northernmost peninsula.

Kristin and me *(above)* at our wedding in Rome in December 2010; *(below left)* travelling in Tuscany, Italy, in 2016, the only way to do it – the Fiat way!; *(below right)* enjoying the Croatian summer with our three children, 2018.

Signing the letter of intent with Huawei at the Palace of Heavenly Peace in Beijing in 2005 during an official state visit by Iceland to China, with the presidents of both countries looking on.

Emerging with Mikhail Gorbachev from my private Challenger jet after a flight from Germany to Iceland in 2006.

Kristin and me with former US president Bill Clinton in London in 2014. Clinton had a strong affinity with Iceland and confidence in its economic recovery.

In my penthouse office suite on Park Lane in London.

My private jet, painted in the Novator livery, taking off from St Moritz in 2007 with me and all my family aboard. (Photo: Hans Domjan)

Leaving prime minister Geir Haarde's office in Reykjavik after late-night crisis discussions in 2008, the day after the government had dramatically decided to nationalise Glitnir – the catalyst for the crash of the Icelandic banking system. (Photo: Daniel Runarsson, *Frettabladid*)

Protests and paint: The prime minister and I were blamed most for the financial crash in Iceland. *Above left:* My image, with year of death given as 2008, spray-painted on to my house. *Above right:* Graffiti on the same wall saying I had ravaged Iceland and should pay. *Right:* My four-wheel drive covered with red paint in August 2009.

Brothers in arms: with my partners in Novator, Birgir Mar Ragnarsson (at left) and Andri Sveinsson (at right). (Photo: Charlie Strand)

Kristin and me in Italy after a motorcycle trip through the Alps in 2010, riding one of the first new Indian motorcycles to be produced after my partners and I rescued the iconic company from bankruptcy.

Giving the opening address at a conference hosted by the American magazine *Wired* in 2016.

Rómeó og Júlía sett upp á fjölum Young Vic-leikhússins í London

„Íslendingar eiga erindi á stóra sviðið"

ÍSLENSKI leikhópurinn Vesturport frumsýnir Rómeó og Júlíu eft-
ir William Shakespeare á miðviku-
dag í hinu kunna leikhúsi
Lundúnaborgar, Young Vic. Er
þetta í fyrsta sinn sem íslensk upp-
færsla með íslenskum leikurum fer
á fjalir eins af stóru leikhúsunum í
Lundúnum. Íslenskur leikhópur
hefur ekki áður sýnt fullmótað verk
í einu þekktasta leikhúsi Evrópu án
opinberra styrkja.

Hið kunna leikrit Rómeó og Júlía
er hér í leikgerð Gísla Arnar Garð-
arssonar, Hallgríms Helgasonar og
Tanya Ronders. Verkið verður sýnt
sjö sinnum í viku fram til 25. októ-
bers nk. Sýningin er ein af aðalsýn-
ingum leikhússins þetta leikárið.
Auk þess að vera einn aðalleikari
sýningarinnar er Gísli Örn leik-
stjóri ásamt Bretanum Rufus Norr-
is. Um tuttugu Íslendingar hafa
dvalið í Lundúnum síðustu tvær
vikurnar við undirbúning og æfing-
ar.

Hefur mikla trú á ungu íslensku listafólki

Björgólfur Thor Björgólfsson,
kaupsýslumaður, sem búsettur er í
Lundúnum, styrkir uppfærsluna og
kemur að ýmsum þáttum hennar.
Björgólfur Thor segist hafa mikla
trú á ungu íslensku listafólki og er
hann sannfærður um að það eigi
fullt erindi á leiksvið í borg leikhús-

Björgólfur Thor Björgólfsson og Gísli Örn Garðarsson fagna undirritun samstarfssamnings á sviði Young Vic-
leikhússins. Leikararnir Björn Hlynur Haraldsson og Nína Dögg Filippusdóttir sveifla sér í rólunum fyrir aftan þá.

In 2003, Kristin and I sponsored a unique and acrobatic production of *Romeo and Juliet* by the Icelandic theatre company Vesturport at the Young Vic theatre in London. Kristin also both produced the show and made a documentary about the entire adventure. Here I shake on the deal with Romeo himself, the actor and director Gisli Orn Gardarsson.

50 Cent was one of the artists who performed at my 40th birthday party on the island of Jamaica in March 2007. Eighteen months later I had lost 99 per cent of my fortune.

Kristin and me with (left to right) George Clooney, Matt Damon, the late Jerry Weintraub, Brad Pitt and Don Cheadle at the premier party of the movie *Ocean's Thirteen* in 2007.

With my good friends David Beckham and Guy Ritchie in 2018 at London's hottest Christmas drinks event, hosted by Beckham at the Haig Club House in west London. (Getty Images)

Kristin arriving at sunset at the 2016 Burning Man festival in the Nevada desert, after a 1,030-km two-day ride from Los Angeles – of course driving an Indian.

A kiss from my daughter, Bentina, on holiday on the French Riviera, 2016. Life doesn't get much better.

Celebrating five million WOM customers in Chile in 2019.

On the cover of Colombian *Forbes* in February 2021, just before WOM was launched in Colombia after five successful years in Chile.

Me with (on my left) the larger-than-life Chris Bannister, then CEO of WOM, and the team from Novator (left to right: Bruce McInroy, Serdar Cetin and Thomas Leslie) heading into a meeting with the president of Colombia in the presidential palace in Bogotá, February 2020.

In Oaxaca, Mexico, with Don Fortino Ramos, a master mezcalero with 40 years' experience. David de Rothschild and I founded The Lost Explorer Mezcal in 2020 with the aim of establishing a sustainable Mexican enterprise, as well as protecting the ancient artisanal craft of mezcal making.

Kristin and me at the World Economic Forum annual meeting in Davos in 2020, just after my first meeting with Iván Duque Márquez, the then president of Colombia.

Kristin (at left) co-chairs the film committee of the Serpentine gallery. Here she is interviewing Maya Sanbar, the director of *Footsteps on the Wind*, an animation film about child refugees, in 2023.

With my mother, Thora, not long before she died in 2020 at the age of 90.

At the summit: I treasure this picture with my father, aged 83, in Courchevel, France, on New Year's Day 2023. It epitomises us coming out victorious from all our highs and lows. He was very proud of being able to join Kristin and me at the peak.

Kristin and me with our son Daniel at his graduation from Wellington College in 2023.

The family at son Lorenz's confirmation in Iceland in summer 2023. We are standing outside the wooden villa at Frikirkjuvegur 11 that was built in 1907 by Thor Jensen, my great-grandfather. In 2008 I bought the house from the city of Reykjavik and had it fully restored to its original appearance.

In 2023 a trust which I have set up for the benefit of my family acquired Bramshill, a Jacobean palace in Hampshire. Restoring the house and estate is an exciting challenge for both Kristin and me.

The grand entrance to Bramshill house.

Kristin in the grounds of Bramshill, with the house in the distance.

Kristin and me celebrating her 50th birthday in 2022.

8

AFTERSHOCK
2009-2010

Everybody knows the dice are loaded
Everybody rolls with their fingers crossed
Everybody knows that the war is over
Everybody knows that the good guys lost
Everybody knows the fight was fixed
The poor stay poor, the rich get rich
That's how it goes and everybody knows

Leonard Cohen, 'Everybody Knows'

It was no surprise that the biggest crash in history elicited the largest ever post-mortem and, as someone who lost the best part of €4 billion in the events of 2008, I should probably have had a ringside seat at the inquisition. However, I was not asked to participate and had little interest in the government commissions, regulatory reviews and countless books probing what went wrong with the system and how it needs to be fixed. Cracks in the system have always existed. They may move around, die down and later emerge in a different place, just as the Earth's geological core is constantly shifting, but we will always have the financial equivalent of fissures and faults in any system. Could the world's financial system be better?

Could some flaws be eradicated? Should it offer more protection to those least able to cope with financial losses? Yes, yes and yes again. But am I interested in wholesale revolutionary systemic changes? Do I want a new era of much greater regulatory oversight and do I think they would make a great deal of difference to the boom–bust cycle that countless politicians have unsuccessfully pledged to abolish? No, I do not. I have made my money from the cracks in systems. And that's partly how I lost it as well.

That is not to say that I have as harsh a view of life's realities as the Leonard Cohen song 'Everybody Knows'. Everybody does or should know these things, but everything is also temporary: for Iceland, for international financial markets and obviously for myself. Within just 12 months, I lost 99 per cent of my wealth and life's work, while Iceland saw the bursting of a ten-year bubble, the likes of which I do not expect to see again in my home nation. It has taken much longer for the global economic tides to turn, but turning they most certainly are. Just as the past 100 years have been called the American century, the one we are in now will probably go down in history as Asia's. In the West, we have grown up with an intrinsic belief that life inevitably gets better with every generation. The quality of life increases, life expectation grows longer and we all become a little wealthier. This may be true in a general sense, but will it always be? Who knows? But in striving for better times it is sensible to try to learn lessons from the past, even though human fallibility means that the mistakes of the past will almost inevitably crop up again somehow, somewhere. One just has to watch the cryptocurrency space and day-trader activity over the next few years for fresh evidence of that.

So what lessons can be learned from the crash? The first, I guess, is to look out for history repeating itself. In 2003 in Iceland, for example, I could see clear parallels with the leveraged boom in Russia of a decade earlier, although my vantage point had changed markedly. Instead of being young, poor and mustard-keen in a freezing Khrushchev-era apartment block, I had made my first fortune, was living and travelling first class and had an office in Park Lane. Still, I could not resist grabbing another piece of the action. Five years later, I experienced a familiar feeling. Iceland's boom was not going to last any longer than Russia's had but, while the merry-go-round kept turning, it was tempting to stay on for the ride. 'When there's so much money available, you should take it while it lasts,' was the prevailing sentiment at the time. It was another land-grab situation.

I thought the difference was that in Iceland things would slow down gradually, rather than come to an abrupt halt as in Russia in 1998. Arriving in Russia in 1993, I had felt there was a window in which foreigners could make money before the shutters came down, restrictions were imposed and Russians became much more entrepreneurial themselves. I also saw this kind of situation in Iceland in 2007 but felt that financing would be plentiful for a period before slowly subsiding. I didn't expect it to drop off a cliff, and when it did my reaction was: 'How did I get here again?' I had seen Russia crumble in 1998 and now I was seeing another system falling ten years later. I had a strong hunch that the situation in Russia could not be sustainable, yet when the crash happened it took me by surprise. A decade later, most of Iceland's banks were clearly lending too much to the same groups and the money was just being recycled around the financial system. I remember thinking to myself that the situation was crazy. Small investors were joining together with friends to form companies, guaranteeing each other so they could put up more to invest. Seemingly everyone was borrowing money to buy cars and property, or go on golfing or skiing trips – all against the security of absurdly pumped-up asset prices. That people admitted to being less focused on their day jobs because they could make a lot more money doing something else was a clear danger sign.

Looking back, Iceland's demise had much to do with its immaturity as a society. A migrant nation of just 320,000 people, it had been an independent country for less than 100 years, yet at the turn of the century it had such big ideas. For a few short years it stood tall and attracted global attention, even respect, but it was not long before it became clear that Iceland as a nation did not have the history or, more importantly, the infrastructure to support its own rhetoric.

In a talk in Reykjavik in October 2011, the chief economist at Citigroup, Willem H. Buiter, likened the talent pool in Iceland to that in a mid-sized city such as Coventry in England. The nation couldn't therefore logically expect to provide good people for the Treasury, the Central Bank, the FSA, the courts, the parliament, the Foreign Office or the business sector. Buiter told his stunned audience that he had never witnessed such collective stupidity in any developed country as was so dominant in Iceland during the last fifteen years before the crash of 2008. Strong words indeed, but he had a good point.

*

When Iceland's banks came under severe pressure at the beginning of October 2008, the nation's financial system unravelled very rapidly. The end began with Glitnir being the first bank to go. My involvement started when I received a phone call on 2 October from Geir Haarde, Iceland's prime minister, only four days before his famous declaration that Iceland's banks were bust. 'We are very worried about Landsbanki, its Icesave internet account,' he told me. 'Why?' I replied. 'Icesave's deposits are a great strength to Landsbanki and to the Icelandic banking system.' He just repeated: 'Well, we're greatly concerned about it.' I could not see how this online savings account in the UK could be a problem. Icesave had emerged from Heritable Bank, a small Mayfair-based outfit that Landsbanki already owned when my father and I bought our stake. Heritable was a niche bank with an excellent track record and no write-offs. A new managing director, Mark Durrant, had taken over and it was his idea to go into internet deposits. Icesave was set up in 2006, as a means of attracting more business.

At that time, one of the main criteria analysts used when looking at a bank was how much of its asset base was funded by deposits. This became even more important after the collapse of the UK's Northern Rock in August 2007, so Landsbanki put more emphasis on getting deposits. As Iceland's population was not big enough to raise the deposits it needed, Icesave increasingly fulfilled this need. At the time this was seen as a highly prudent strategy. A deposits-to-assets ratio of anything above 50 per cent was considered good and Landsbanki's ratio in 2008 was 60 per cent. This wasn't a surprise. Landsbanki had deliberately targeted the UK savings market with highly competitive interest rates and £5 billion of deposits flooded in, mostly between January 2007 and October 2008. From a shareholder point of view, I saw this as de-risking the business, using money from small depositors to pay off the international bond markets so that we were less exposed to market volatility.

After the collapse of Northern Rock in August 2007 and subsequent concerns about other UK-based banks, what I had seen as a secure deposit base and a strength began to weaken. After the collapse of Lehman Brothers a year later, UK investors

began a general run on bank deposits which was to pose juris-
dictional questions in previously uncharted waters. Icesave
became a problem because its UK deposits were held by a UK
branch of Landsbanki, rather than by Heritable, which was a
British bank wholly owned by Landsbanki. In hindsight, this
was a major mistake by the management. I have to admit that,
right up to the weekend of the collapse, I was unaware of such
technicalities. It only started to dawn on me that this could be
a difficulty when I spoke to the prime minister on 2 October.
I can see it clearly now. Iceland is not a member of the EU,
but an Icelandic bank had opened a branch in the UK, under
EU regulation, and accepted deposits. So there was a jurisdic-
tional issue – an issue that came to the fore over the weekend
of 4–5 October 2008, as Iceland's financial crisis unfolded.

At this time, all rating agencies were recommending banks
to fund themselves more with deposits than by issuing bonds
in the markets. We were simply following an international
trend.

After Haarde had raised the issue with me, the German
chancellor, Angela Merkel, made a public statement that the
German government would guarantee all German depositors' money. The same thing happened in Ireland, so we took
that to mean that a sovereignty guarantee on depositors is
not automatic but needs extraordinary action from governments. The problem was that the deposit insurance scheme in
Iceland catered for a country with just 200,000 bank accounts.
Icesave now had more than 400,000 depositors in the UK and
the Netherlands. So it went from being our greatest strength
to something that has haunted me ever since.

At the time, the panic about the effect that the Icesave
episode could have on the nation's future led to outlandish
claims that Icelanders would toil for years to pay off the debt,
with their children and grandchildren facing impoverished

futures. A well-known singer decided to make his own radio ads, babbling nonsense about how Icelandic children had been sold into slavery in other countries in the sixteenth century and that it must not be repeated. In this climate of fear and exaggeration, I was regularly accused of having stolen the Icesave money for myself. There were even pop songs written about the criminal few who had ripped the nation off. I always believed that ultimately nobody would lose money on Icesave, although it would take several years to sort out. The Bank of England's guarantee scheme covers up to £50,000 for each UK depositor, and the bank had a claim on the Landsbanki 'estate' for monies that it had paid out. And for monies not covered by the Bank of England's guarantee, individual investors could claim against the Landsbanki estate. The UK government wanted Iceland's government to guarantee payment of the uncovered balance plus interest, but that was voted down in a referendum. One can hardly blame Icelanders for that, as the sum worked out at $6,000 for every man, woman and child in the country. And all the self-proclaimed experts forgot to look at the value of Landsbanki's assets.

The case came before the European Free Trade Association (EFTA) court, where the EFTA Surveillance Authority claimed that Iceland was in breach of the EEA agreement, as it had breached the Deposit Guarantee Directive or had discriminated against depositors contrary to EEA law. On 28 January 2013 the court rejected all claims. The court held that the directive did not envisage the alleged obligation of result to ensure payment to depositors in the Landsbanki branches in the Netherlands and the UK in a systemic crisis of the magnitude experienced in Iceland.

In a statement at the time, the Icelandic Ministry of Foreign Affairs pointed out that the Landsbanki estate had already paid 'over 90 per cent of the total which the UK and

Dutch authorities advanced to cover the minimum deposit guarantee'. The Ministry wrote:

> It is important to bear in mind that payments from the estate of the failed Landsbanki will continue regardless of the ruling of the EFTA Court. The assets of the estate are now estimated to be 1,517 billion krona, which is approximately 200 billion krona more than the priority claims which amount to 1,318 billion krona. Of these priority claims, 1,166 billion krona result from the Icesave deposits, while just under 150 billion krona result from wholesale deposits, including those from municipalities, charities etc. The sum of 660 billion krona has already been paid out of the estate against priority claims, i.e. around 50 per cent of their total value. Of this, 585 billion krona have gone to claims resulting from the Icesave accounts. This sum amounts to over 90 per cent of the total which the UK and Dutch authorities advanced to cover the minimum deposit guarantee.

My belief that the estate would make good was thus eventually recognised officially. And the final sentence of the Ministry's statement said it all:

> It is expected that the Icesave claims will be paid out in full by the actual debtor, the estate of the failed Landsbanki. This outcome results from the implementation of emergency legislation in 2008, according to which deposits were given priority against unsecured claims.

Many acted as though they were hearing for the first time in January 2013 that Icesave would never be the problem it had been made out to be. Others, however, had acknowledged earlier that this was indeed likely. In his May 2011 blog, Egill Helgason, an influential Icelandic TV personality, had a classic 'wtf' moment and wrote:

> One is flabbergasted after two Icesave referendums – and some of the fiercest clashes in Icelandic politics. Was it really so the whole time that the Landsbanki estate fully covered this at hardly any cost for the nation? What were we fighting for?

For me, it has been a bit like being a murder suspect about whom all kinds of wild statements and half-truths have been made, and for that to be capped in the end by finding that the murder never actually took place when the victim shows up alive and well.

How, then, can this saga be viewed in hindsight? Clearly, the first decision to honour only the Icelandic deposits was idiotic and self-serving. All of a sudden, people were being discriminated against according to their passports. Foreign creditors lost €48 billion in the Icelandic crash. The emergency law passed on 6 October 2008 dictated that all domestic assets be secreted in new, publicly owned domestic versions of the banks, while the foreign versions went into receivership and liquidation. Domestic residents would not suffer any losses from the fall of the banks. Deposits took priority over bonds and other claims, which meant that foreign creditors were hit hardest. It has been pointed out that a third of all the capital flowing into Iceland came from German banks. Bayerische Landesbank was one of the largest creditors and became the first German bank to turn to the German state for support when the global financial tsunami hit. Members of Iceland's parliament jokingly called this 'Operation Fuck the Foreigners' when they were drawing up the bill for the emergency loan. *Island Ehf*, a book about the years after the crash by Magnus Halldorsson and Thordur Snaer Juliusson, contains a chapter with this title about the decision to honour only Icelandic deposits. The next chapter about the reaction of foreigners is entitled, appropriately: 'Fuck You Too'.

There were people running about like headless chickens after the crash, saying that the state should stand behind this without having an inkling about its ability to do so. Iceland's parliament should have stood its ground and said: 'This is a commercial enterprise and you will have to deal with the estate.' I talked to one of the JP Morgan bankers flown in by the government on that October Saturday afternoon with a simple instruction to 'come and help with the economy'. He has told me that it was chaotic when they got there. Nobody knew what was happening. The level of incompetence and amateurism was incredible – perhaps unsurprising, considering that Iceland, with only 320,000 people, does not have a deep talent pool for dealing with financial crises.

Over the crisis weekend, the Bank of England told Landsbanki to move the supervision of the deposits to Heritable so the Financial Services Authority (FSA) and the UK's deposit protection scheme would cover and stabilise them. Landsbanki had discussions about this with the FSA and started to make progress. Hector Sants, the FSA's chairman, gave Landsbanki a week to ten days to switch the assets and, as a measure of good faith, deposit €300 million with the Bank of England on Monday 6 October. To do that, Landsbanki needed a loan from the Icelandic government and, after a frantic weekend of talks, the message about what was needed finally reached Haarde's office at midnight on the Sunday. 'Don't worry about it' was the message from the prime minister to Landsbanki in a phone call, and we went home with a sigh of relief. Having slept terribly on Friday night and Saturday night, I slept well that Sunday, safe in the knowledge we were going to make it.

As it turned out, we didn't. For some reason that I have never understood, the prime minister's view changed overnight. The Icelandic Central Bank refused to give Landsbanki that €300 million. It didn't even give an answer until 4 pm, close to the end of the working day in London. That was the final straw, I believe, for the UK authorities, who had noticed a Kaupthing transfer from London to Luxembourg at around this time so were already worried about Icelandic funds moving out of the UK. Lehman had transferred more than £8 billion from the UK during the week before the bank filed for bankruptcy, and the UK authorities wanted no more of that. The UK government reacted by invoking anti-terrorism legislation, which was originally intended to allow it to seize funds from money launderers and terrorists. This still seems to me to be an afterthought by the UK government. It had been dealing with the collapses of HBOS and RBS that weekend and was busy injecting billions of pounds into them. Then Icesave came up as an additional problem; the government had the anti-terrorism legislation and decided to use all the powers it had. After all, the sharpest minds in the UK and the US were making monumental decisions that weekend, calculating and arranging what to do, while Iceland's government was running around helplessly, not knowing what was going on. It didn't even have a spokesperson.

In Iceland, the government did not have the option of bailing out the banks as the UK government did with RBS and HBOS because the krona was too weak and foreign reserves were not available to prop up the nation. In my view, however, Iceland's government was unprepared and completely out of its depth. I was in London watching Sky TV when the UK chancellor, Alistair Darling, announced the enacting of the anti-terrorism legislation. 'I knew it,' I told a colleague. 'The government has not just completely botched it in Iceland; it has crossed the line internationally.'

After learning that Landsbanki would not be receiving the amount needed, the board held a meeting in the evening where the decision was straightforward. Without the €300 million, the bank could not survive. It called the FSA to say that it could not continue with the plan, and 6 October 2008 was the last day of operations for Landsbanki as it then was. It was hardly alone. Tuesday 7 October was the last day of trading for Glitnir, which had seen the government attempt to nationalise it a week earlier. Wednesday was the last day for Kaupthing. The chain of events still leaves a bitter taste. All three banks asked for assistance from the Icelandic government. Glitnir asked for €600 million and got it. Kaupthing asked for €500 million and got it. Landsbanki asked for the smallest amount and was the only one of the three banks to receive nothing.

I still find it astounding that Landsbanki was the bank that the government chose not to support, considering that it was offering security of €2 billion for the loan, made up of €1 billion in government bonds, €500 million in housing bonds and €500 million in debt from the Icelandic pension fund system. These were rock-solid assets and the loan-to-value ratio was 15 per cent against the security, meaning there were sufficient funds to cover the loan six times. So why was it not given what it needed? I believe it was a purely political decision, nothing to do with economics. It is a fact that the governor of the Central Bank and the prime minister had a phone call to discuss the loan to Kaupthing, but what the two men said has never been revealed, even though the call was recorded and the parliament itself asked for the information. The prime minister, who didn't know at the time that the conversation was being recorded, has vetoed all requests to make it public.

It's tragic, but the government perceived Kaupthing to be the strongest bank. This was mostly because Kaupthing had made two totally false claims that on the face of it certainly strengthened the bank. The first was that the bank did not have any subprime loans on its books. That turned out not to be true: Kaupthing did have subprime exposure through its subsidiary Onca, which it had hidden in this shell company in order to paint a rosier picture of its financial health. The second claim was made a few weeks before the collapse, when Kaupthing announced that Sheikh Mohammed Bin Khalifa Bin Hamad al-Thani had bought a 5 per cent stake in the bank, commenting that this was a mark of confidence in the bank. Later it turned out that the bank had financed the deal itself. Basically, Kaupthing committed the most serious economic crimes in Icelandic history, and the people running it at that time were sentenced to the harshest punishments that the nation has ever handed down for such matters, with hard prison sentences of 4½–5½ years for the four men who created that fake deal and misdirected the authorities in the middle of the crises.

The man behind the S-Group in the privatisation, industrialist Olafur Olafsson, was sentenced in 2013 to three and a half years' imprisonment for market manipulation. Kaupthing's former CEO, its former chairman and the former CEO of Kaupthing's Luxembourg Bank also received heavy sentences. And in 2020 the CEO of Glitnir was sentenced to five years of probation for agency fraud.

Following the banking collapse, both the general public and politicians started demanding that those deemed responsible for the banks' downfall be held to account. In response to this widespread concern, a dedicated special prosecutor's office was established in 2009, tasked with investigating suspected criminal activities leading up to, coinciding with and subsequent to the events that triggered the banking crash in Iceland.

Kaupthing's four directors with their jail sentences, as presented by the Icelandic newspaper *DV* in 2014. *Left to right:* Magnus Gudmundsson, former CEO of Kaupthing Luxembourg; Olafur Olafsson, the second largest shareholder at the time; former chief executive Hreidar Mar Sigurdsson; and former chairman Sigurdur Einarsson.

The special prosecutor's office operated until 2015, when its responsibilities were transferred to the district prosecutor's office. Investigation of the final criminal case related to the economic collapse was concluded in December 2018. In all, 202 cases were comprehensively examined: of these, sixteen went to trial, with thirteen resulting in convictions.

In all, 35 bankers were found guilty and 27 received prison sentences. Five were sentenced for more than one case, but as the maximum sentence for fraud in Iceland is six years some individuals evaded the longer punishment that multiple convictions might otherwise have incurred. And although not all of those sentenced served time behind bars there was still for a time a significant number of white-collar criminals in Iceland's open prisons.

Eight of these cases were referred to the European Court of Human Rights (ECHR) with one case resulting in the Icelandic state being directed to provide compensation for damages. In 2021 the Icelandic state also acknowledged that five individuals had not received a fair trial and agreed to pay them compensation, leading to their cases being dismissed by the ECHR and resumed in the Icelandic courts. One case still awaits resolution by the ECHR.

In the end the bank I invested in, Landsbanki, had the fewest cases and convictions out of the three banks during the judicial 'purge' of the banking and business sector following the crash.*

The government opted to support Kaupthing because it was much closer to the smaller party in the coalition, which was strangely the strongest force in the government's crisis meetings over the weekend of the crash. I have been told that, on that Sunday night, 5 October 2008, Haarde was in such a state of shock that his hands were shaking and he could hardly speak. I was speechless, too, when I heard the news some 16 hours later. This decision will always be a 'sliding doors' fate-changing moment of life. We will never know if

---

*Only three criminal cases relating to the activities of Landsbanki were brought to court. In one, all parties were acquitted. In the other two. however, the defendants were wrongly sentenced by a panel including a supreme court judge who was later deemed to have lacked the required impartiality due to the loss of his significant shareholdings in the bank. The state acknowledged this with a special declaration, and the ECHR recognised that the convictions were delivered by a court that included a judge who lacked the required impartiality, while also considering the treatment of the defendants to be in violation of due process for other reasons. As a result, after subsequent retrials, either partial convictions with reduced sentences were handed down, or the defendants were acquitted altogether.

Landsbanki would have made it if it had got the loan. But we know that Kaupthing did not make it.

In their 2016 book *The Icelandic Financial Crisis*, Ásgeir Jónsson, economist and current governor of the Central Bank of Iceland, and Hersir Sigurgeirsson, associate professor of finance at the University of Iceland, say there is some variation in the average recovery figures of the Icelandic banks. It was lowest for Kaupthing's estate (40 per cent), while the estates of Glitnir and Landsbanki recovered 44 per cent and 58 per cent respectively.* They go on to say:

> The final payout for general creditors of Kaupthing and Glitnir were 30 per cent and 30.2 per cent respectively. These statistics refer only to the parent companies; given the high recoveries of the banks' subsidiaries (e.g. KSF, with at least 85 per cent and Heritable bank with about 98 per cent), the recoveries on a consolidated basis are higher.
>
> The variation in recovery rates can be explained partly by differences in the banks' structures and the jurisdiction where their foreign assets were controlled. As a rule, foreign recovery was much better abroad than at home, as domestic assets were engulfed in the financial crisis. Kaupthing was organised into a number of subsidiaries. In contrast, foreign lending at Landsbanki was to a much greater extent carried out from the mother company in Iceland. Hence, the resulting assets came under Icelandic jurisdiction, which led to an overall higher recovery ratio for Landsbanki than the other banks.

*

---

* Recoveries for general creditors were lowest on Landsbanki's estate (14.38 per cent), which can be attributed to the large amount of priority claims due to Icesave.

The hysteria that arose around the issue of the Icesave international internet savings account that Landsbanki had operated
was something I had never experienced before. Icesave
dominated politics for several years, diverting government
from dealing with such key issues as ownership of the fish
stock in Icelandic waters and much-needed constitutional
reforms.

The 'Icesavestein monster', as it was sometimes referred to,
was a bit like the Y2K (Year 2000) millennium bug and Iraq's
weapons of mass destruction (WMD): a lot of fuss and fear
about something that turned out to be nothing, or at least not
very much. And, like the Y2K bug and Iraq's WMD, it was
used to further the interests of those who were busy stoking
the flames of fear.

The main strand of the claim that made up this issue was
that an enormous sum invested by UK and Dutch savers
would now have to be paid back by the Icelandic taxpayer.
It was an incendiary idea, which, by virtue of being repeated,
became an accepted truth. In fact, for the Icelandic taxpayer
to have to foot the bill, Landsbanki's assets would have had
to have been worthless or to have fallen at least 50 per cent.
Neither was ever the case. Landsbanki did not go bankrupt
because it had lost its assets. It had simply not been able to
change Icelandic krona for foreign currency. It was a liquidity
crisis, rather than any fraud or malfeasance, that forced it
to stop. Furthermore, no one had previously suggested that
the Icelandic state was responsible for debts of a commercial
enterprise, so it was extraordinary to do so now. The problem
was some ambiguity over the responsibilities in such situations of EFTA countries (Iceland, Norway and Switzerland)
vis-à-vis EU member states.

My legal adviser had been working in the financial markets
division of the Ministry of Commerce, which was responsible

for banking and deposit insurance regulation and the implementation of EU rules into Icelandic law. He knew these rules at first hand and was adamant that the argument that the state had to pick up the bill was completely wrong. Landsbanki itself had various legal opinions of the same conclusion. Essentially, the disaster of 2008 was a global crash and contagion, not some isolated little island affair. This was therefore always going to be a matter for the international courts, which resolved the issue in exactly the way that I anticipated.

Icesave was a complicated issue that arose at a time when the nation was confused and anxious, and it became the focus by which that anxiety and fear were stoked in the press, through social media and in everyday conversation. It was intense and immensely harmful. In the end, as a result of pressure from the UK and Dutch governments that Iceland should pick up the bill for any shortfall in the repayment of the debt, Iceland took the extraordinary step of holding two referendums on whether it should, and twice the Icelandic people voted 'no'. Only once before in the republic's 60-year history had the president of Iceland used his special power to call a national referendum to affirm or block parliament's actions.

As for me, I had invested my own capital in Landsbanki and had only myself to blame for my own losses, but being held responsible for the collapse of an entire economy was something I found hard to swallow. It was the worst of times for me – and really quite frightening. Icesave and Landsbanki were toxic, and anyone connected with them, from employees to advisers, was almost a social pariah. I was beset by depression over it all. In the media I was asked if I was going to pick up the bill myself, and it was suggested that it was 'prudent for me not be out and about in Iceland these days'. I was as afraid and angry as anyone there, but nobody was interested in listening when I came out publicly and said that I was certain that Landsbanki's estate would totally cover its Icesave exposure and that it would never be a cost to anyone outside. I was desperate to get the position clarified, but the confusion seemed to drag on for ever. To many Icelanders, I was instrumental in bringing about Iceland's sorry state; I was a troublemaker who had no right to be heard.

Were the banks reckless in their aggressive expansion? Perhaps? But did that description also apply to the actions of the Icelandic central bank or the government? You could say that recklessness had crept into the entire way of operating in Iceland at all levels in the crazy boom years. One thing I am fairly sure about, however, is that the Icesave fallout affected Landsbanki's standing when we were rejected for the state help that would have saved the day. How else can the decision be explained? The Icesave debacle ruined my reputation – and yet no depositor lost any money. The UK insurance scheme lost nothing on it, and the Netherlands has recovered the full €1.4 billion that it paid to depositors of Landsbanki's Dutch Icesave unit after selling the rights to proceeds from its bankruptcy to an unnamed buyer in August 2014.

*

All this was spinning around in 2009 when I fulfilled a long-standing engagement to give the graduation speech for the Stern Business School of New York University, my alma mater. I had accepted the invitation gladly, but by the time the graduation ceremony came about in 2009, my world had crumbled. I contacted the university and asked if they wanted to reconsider their choice of speaker, given that the global financial markets crash had also seen almost my entire business empire come crashing down. The university's president, John Sexton, replied swiftly. 'Thor,' he said, 'of course we want you to do it – now more than ever. The business world has its ups and downs and we need to remind people of that, so it's ideal for someone who has just gone through a perfect storm to share his experience.' I was grateful, but at the same time unsure of how well I would cope with giving the speech. With all that was happening, I was in limbo in so many ways.

The night before the event, I was still unsure what I was going to talk about. These young people had invested years in educating themselves in business, and instead of heading straight for a promising career on the back of their degree, they were almost all facing the prospect of no jobs in a sector that was bombed out and more preoccupied with firing than hiring. It was a horrible time to be graduating, and I had to find out what I could say to inspire this crowd or at least come up with some advice to help them figure out what to do next. As I pondered this, Kristin pointed out a reference to Charles Darwin in a magazine in our hotel room and I was struck by its relevance. The devastating crash we had all just gone through was like some force of nature that forces evolution to happen in the animal kingdom. It was a catalyst for change. I did not know what the changes ahead were, but a transformation was undoubtedly under way and so I decided to focus my speech on the process of change itself. To do this, what better to consult than the works of the originator of the theory of evolution?

The next morning I went hand in hand with Kristin to the event and stood at the podium at the graduation ceremony in New York's enormous Radio City Music Hall, addressing a full house of graduates and their families along with the professors. I spoke for a few minutes and gave the highlights of my career from leaving NYU to that point in time. I finished with the following words, inspired by the great evolutionist himself.

I know many of you here are worried about the current global financial crisis and its effect on your future career. I have strongly advocated that this crisis is not an isolated event that will sort itself out and go back to the way things were. I believe that this is fundamentally a process of real evolution of the financial system with profound changes taking shape now and in the near future. Therefore as you plan your future, I would like you to consider carefully what Darwin said about evolution, and I quote: 'It is not the strongest of the species which survives, nor the most intelligent, but the one most responsive to change.' You need to be very flexible in the future and embrace change. In my case, for instance, the road from graduation to my current job is almost too unreal to be true, but it is basically a story of how things never go as you plan – but may still turn out as you want.

To sum it all up, I probably do things the same way as most of you. I attempt to organise resources in an intuitive way. I have to be passionate about everything I venture into. I accept full responsibility for the outcome. And if everything will turn sour in the end I can always say: 'I started out with nothing, and I still have most of it left.' So I cannot be other than happy, grateful and optimistic. Therefore, I say to you: never be afraid to lose out. That fear can keep you from betting big on your own intuition and reaping the rewards of your passion in work. This is what I want to leave you with as a thought, and I want to challenge you to bet on yourself, your intuition and your own talent at all times and especially if it is against the odds.

It was a great moment for me, and I honestly felt that I had hit upon a way to look upon the uncertainties of the time in a positive way, and hopefully I managed to inspire a few young people in the process. Later that day I went with Kristin to a late lunch to celebrate the event, and we were sitting in a nice hotel restaurant on a fine spring day in Manhattan when I got a call from my office in London. My two colleagues were on speakerphone and proceeded to summarise for me the meetings that had taken place with Deutsche Bank in London that day, which were the culmination of very lengthy and stormy confrontations over the previous eight weeks. It was very bad news, and I felt as though I had been doused with a bucket of iced water. Deutsche Bank, my biggest creditor as a result of its loans to Actavis, had finally spelled out its terms. They were completely unacceptable. The scale of my Actavis problem finally dawned on me.

The day had started so perfectly with the speech and then been turned totally on its head with this news from London. But after a few hours of fuming with anger, I had what recovered alcoholics refer to as a 'moment of clarity'. The key to my future was embedded in the speech I had just delivered. I needed to adapt and roll with it instead of fighting. It was not my time to be strong, nor to be clever, but to adapt to this new world and learn to play the game again from scratch. The creditors were the ones setting the rules, and I had to adjust to their thinking and their agenda. I had to stop fighting with them and do things their way. My incentive was that by doing so I would buy time to work things out. Ever the optimist, I always believed I could help turn Actavis around and help it to become one of the biggest companies in its field. At that time, it looked far from promising to the bankers, but I thought to myself: 'That's exactly it. They're looking from a different angle, and I need to work out a special situation that will enable us both to get our desired outcomes, even though they are totally different.'

This became the genesis for my new business platform, and

although I knew I could end up with nothing if things stayed the same or got worse, there was also the chance to make a healthy return. The world was worrying about sovereign defaults, and Portugal, Italy, Greece and Spain, the so-called PIGS economies, were being bailed out. But I had bet my life's work on a similar structure after the Russian crash and I was now prepared to do that again. The similarities between the bet I made on the Russian brewery with my American investors and what I was doing now with Actavis were striking. It was no less than a game of double or quits.

Actavis was in a bad state after the health and safety incident which led to a Food and Drug Administration decree. With a whole division shut down and the need to recall more than sixty products, the company's underlying earnings shrank dramatically overnight. The debt of the leveraged buy-out was crushing the company, in part because the original management projections for the deal had proved to be unduly optimistic. We also had enormous price pressure in key markets like Germany. The economic meltdown following the Lehman Brothers crash was also hindering business confidence in all our markets. To top it all, because of the FDA decree and other problems we had had to replace the chief executive and were working with management to try and keep the company's head above water.

Deutsche Bank, which had a lot of money at stake, insisted that I do two things. First, I had to put more money into Actavis. This was bad news, but I used all my remaining funds and injected €150 million into the company as fresh equity on top of the roughly €1 billion that I had put in initially. Second, Deutsche Bank insisted that I look for a buyer for Actavis, which I duly did with the help of Merrill Lynch Bank of America. Needless to say, trying to sell the company in this environment and with these internal issues proved futile.

The indicative offers we received reflected the parlous state of the company and were very disappointing. We abandoned the sale process and set about coming up with a rescue plan. My Novator investment company presented a six-point plan, but getting Deutsche Bank to engage in discussing this and making a decision proved difficult.

I had a meeting with Michael Kors, who was joint head of Deutsche Bank's investment banking arm at the time. He said it was happening in his division and having a horrible effect on the board and on bonuses and everything there. At Deutsche Bank credit control meetings, it was a standard routine for bankers to take executives through the company's ten biggest debtors. Lately it had been somewhat skewed with the US government at number one, the UK government at number two and me at number three. That was far from normal for the bank. His words demonstrated how uncomfortable Deutsche was with its loan position, and I felt bad about it, too; the scale of my problem was gargantuan.

However, if I thought that dealing with Deutsche on an Actavis rescue plan was difficult, that was nothing compared to dealing with the bankrupt estates of the Icelandic banks run by so-called 'resolution committees'. When the dust had finally settled on the restructuring agreement with my creditors (of course I had to call it 'Darwin'), I wanted to know how much we had spent on the hordes of lawyers and consultants. I was astonished when the final bill for putting the agreement in place arrived: €45 million, plus a huge amount of blood, sweat, tears and time. In the final hours of getting everything signed, the team worked on it for 56 hours non-stop.

As the signature pages were lined up, I walked around an enormous meeting table in the London offices of law firm Clifford Chance and tried to lighten the mood by playing a song on my iPhone as I signed. It was 'Release Me' by Engelbert

Humperdinck. I felt the words 'Please release me, let me go – so I can live again' summed up my feelings perfectly, as I had finally staved off the threat of personal bankruptcy. It was a great moment.

History will judge us not on the crashes we avoid, but on how we deal with the ones that inevitably happen.

9

NEW HORIZONS
2014-2023

Rising up, back on the street
Did my time, took my chances
Went the distance, now I'm back on my feet
Just a man and his will to survive

So many times it happens too fast
You trade your passion for glory
Don't lose your grip on the dreams of the past
You must fight just to keep them alive

Survivor, 'Eye of the Tiger'

After everything I had been through and the amount of things I had rectified or put in order in my affairs after all those years of running too fast and carelessly, I suddenly found myself facing a very interesting question. Why was I still not married? Kristin and I had been together for many years and – after a long struggle and finally with the help of IVF – we now had two boys. We had a wonderful family together, and yet I had always postponed marriage for some reason or other.

By autumn 2010, however, I had recovered my confidence and stopped looking over my shoulder for the next crisis creeping up on me, and I asked Kristin to come away with me to an exotic and romantic place to get married as quickly and with as little fuss as possible. I felt energised and wanted to ride this wave of liberation into a new era with my wife officially by my side. She was more than happy to finally get married and we had a laugh that we had somehow never got around to it.

We decided on a civil ceremony in the most beautiful city we knew of and which coincidentally we had never been in together – Rome, the eternal city. We also decided not to tell anyone and to make it as intimate as possible. I contacted a friend of mine in Italy to help us make the arrangements after jokingly swearing him to secrecy. He agreed to be one of our witnesses and suggested his father as the other. We booked a time with the notary public for the ceremony and off we went to Rome. It all happened very quickly, and we told our boys and our families that we were just going for a short weekend break, nothing special at all. We didn't even buy any new clothes.

Kristin did have a few conditions, which were non-negotiable. She said that this was one of the most special days of any woman's life and that she wanted to bring her hairdresser to make sure she was looking her best and, being a film producer, she also recognised the importance of having a great photographer to record this occasion, especially since none of our family would be there and pictures were crucial to sharing the moment with them.

It was a chilly, rather grey late November day when we woke in the Hotel Hassler overlooking the Spanish Steps. Our wedding was booked for 3 pm and the ceremony was in the famous Campidoglio fortress in the centre of Rome, designed by Michelangelo. Our chariot for the very special day was an old Rolls-Royce in which I had installed a speaker system for the extensive playlist Kristin and I had compiled of songs that had significance to us from the twenty years we had known each other. We arrived in style at the Campidoglio, where our notary turned out to be the head of the department, with an uncanny resemblance to Mussolini (right down to the assortment of medals on his sash), as my 87-year-old witness pointed out. 'I remember him, I was here when he was,' he whispered with a smile. The ceremony was carried out in Italian with our two witnesses and a translator at our side. It was magical and so much fun as well. It felt incredible to walk out into the piazza in front of the palace hand in hand with Kristin and chat to all the locals who were congratulating us. It was the perfect day in all respects – without question the best day of my life. We rode around Rome in the Rolls-Royce all afternoon drinking champagne with the music playing and the windows open, being greeted by smiles and calls of 'bravo' from those we passed. We glided between Rome's greatest locations and monuments, savouring the moment. It was just the two of us, with not a care in the world and a fantastic new beginning. And to set the seal on our happiness, ten months later a little princess found her way into our life as well. Life was very good – there for the seizing.

My major business investment was about to get a second chance too. When at the airport about to depart on honeymoon to the Maldives, I was called by a former colleague, Sigurdur Oli Olafsson, who had previously been CEO of Actavis. Siggi Oli told me that his new company, US-listed Watson Pharmaceuticals, was interested in buying or merging with Actavis. He wanted to know if there was any way to achieve this in a low-key fashion, as the company was not interested in going into an auction. He said that Watson wanted to act soon, but understood from Deutsche Bank that a sale of Actavis was off the table for two years. He and his colleagues believed that a lot was going to happen in the world of generic pharmaceuticals in the following 24 months and the group had to move fast to be an acquirer instead of becoming a target.

I was of the same opinion and was keen to get involved in the giant game of musical chairs that I felt would start in the industry and in which I believed Actavis could be a key player. However, I had a problem, due to the agreement with Deutsche Bank. It had provided me and the company with welcome breathing space in which to rebuild the company and reduce its debt, but if we stuck to executing the four-year agreed rescue plan there was a risk we would get marginalised by consolidation among other firms in the sector. It was tricky to decide what would be the best course to follow, and of course Deutsche Bank was instinctively risk-averse and had finally got into a comfortable position with its loan to Actavis. It didn't want the boat rocked, so I needed to come up with a new plan – and fast.

In my dealings with Deutsche I knew I had available the help I had been offered by a senior board member in getting through to the head of the bank and other decision-makers if there was a communication problem or if something special came up. I had never taken up the offer, preferring to wait until I really needed it. This was a one-time favour that I knew I had to use carefully. Finally, I felt that time had come.

I was in New York for a board meeting and I met up with Siggi in the Waldorf Astoria Hotel to flush out what Watson's ideas were. Joining us in the meeting was Watson's chief executive Paul Bisaro. As they began to describe their vision for the company and the sector, I couldn't help but smile at the irony of it. Paul and I had crossed swords before in the very public battle for the Croatian pharma company Pliva, where we had each fought with every trick we knew. He had won and I had lost. That was water under the bridge, and I explained the situation for each of the stakeholders in Actavis. Deutsche Bank was looking for no risk at all, while my Novator vehicle was willing to look at the big picture in terms of future value creation. Watson's idea was to pay with cash and stock, and clearly that would not work for Deutsche, even if it could work for us. I needed to find a way to make this work for both the bank and Novator. As they say, the devil is in the detail.

After the meeting finished, I headed four blocks up Park Avenue to the Deutsche Bank building and met my friend there. I told him that all was well with the company, and our working relationship with Deutsche was in good shape. However, there was now an opportunity presenting itself and I needed someone to take a key strategic decision for the bank. I reminded him that the last time I looked for that, it had taken a year and a half. In this situation, we did not have anywhere near that much time. Deutsche had a choice between sticking to the current plan of growing Actavis or trying to cut a deal with Watson that would satisfy both them and us. I asked him to take this up with the head of the bank, and flew back to London.

The next day, I received a call asking me to come to Deutsche's headquarters in Frankfurt to sit down with its chief financial officer and his team. I had woken the giant and now had its full attention. The game was on.

In Frankfurt, I agreed with Deutsche Bank that I would continue to explore the Watson opportunity and try to crystallise it into an offer that we could work with, based on our different motivations. The weeks rolled on and I sensed that the Americans at Watson were also trying to be opportunistic and buy Actavis on the cheap through the bank. I knew, however, that Deutsche Bank had a clear pain threshold, from which it could not budge. Its absolute minimum was €4 billion in cash – more than the Americans were offering. I needed to make sure that this would not turn into a game with no outcome. This was truly a unique chance for us all.

At first, the Watson people were very enthusiastic, and then some fatigue crept in. I sensed that we were losing momentum and had a suspicion that they were looking at another company simultaneously, so I took measures to have a backup bidder on the side should they disappear. It was tricky to manage this, but it worked. I had to get people back to being laser-focused on this deal.

On 26 September 2011, at a meeting with the Watson executives in my office, I extrapolated the numbers and hypothesised about what the stock price of a Watson–Actavis combination could be over one-, two- and three-year frameworks. It was a persuasive argument and the main players all now agree that this was the point at which we all set ourselves on a mission to finish it one way or another. As it turned out, I had other matters to think about. The meeting was abruptly cut short when Kristin called to say she was going into labour prematurely and needed help immediately. I ran straight out of the meeting, shouting at my PA to call an ambulance to my home, and drove myself home like a madman, fearful for Kristin and our unborn child. Mercifully, a few hours later Kristin successfully gave birth to our little girl in an emergency procedure. I, however, still had another deal to deliver.

I would get very little out of a Watson transaction if it were all cash, so I saw an opportunity emerging in the form of a riskier contingent payment which would be paid entirely in Watson shares. I saw a potential trade between Deutsche Bank and myself in the method of payment. Once again, I would have to double up on risk in order to have a shot at the upside that my intuition was telling me was there to be had.

What happened in the following week was a trilateral negotiation between Deutsche Bank, Novator and Watson which ended with an arrangement that suited each party. Watson got Actavis. Deutsche got what it wanted, all in cash. I assumed the risk of the Actavis business not performing to an ambitious plan the next year, as well the risk of an adverse movement in the price of the Watson shares that my future payment would be made in.

It was by no means a guaranteed success, but I believed in my people and my company and I had faith in the Watson guys. It would take a few years to play out, but I rolled the dice and took a deep breath.

*

According to some measures, Novator and I owed $10 billion in 2008, and I had personally guaranteed $650 million of this debt. Since then, I have repaid my entire obligations. It was slow going at first, but then the tide started to come in.

After five moribund years in which I could see little on the horizon, events began to turn quickly. It didn't happen as rapidly as when things turned bad in the autumn of 2008. Nor did it appear in the way I expected. As an optimist, I always expected to emerge from the wreckage of 2008 at some stage, and I saw myself operating a more subdued version of the financial and business value management model that brought me so much success on the way up. And there were opportunities to do some deals. A consortium involving my investment company Novator was shortlisted to repurchase BTC, the Bulgarian telecoms company that we privatised and listed so successfully in the first decade of this century. It would have been extremely satisfying to pull off another deal there, but it didn't happen and little else stuck in those five years on the sidelines. The little leeway I had to conduct new business under the terms of the 2010 agreement with my creditors never came close to being used. I was a business pariah. The phone stopped ringing. No one wanted to know me. But I took comfort from the fact that the underlying business of Actavis and Play was doing well.

But of course the moment I was seen to be back in the game,

the calls began again. For me, it happened suddenly, almost as if it was on the flip of a coin. In late 2013, Jamie Dimon, chief executive of JP Morgan, rang me and said that he was personally at my disposal if I needed any help with a $1 billion bond issue being undertaken by Play, the Polish telecoms operator that I had set up back in 2005. The bank was very keen to handle it, and we were glad to oblige. Then I got a call saying the same thing from Brian Moynihan, chief executive of Bank of America. JP Morgan and Merrill Lynch ended up getting the mandate to act for Play on the bond issue. And as part of the process, which other global bank should be back at my office offering to lend us $1 billion but Deutsche Bank? That was ironic. Some of the bankers we dealt with this time were the same ones who had put all that debt into Actavis, very nearly losing a good deal of it. I rang them to say that they weren't going to get the bond issue mandate, and then got a text message back saying that they were prepared to underwrite the whole issue. I couldn't believe they were prepared to do the same thing that ended up with us both in trouble the last time we did a deal together.

By mid-2014, I had finally paid off all my creditors under the Darwin agreement. Ironically, in the end less than 10 per cent of the overall amount was actually owed to local Icelandic banks. But it was done and I finally had carte blanche again to make my way in a new world of investments. As the leverage bubble had burst, that was now a no-go zone for me. I needed to find a way to generate outsized returns without using debt as the main driver. All the action seemed to be heading into the tech investing arena, with a consensus that the classical business models were going to be fundamentally challenged by disruptive new models as technological advances made customer interaction fundamentally different from how it had been before. The advent of the super-apps like Uber, Spotify,

Instagram, Netflix and Deliveroo had radically changed consumer behaviour in a major way.

I took to that market like a fish to water. I had some experience of the tech sector through my gaming portfolio companies. One such business was CCP, an interesting company founded in Iceland by a team of developers and gaming enthusiasts with investments from an Icelandic pension fund. These two very different groups did not see eye to eye at all, so the founders approached me to buy out the institutional investor. They presumed someone like me who had founded and built several businesses would speak their language and be a better fit to expand the company.

The founders and management had massive ambitions that I took with a pinch of salt, but there was an incredibly loyal fanbase of customers who paid a monthly subscription fee. The company's stated goal was to create another world outside the real one: to their users, the creation was more important than the actual world! They called it the 'Metaverse' and they were actually the first real players there, years before Facebook's Mark Zuckerberg called it out as the next level of social networks and renamed his company Meta. CCP's EVE Online game was and is a space-based sandbox 'massively multiplayer online' (MMO) game known for its player-driven economy, vast universe and complex gameplay mechanics. It allows players to explore, trade, engage in player-versus-player combat, and participate in large-scale battles and political events within the game's persistent universe.

I saw CCP grow from one office in Iceland to large offices in the US, Shanghai, the UK and elsewhere. As most of EVE's players were inside that sandbox world for hours each day, it really felt that it was becoming the most important place for many of them. The annual EVE Fanfest attracted thousands of people from all over the world, and often people from different countries who had met inside the game would get married there in reality. It was astounding to watch this community as it grew, and I really felt that if this was a guide to the future, then technology was changing the social fabric in more fundamental ways than most people realised.

I decided that I had to focus more of my time and effort on being part of that future, while still keeping half my bets on the old industrial world with my investments in telecoms. After all, the telecom companies operate the key infrastructure that allows all of these internet-based businesses and communities to stay connected and blossom. I figured that it would be a wise move to have one foot on each side of the equation: the content on one side and the delivery system on the other. I knew that these new tech companies about to change the world were inherently risky investments, as well over 75 per cent of start-ups fail. So I needed to adjust my investment style for this sector, to allow for smaller stakes in more companies to diversify risk, instead of my old mantra of taking by far the biggest stake in a company in order to have more influence on its direction and control in case management was off-course. As a result, I started to get involved in a smaller capacity with many tech companies, which was a fresh direction that I liked.

CCP never managed to go mainstream and remains a producer of a cult game with a small but extremely loyal fanbase compared with the big computer-game names most of us recognise. I also invested in other exciting ventures, including Zwift, a global multiplayer videogame platform developer for the indoor cycling and fitness community. This was based on our vision of the gradual computer 'gamification' of popular sports, as the physical exercise regimen fuses with interactive social media and virtual reality. Zwift is really a groundbreaking player in this space and has taken the cycling community – professional, semi-pro and amateur – by storm. Zwift is popular because it turns indoor cycling into an addictive, social and competitive game with immersive worlds, real training benefits and year-round riding freedom. Zwift took the typically boring indoor trainer experience and turned it into something genuinely enjoyable and motivating.

Interestingly but not that surprisingly Zwift did exceptionally well during the Covid-19 pandemic when people had to stay at home and exercise there. It provided a social context and community during those strange times.

Another investment was in Klang Games, a Berlin-based studio building a multiplayer online game called Seed, in which AI will complement and take over a participating gamer's roleplay in a virtual world when he is offline, copying his playing habits in a such a way that he never has to reboot into the game: it is non-stop and in real time.

We also went into a classic founder-led gaming start-up called Steel City Interactive. The company was founded in 2020 by the three Habib brothers from Sheffield, England, who are boxing fanatics. Despite having no prior experience in video game development, they taught themselves the necessary skills online and collaborated with the boxing community to create 'Undisputed', a hyper-realistic boxing game. They landed more than £15 million of funding led by Novator Ventures and London Venture Partners, with backing from boxing insiders Egis Klimas and Jose de la Cruz. Featuring over 70 licensed fighters like Oleksandr Usyk, Manny Pacquiao and Tyson Fury, 'Undisputed' launched in 2024 across major platforms, sold over a million copies, and has carved out a serious spot in the sports gaming arena.

We also backed a great unicorn in cybersecurity called NordVPN, started by two classic scrappy founders from Lithuania. Tom Okman and Eimantas Sabaliauskas turned NordVPN into the world's leading virtual private network, trusted by more than 14 million users. With zero outside backing at the start, they built a global powerhouse known for unmatched security, speed and innovation – outpacing all rivals and redefining online privacy worldwide. I sold back my shares to the founders recently at a good profit, and in my opinion they will continue to do well

My first foray into e-commerce was in Rebag, based in New York, which has the wonderful idea of trading used luxury handbags and jewellery. This company was well ahead of the trend for environmental, social and governance (ESG) engagement by recycling and finding new homes for unwanted fashion items, thereby reducing the volume of new manufactured goods. I also made investments in Deliveroo (which went well) and the UK used-car internet retail platform Cazoo (a disastrous investment). We also branched out into healthcare technology. I took part in fundraising for the Cambridge, UK firm Touchlight which is revolutionising the manufacture of DNA-based drugs by making artificial DNA as the raw material for them. This is a game-changer in speed, quality and delivery for the next generation of blockbuster drugs. I also funded Sidekick Health, a digital therapeutics company helping people to prevent and combat chronic diseases.

Play is itself quite a story. I founded it in 2005 at a time when in my opinion the Polish telecoms market was badly run, being dominated by big European companies, each of which was having to deal with tussles between its shareholders. Vodafone had a dispute with its Polish partner that ended with its Polish operation being bought by Polkomtel; France's Vivendi and Deutsche Telekom's T-Mobile were fighting over their asset in Poland; and France Telecom's Orange was having a problem with its local partner. We saw an opportunity for a fourth player to start afresh and try to capture market share, so we sneaked into the market by buying telecoms licences. We didn't bother with 2G and decided to bid only for 3G licences. It was unheard of for a private equity company to buy licences without any experience in building the infrastructure. But we found Netia, a small fixed-line independent, to help us as a local player in the Polish market. We ended up outbidding 3, the mobile phone provider backed by Hong Kong's Hutchison Whampoa. The key to making this work was getting funding, which we did principally from China Development Bank. We had spotted in our privatisation and tender processes for upgrading Bulgaria's telecoms that the Chinese government has a long-term strategic plan to become a major player in telecoms infrastructure. We saw that the best kit was coming from Chinese subcontractors, so we went straight to them and found that they had big plans.

We had big plans too and suggested that we work together, building a new mobile telecommunications infrastructure in eastern Europe's biggest country, with a population of 40 million. The Chinese like to take a long-term view, so we signed a letter of intent in China at the same time as we were bidding for licences. I used the occasion of an official state visit from Iceland to China to get the deal rubber-stamped, and so in the Palace of Heavenly Peace in Tiananmen Square there was an official signing ceremony as the climax of the state visit. We signed a letter of intent to buy all the equipment from Huawei, which has since emerged from the shadows as a dominant player in global telecoms, and which lobbied China Development Bank to make its first ever major loan in Europe. In total, this loan amounted to more than $1 billion. I have a great picture of the deal being signed by us and Huawei with the presidents of Iceland and China standing behind. It was an occasion that I am sure went a long way towards getting China Development Bank's support and resulted in Huawei sending an army of Chinese engineers to Poland, where they helped us set up the towers, transmission and other infra-structure from scratch. We entered Poland as outsiders and targeted the youth market. It was tough going for the first two years but our patience paid off, and after about four years we broke even.

I came within striking distance of losing Play completely in the 2008 crash. As part of the deal with China Development Bank, we were to feed in equity funding as it was needed as part of our expansion plan and the bank would match that with loan funds. Typically, we would do that at the end of each year, but the events of 2008 meant that when the call came to put in €150 million at the end of that year we could not come up with the money. Novator and Straumur jointly owned 75 per cent of Play at the time, with the remainder having recently been acquired by a Greek entrepreneur, Panos Germanos, in return for injecting his business into ours. Germanos had built a major mobile phone retail network in Poland and elsewhere in eastern Europe, with more than 1,000 shops and the best sales network of any telecoms operator in Poland. Having that available to us meant that we now had a better retail presence in Poland than any of the big incumbent players, which helped us grow at a phenomenal pace. At the end of 2008, Germanos could see that his quarter of the required €150 million would get Play nowhere if we were not able to finance our portion. He managed to come up with the entire €150 million, which he put into the business in exchange for us giving him a further 25 per cent stake. The way I saw it was that it was better to have 50 per cent of something than 75 per cent of nothing.

A few months later, the Greek economy imploded. With the kind of global economic event timing that I should be used to by now, there was just this narrow window between the fall of Iceland and the financial collapse of Greece in which Germanos was able to help us. On a state visit to Iceland in 2007, the Greek president had given me the highest order possible for a foreigner in Greece, making me a Grand Commander of the Order of the Phoenix. I didn't think about it much at the time, but the phoenix seems a suitable bird for me. It was a Greek who recognised before anyone else that I had the phoenix in me. He came to the rescue in my darkest hour in Poland and we have remained partners ever since. The 50 per cent holding in Play was held partly through Novator and partly through Straumur, and in 2014 Novator bought out Straumur. It was widely thought in Poland that we would be a distressed seller following the crash – it was a loss-making start-up telecoms company owned by an Icelander and a Greek, after all. However, we managed to pull it off and keep control, and when we came to refinance in late 2013 some of the biggest names in banking were quick to knock on our door.

Under our stewardship Play became the fifth-most-valuable brand in the country, greatly increasing the value of my 50 per cent holding. In the ten years since launch, Play gained more than 15 million subscribers, becoming Poland's biggest mobile phone operator, with a 28 per cent subscriber market share. Novator led a flotation of Play on the Warsaw Stock Exchange in July 2017, with a market capitalisation of €2.2 billion. The company distributed more than €330 million in dividends over the following three years, and Novator fully exited in 2020, selling its remaining stake to French investor Iliad Group, led by Xavier Niel.

The other main reason for the sudden revival in my fortunes related to Actavis, which since 2008 had been my biggest piece of unfinished business. For much of that time, it struggled to be worth anything near the €5.3 billion that we had paid for it just before everything went wrong in the financial markets. Write-downs were taken and the company went sideways, but the logic behind the deal remained intact. In a world where the truly big drug discoveries are thought to have been made, generic pharmaceutical companies have the attraction of a much lower cost base, with plenty of off-patent drugs to produce. Generics were one of the last unconsolidated parts of the pharmaceutical landscape and when the mergers and acquisitions market started to recover in 2013, generic pharmaceuticals was one of the first sectors to benefit.

Actavis got over its 2008 management and operational problems and is now a good company with an excellent research and development pipeline. Its recent success has been driven by mergers and acquisitions. First, Actavis was taken over by America's Watson Pharmaceuticals for €4.25 billion in 2012. The following year, the combined company merged with Ireland's Warner Chilcott in a deal valued at $8.5 billion. In July 2014 it completed the acquisition of Forest Laboratories for $25 billion. Then Actavis bought Allergan, the manufacturer of Botox, for $70.5 billion, assuming the acquired company's name. A $160 billion merger with Pfizer was abandoned and Allergan later sold its generic drugs business to Teva Pharmaceuticals for $40.5 billion before being acquired by America's AbbVie for $63 billion in 2019. Not bad for a company that I bought at a valuation of $20 million in 1999. I originally put only $4.5 million into its privatisation when it had revenues of $100 million. By 2016, when I finalised the sale of my last remaining stake, I had made $1.1 billion from the company. But even before this, after five years in which the financial markets were effectively closed to me, the combined growth of my investments in Play and Actavis had by February 2014 made me – on paper, at least – a billionaire again.

Unlike last time, there was no fanfare or front-page magazine appearance, and that is how it should be from now on. I would like to think I have learned a lot from my experiences since

2008, though I do reflect ruefully on the irony of my downfall. The Landsbanki investment that brought me down was to my mind the safest and most stable of all my investments and risk-taking financial gambles. I remember explaining to Kristin that this was a 100-year-old institution that was monitored by Iceland's stock exchange and Iceland's premier financial regulator and advised by international rating agencies. There were a lot of outside checks and controls and I took comfort from these, wrongly as it turned out. I thought Landsbanki was the one investment that I didn't need to worry about since it was being externally monitored. At the beginning of 2008, only 18 per cent of my estimated personal net worth of $3.4 billion–$4 billion was accounted for by my interest in Icelandic banks, which I had acquired for just €150 million.

Despite all this, Landsbanki ended up being the only one of the companies I have been involved in that has gone bankrupt. This was more a consequence of Iceland's entire financial system collapsing than of the bank crashing, but it brought the rest of my business interests crashing down too. This was because after the crash I found myself with €650 million-worth of personal guarantees. My advisers in London said that this was the biggest personal guarantee they had ever come across. I got to that figure by reckoning that I could enter into personal guarantees for 10 per cent of my net worth. At that point my net worth was about €3 billion, so I could go up to €300 million if I had to. I never thought that the financial affairs of my father, who was my partner in those guarantees, would blow up, but when he went bankrupt these guarantees became my responsibility, as had been agreed. And those personal guarantees were mostly given in the months before the 2008 crash. When other people were making exit plans, we were stepping up and taking personal guarantees. We withstood the first six months after the October 2008 crash, but then Straumur was taken over by the authorities and Deutsche Bank called to say that my rescue plan for Actavis was not working. For the bank not to repossess the company, we had injected another €150 million of capital in the late summer of 2008. It had not been enough to cover all the interest payments, but it was sufficient to pay salaries and keep the company running for the next few years, which was very important.

I believe that all this has to be seen in the context of the Icelandic banking bubble of the first decade of this century being effectively one big casino. The political elite of Iceland made a bet that it was a good time for bank privatisations which would make everybody money. The ruling party's cronies were the first in line. Then came its backers. All the party's backers and voters were supposed to make money, as long as they had the will to go with free-market reforms. So they privatised Iceland's biggest money-making machines but failed to consider how all this could be regulated. To compound the problem, the newly privatised banks set about inflating the asset bubble by injecting the incredible amount of debt that was available worldwide. When the genie was released from the bottle, no one foresaw that the international market forces of a record-breaking supply of debt capital would hit a willing, eager and novice investor community in Iceland like a tidal wave. And no one came up with a plan of what to do if it didn't work. Two days after the publication in April 2010 of the Icelandic government's report on what happened in the financial crisis, I issued a public apology for my role in it. On the front page of *Frettabladid*, Iceland's largest newspaper, I stated:

> I the undersigned, Bjorgolfur Thor, apologise to all Iceland-
> ers for my role in the asset- and debt-bubble that led to the
> collapse of the Icelandic banking system. I apologise for
> my complacency towards the danger signs which arose. I

apologise for having not succeeded in following my instincts when I realised the danger. I request your forgiveness.

I had hoped that others would follow my example and apologise for their role in events leading to the crash. But no one did. And therefore no reconciliation ever got off the ground.

That is history now and I'm glad to say that I have made good on my promises to repay my creditors and stick to the terms of the restructuring settlement that was reached in 2010 between myself, my investment company Novator, and all of our creditors. This agreement was projected to take approximately five to six years to fulfil, and an army of around 100 lawyers, accountants and other specialists worked tirelessly on it. The forensic accounting process was immense and spanned nearly a year and a half, and I am sure that such thorough practices were not employed in the cases involving others connected to the Icelandic banking system. As part of the settlement, I relinquished most of my personal assets, including various apartments and holiday houses, a private jet and a yacht. Moreover, I granted creditors complete access to all of my bank accounts to ensure that all my assets were on the table.

I was determined to ensure that these agreements would achieve the goal of paying everything I owed to the bank group and winning me back my freedom. This required relentless efforts to maximise the value of assets, including my shares in Actavis, Play, CCP and Verne Holdings, which operates a data centre in Iceland.

I am proud to say that I kept my word, and the commitment I made to fully repay all debts came true ahead of schedule. In August 2014, the comprehensive settlement between myself, my investment company Novator, and the Icelandic and international creditors was successfully concluded. A total of 1,200 billion Icelandic krona had been paid, with 100 billion krona specifically allocated to Icelandic banks and their subsidiaries, marking the completion of the settlement process. It´s interesting that Icelandic banks had less than 10 per cent of the claims, because of the international nature of my business dealings.

I have expressed the belief that debts cannot be settled unless individuals possess real assets to repay them. During the time of the bank crash, it is true that my debts were substantial, but so were my credits. The Icelandic banks indeed extended loans excessively to a select few individuals. The most concerning aspect was that most of those who borrowed the most did not possess tangible assets, but rather virtual assets on paper that were acquired through virtual business dealings with their colleagues. It is therefore not surprising that the bank recovery from them was pitiful.

For me, I had my freedom and reputation back, especially in the wider banking community. Bankers love nothing more than a troubled borrower who makes good on his promises and gets them repaid. Now it was time to start again from a fresh footing.

There has also been a verdict on Icesave in the European courts, clearing Iceland of responsibility for the UK online bank's deposits and blaming an EU legal error for the bizarre situation that resulted. I feel that this validates our assumptions about the situation we were working in on that fateful weekend in October 2008. Since then, the British government has been widely criticised for its use of anti-terrorism legislation in that context.

A remarkable report, 'Costs and recovery of the Treasury from the collapse of the banks', was published in 2016. Commissioned by the Ministry of Finance and Economy, it was written by Ásgeir Jónsson and Hersir Sigurgeirsson, authors of *The Icelandic Financial Crisis*. According to the report, the Treasury of Iceland's net costs were fully

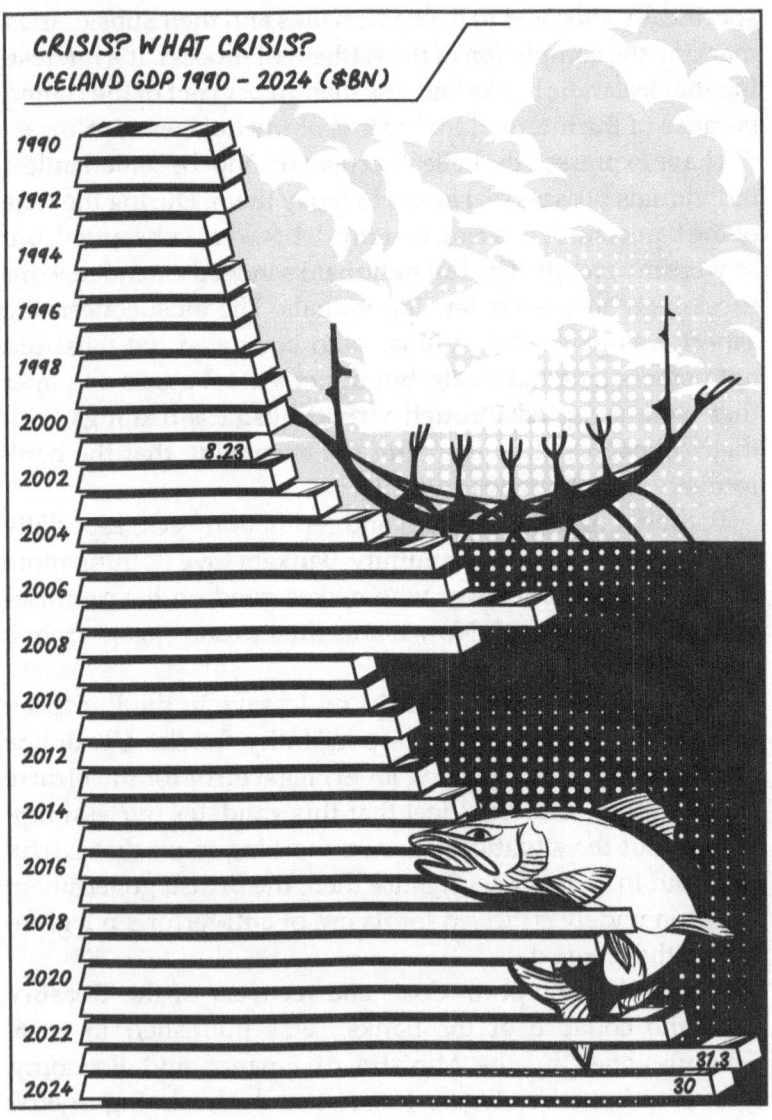

recovered, resulting in a surplus. It is therefore safe to say that the Treasury benefited from the collapse and restoration of the banking system.

In the end Iceland turned disaster into an unlikely fiscal victory. When its oversized banks collapsed in 2008, the government let them fail, shielded domestic savers, and locked in foreign creditors with capital controls. Later, it forced those creditors to pay hefty exit fees, netting a huge windfall of around 17 per cent of GDP. That cash, plus profits from the second bank sales, covered all crisis costs and slashed public debt. Iceland sold its banks not only once, but twice. It privatised them first time and took them back in the crash and sold them again a decade later to new buyers. By the end, Iceland's Treasury didn't just recover – it came out ahead with a significant fiscal surplus. In a rare twist, the state profited from its banking collapse, while foreign creditors footed the bill. The biggest losers were UK, Nordic, German and Dutch institutions. Interestingly the hedge (vulture) funds that bought these debts and held on to them profited highly in the post-crash years, so there were profits going back to the international system through hedge funds as well as the Icelandic treasury.

Iceland has gone some way to being rehabilitated in the global economy, aided hugely by a resurgent tourist economy. I recall Bill Clinton telling me in May 2014 how impressed he was with Iceland and how the country was a shining example of how to beat a crisis. It's a common misconception that Iceland is a miracle story of sorts. But the fact is that the 'miracle' is questionable, to say the least. The miracle is basically due to the fact that Iceland is so small in the global financial system. The country got away with ringfencing domestic interests from foreign creditors in a defensive move and then strong-arming them through very punitive capital controls over a lengthy negotiation period. Iceland was small

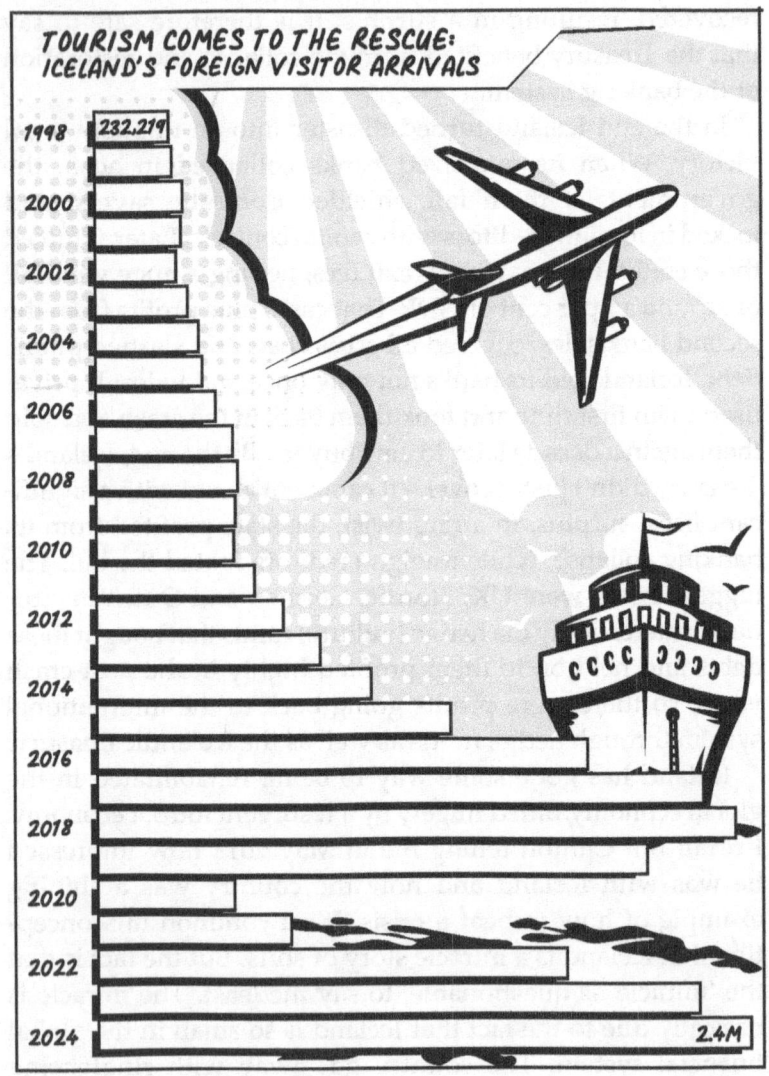

TOURISM COMES TO THE RESCUE:
ICELAND'S FOREIGN VISITOR ARRIVALS

1998 232,219
2000
2002
2004
2006
2008
2010
2012
2014
2016
2018
2020
2022
2024 2.4M

enough to go bust and play hardball internationally in the aftermath without any serious long-term consequnces. It would be hard to see other bigger nations pull something like this off in a similiar situation.

The immediate crash hangover period of 2008–12 was characterised by mass confusion and real hysteria in Iceland. This hysteria in the public discourse was hyped up by the political parties in power and by the media, exaggerating the damage done to the economy and the risks ahead. It was an uneasy time, but the economy actually recovered very quickly, largely because of an unexpected factor – tourism.

As the surge in tourism began to drive economic recovery, and with few villains found to punish, most Icelanders started to become weary of the negative discussions and media coverage. In fact it became quite common to hear well-informed people say that in order to safeguard their mental well-being they no longer followed the news.

Well-funded international marketing campaigns by the government, followed by two volcanic eruptions in 2010 and 2021 – regarded by locals as 'tourist eruptions' because they posed little threat to infrastructure or human safety but provided a breathtaking spectacle – resulted in a huge boom in tourism. During the year of the banking crash, approximately half a million tourists visited Iceland. A decade later, however, the number had increased by almost five times, to two and half million. Key to this, and often overlooked, is that the Icelandic krona had fallen dramatically in the crash. Previously Iceland had been prohibitively expensive to visitors, with the artificially high krona making the country one of the most expensive in the world. Now it was available to foreigners at effectively half price, making the country an affordable destination for the first time. The moral of the story here is that in each setback we encounter, there may actually be the seed of a later comeback. So when the krona lost 50 per cent of its value, Icelandic nature became the key resource for economic recovery rather than the traditional fishing export industry.

For a small island nation like Iceland, a tourist influx six times its population each year inevitably leads to cultural transformations. The presence of visitors from around the world has brought the global sphere directly to Iceland, with tourists engaging in daily interactions with locals and engaging in small-scale business transactions by spending money on food, drinks, activities and souvenirs. This shift contrasts significantly with the past when major financial transactions dominated, such as hedge funds trading government bonds or Icelandic financiers acquiring airlines and high-street toy stores. The prevalence of smaller and more numerous transactions has resulted in a more evenly distributed economic impact and has laid the groundwork for a more stable economy, fostering a departure from the previously fragile economic 'monocrop' landscape of fish exports.

As the events of 2008 gradually recede, the impact of the word 'crash', or *hrun*, which gained infamy during the banking collapse, has significantly diminished along with its relevance. Today's university graduates were merely young children during that period of turmoil – to Generation Z, the subject is uninteresting and simply a strange time when Iceland 'lost the plot'. Their focus and concerns are on other and more global issues than seeking individuals accountable for an economic crisis that occurred more than fifteen years ago.

Hindsight is not a negative concept. Only by looking back can we learn for the future.

10

ADVENTURE CAPITALISM 2.0
2014-2023

Upside, inside out
She's livin' la vida loca
She'll push you and pull you down
Livin' la vida loca

Ricky Martin, 'Livin' La Vida Loca'

As I emerged from my restructuring agreements in Iceland,
the future began to look full of opportunity again, but where
should I focus? Iceland seemed too small a pond to fish in,
while eastern European privatisations had had their day.
The US is a legendary graveyard for many European brands
whose owners thought they could simply globalise. None of
these markets seemed appealing.

No. My return to adventure capitalism needed to bear the
hallmarks and characteristics of my past ventures: a business
opportunity in a sector like telecoms that I knew something
about, but in a territory that constituted a great unknown and
fed my curiosity for the new. Asia was enticing but too far
away for me to make any meaningful inroads. Africa is going
to be a major opportunity but, with all the ventures I looked

at there, I decided it was too soon; the necessary infrastructure was simply not there yet. Then I travelled to Latin America and decided that this was a place where I could do business.

As so often happens, the first opportunity was not the most interesting. When I flew to Ecuador to conduct personal due diligence on a potential oil investment, it was the first time I had set foot in South America. Like most visitors, I was captivated by the colours, energy and vitality of this rich cultural continent. Although that investment opportunity was indeed a 'special situation' and I knew the key players, investing in oil was not where I wanted to be ethically, and other potential geographical choices seemed fraught with danger. Brazil was undergoing a boom as the B in the BRICS, but there were already serious questions about how long the good times would last. Argentina was a great place for a holiday but its infamous inflation and habitual political and economic crises still made it a terrible place to start a business. Ecuador didn't feel right. In Peru, we made enquiries but nothing ever really got off the ground. In Bolivia and the Dominican Republic, we tried but could not get telecoms frequency. Then the Chilean offshoot of US telecoms player Nextel came on the radar and I quickly realised that it was just my kind of distressed opportunity.

Nextel Chile had seemed like a good idea to the founders of its US parent, Nextel Corporation, which was founded in Virginia in 1987 and quickly became one of the first telecoms providers in the US to offer a national digital cellular coverage footprint. By 2015, however, the parent company had merged with Sprint and the Chilean business was in trouble, with only 200,000 subscribers in a nation of 19.5 million people and just days away from seeking protection from creditors under America's Chapter 11 bankruptcy code.

Mobile telecoms was a sector I knew well, having grown

Play, my start-up in Poland, into a top-four independent challenger brand, and although Chile was on the other side of the Atlantic, it did bear some similarities to Play's Polish homeland. Both were Catholic cultures with a high degree of conservatism. Another element they had in common was their domination by international behemoths. While Play in Poland was up against France's Orange, Deutsche Telekom's T-Mobile and Polkomtel, whose Plus brand was 24 per cent owned by Britain's Vodafone, Nextel Chile had to contend with Entel, the former nationalised Chilean telecoms company whose 127-metre Torre Entel literally towers over central Santiago. Entel controlled about 30 per cent of the Chilean mobile telecoms market. Then there were Movistar, owned by Spanish giant Telefonica, which held a market share of around 28 per cent, and Claro, part of the America Movil telecoms giant, famously fronted by Mexican billionaire Carlos Slim, which had 23 per cent. Nextel Chile had possessed about 2 per cent of the market as a total underdog, and even that was falling steadily. However, we had grown Play from nothing into the leading mobile telecoms company in Poland with a 27 per cent market share, and we saw a similar potential growth trajectory for this Chilean minnow.

The financial elements of a deal had to be put together very quickly. We completed the whole transaction in about two months and it was only later that we learned how close Nextel Chile had actually been to bankruptcy wipe-out. We refinanced the company with $400 million of equity and $420 million of debt and set about finding a way to rebrand and reposition it as a vibrant independent challenger brand – a far cry from its previous image as a distant South American offshoot of a major US carrier.

Branding is a personal passion of mine, dating back all the way to the Bravo venture in St Petersburg, and it felt exciting and invigorating to be essentially building a start-up again. But what should we call our new baby? After discarding an initial notion to use the Play brand, we looked for a similarly dynamic name behind which to build a challenger, customer-centric culture and asked half a dozen marketing agencies to pitch their best ideas. None of them came up with anything that we liked, but another firm which had not been invited to pitch came up with a left-of-field suggestion that resonated with us straight away. Its concept was to brand the challenger around the 'word-of-mouth', viral way that we wanted to grow through personal recommendations offering great value and customer-centred service. 'Word of mouth' was shortened to WOM and that became our brand.

My idea was to build a new Latin American challenger mobile telecoms brand using the playbook of Play in Poland and Nova in Iceland. I could use the same management team and external consultants who worked on both. The partners at Novator responsible for telecoms, who had worked with me since 2010, focused on financing the new venture and acquiring the necessary spectrum and telecoms licences. Chris Bannister, a personable Brit who became Play's first chief executive in 2005 and had already lived and worked in nine countries, was brought back into the fold as chief executive. And the Icelandic chief technology officer oversaw the technical build-out design, along with his Swedish colleague. Members of our trusted teams from both countries helped in the beginning to transform a failed old-school US telecoms operator into a state-of-the-art 'kick-ass' mobile challenger. None of us spoke Spanish and most had never set foot in Latin America before, let alone Chile. It didn't seem to matter.

When we launched, Chile was the most expensive country in the Latin American region in mobile telecommunication, so we saw a market that was fertile for a new approach.

Conventional new entrants like Nextel and a venture headed by US telecoms billionaire John Malone had failed to crack the nation. We needed to do things very differently. To achieve the maximum impact and truly disrupt the market, we knew that a key differentiator had to be price. Indeed, we priced our services so aggressively that Chile immediately became the cheapest country in South America for consumer mobile telephony. Alongside this value offer, we promoted WOM as an independent challenger offering honesty and integrity. We set out to be brave, innovative, bold and passionate.

The strategy of both Play and WOM was to look for customers who were unhappy with their present mobile telecoms service. When consumers select the brands and corporations they want to rely on, they look for someone who is demonstrably on their side, with the same values and mission. People tend to stick with their telecom brands, and the relationships that are built typically last for decades. We ask customers what they are looking for, what they are not currently getting from their existing provider and what we have to do to win and retain their custom. Our brand message was: 'Nobody gives you more.'

To accomplish all this requires a brand to be worth talking about and recommending to family and friends, so WOM was styled with a rebellious, edgy culture that was not afraid to court controversy and wanted to be talked about. We wanted to have a genuine social impact and to resonate with the issues of the day in order to engage with customers. One of the ways we did that was to acknowledge and address the stark inequalities in Chile and highlight social impact. At the time of our launch, one of the hottest issues in the country centred on various allegations of commercial collusion to the disadvantage of customers. One such allegation involved the forestry and woodpulp industries, with claims that they were artificially inflating the price of toilet rolls, so we filmed an advert featuring someone stealing toilet rolls. Other ads targeted unrest over politics and food. One of our most successful campaigns was based around a popular Argentinian song that proclaimed: 'You have power but you will lose it,' to footage of a scandal alleging collusion in the Chilean fishing industry. Another focused on the empowerment of women. We wanted to expose corruption, inequalities and bad practices.

Some campaigns were really controversial. One featured a 'puking priest' who literally vomited in TV adverts to highlight the homophobia prevalent in Chilean society. This did not go down at all well with the country's Catholic church and some of its politicians. Some TV channels refused to broadcast the ad, while others only showed it after a 10 pm watershed. We also raised eyebrows with an advert showing two girls kissing, and were the first consumer brand advertiser to specifically create adverts featuring disabled people. Equal rights across genders, sexual orientation and all levels of bodily ability were taken for granted in Europe and the US but not in Chile at this time. Our idea was to stimulate debate and create talking points about traditional culture and whether the time was right for a new approach, challenging the status quo in a disruptive manner. Focusing on issues and events that were affecting ordinary people, the aim was to get involved and have a voice. We also targeted media censorship. We really succeeded in putting these issues high on the country's agenda and our advertising positioned WOM as a leading progressive thinker in this area.

This strategy produced exactly the required results, with WOM living up to its name and growing virally through recommendations. Nobody in the Chilean mobile telecoms industry had seen anything like this before. The received wisdom had been that there was no room in the Chilean mobile telecoms market for more than three operators and that nobody would be able to successfully challenge that status quo. We proved this to be incorrect. WOM quickly became an unmissable part of the market, bigger than its Mexican- and Spanish-owned rivals and a close contender for the number one position. What it did and said really mattered to the nation's population. We developed genuine momentum and impact.

When WOM began, it did not have a very viable network. We had only 1,000 telecoms towers in a nation that needed 5,000 and we were up against established national champion telecoms providers who already boasted the kinds of networks we were attempting to build and who based their glitzy headquarters in 50-storey office blocks. Now, the company has grown from a humble fourth mobile market entrant to serve 8 million subscribers as Chile's second biggest telco, with a 25 per cent market share, just behind Entel's 34 per cent and ahead of the Spanish-owned Movistar and Mexican powerhouse Claro. We saw this as merely the beginning, however, as our ambition was always to use Chile as a beachhead from which to attack other South American mobile telecoms markets.

We made our first foray in 2019 when we acquired a majority stake in the bankrupt Colombian telecoms company Avantel, merged it with a vehicle that we had used to buy Colombian mobile telecoms spectrum, and renamed the whole operation WOM Colombia. We then set about investing in infrastructure projects in Colombia over the next five years. Following a bandwidth auction, we won 20 MHz in the 700 MHz spectrum and 30 MHz in the 2,500 MHz spectrum. We then invested in building WOM Colombia's network, installing more than 8,000 antennae and 3,000 additional towers, and created 2,500 direct and more than 5,000 indirect jobs, with an average age of 32 for recruits. We were probably Colombia's largest recruiter, opening 147 stores in one year alone. Altogether, we have invested $1 billion of equity in WOM Colombia. We betted heavily that the strategy that had worked so well in Chile would resonate with customers in the much larger Colombian market. It often surprises Europeans that Colombia is the second largest market in South America, after Brazil but before Argentina and Peru, with an official population of more than 57 million, plus what is reported to be more than 5 million Venezuelans.

I met Colombia's president at Davos and on two other occasions. During our last meeting, he even showed me a signed document as proof that he was going to open up the country's mobile telecoms in the way that we had discussed. We were going to cut the price of mobile phone plans in the nation by 50 per cent, which was going to be good for GDP. He was attracted by that because it would go down very well with voters. I liked him. He was a man of his word.

What we found in Colombia, however, was very different to our experiences in Chile. For a start, it was a pure 'greenfield', setting up a telecoms network from scratch on new spectrum, with no legacy operations to build on. Then our launch momentum was suddenly and brutally interrupted by the Covid-19 pandemic and a national lockdown in Colombia, which inevitably affected our shops. Moreover we were hiring thousands of employees in a new start-up culture, and had to do most of that through Zoom video calls. With hindsight it's clearly impossible to build a strong company culture through such calls, as physical proximity is essential to breed camaraderie and energy levels for a new team coming together for the first time and taking on a David and Goliath fight in a competitive market.

But most fearsome of all was the competition. The mobile

phone sector in Colombia had previously been static, with a concentrated number of players in the market delaying key investments for the development of the country. A market of 66.4 million mobile phone subscriptions was dominated by Claro, with more than a 50 per cent market share, ahead of Movistar with around 24 per cent and local player Tigo with about 18 per cent. WOM Colombia quickly adopted the most aggressive pricing strategy in Latin America. We declared that the country needed a fourth operator to push change and improve access to connectivity for all Colombians. Over our investment period, we set out on a mission to connect the disconnected, bringing together 674 communities across Colombia that did not previously have access to the internet and revolutionising access to remote learning and e-commerce.

WOM Colombia launched at the end of 2020. As in Chile, our promise in Colombia was to democratise connectivity and usher in a truly digital society, lowering prices and massively increasing access. When we entered Colombia, it ranked 15th in Latin America for accessibility. A mere three months later, it was one of the cheapest on the continent. Our target was getting people in the lower strata of Colombian society not just to own a mobile phone, but to use it regularly. We also offered free insurance against handset theft, a measure representative of the value that WOM Colombia could offer.

As at WOM Chile, the branding was independent and quirky. The headquarters building in Bogotá was decked in purple, while in its centre was an enormous sculpture of a hand with the index and little fingers pointing to the ceiling, and the others folded inwards. As in Santiago, the Bogotá head office boasted no executive suites or glass offices, with management working open-plan in full view of colleagues.

I conducted my own due diligence, visiting Bogotá,

Medellin, Cali, Barranquilla and Cartagena shortly before the first Covid-19 lockdown began, and I was hugely excited by the nation's potential and fascinated by how different it is from one side to the other. People work incredibly hard in this nation. With Play, we were asking our managers to open ten new stores every month but actually expecting them to open seven or eight. However, in Colombia our team was opening twelve shops every four weeks. They easily exceeded our expectations.

The real trouble this time around was that this time the incumbent operators were ready and waiting for us. In the first five months after we acquired Avantel, we were hit with no fewer than 38 separate lawsuits challenging our right to exist as a player in the Colombian mobile telecoms market. There was a torrent of complaints from existing mobile telecoms operators to Colombia's Ministry of Information Technologies and Communications, the Commission for the Regulation of Communications and the National Spectrum Agency. In Chile we had taken the competition by surprise and wrong-footed them all. But in Colombia, where the opposition was largely made up of the same players, they put up much more of a fight. The established operators used dirty tactics, waiting for regulators to intervene before agreeing to behave fairly. There were unnecessary problems with networks, bandwidth, service levels and delays with setting up connections and allowing mobile customers to port their numbers. Nobody would give us an inch. It was basically hand-to-hand combat every day in the market.

We also made some mistakes of our own. In order to build our infrastructure, in the 2019 spectrum auction of the 2,500 MHz band, Novator bid about $600 million for one of the 10 MHz blocks – ten times more than the $60 million it was valued at. Weeks later, the Colombian government admitted

Novator's waiver of that block, but forced it to pay a $15 million fine. It was really unfortunate; a human mistake made as participants in the auction. The organisers of the auction also made a mistake. We were extremely disappointed by the outcome of the auction but paid the fine and moved on, regarding the fine as a welcome gift to Colombia. These things can sometimes happen.

A few years later, the Covid-19 pandemic affected our business much worse than we realised at the time, with the effects taking years to trickle down into the business performance and total investment costs. It was basically a knock-out blow, and both businesses required a total financial reboot to get back on their feet again. At the beginning of 2024, I exited both of my Latin American telecoms investments after being impacted by enormous headwinds. In Chile I secured a full exit at a substantial profit by not taking part in new equity injection by bondholders there. In Colombia I sold my majority holding for a large loss as part of a Chapter 11 capital restructuring. Nevertheless I regard both as successful examples of adventure capitalism in a continent that was entirely new to me. The investments did not end how I had planned, but I learned from the Icelandic crisis and this time decided to draw a line under them rather than wait for the situation to improve as I had done in Iceland. I had learned to recognise a crisis, and ending my involvement was the right thing to do.

During 2023 the dynamic in both Chile and Colombia changed in a fundamental way. The biggest part was played by the tower side of the business, the 'hidden' infrastructure part of it as opposed to the more visible consumer operations. Telecom companies are basically service companies, but the 'factory' that makes the goods to sell is comprised of a limited radio spectrum owned by each country. Both these parts are extremely expensive and run into hundreds of billions of dollars. The key difference is that you can sell one of them and not the other. Towers can be sold and a good operator can build them more cheaply than they can sell them, usually to large infrastructure funds. Those funds have been very active over the last decade, and all telecom companies have been selling to them, so in fact this becomes a business line in itself for the companies and is one of the main ways an investor recovers his investment in a telco project. In our plans we had investment banks working for us in such a sales process in 2023 and had done so successfully in our Chilean towers business before. This time in Colombia, however, the market had become very brittle and our buyers walked away from the sales process unexpectedly. This meant that we were not getting the massive cash inflow of hundreds of millions of dollars into either WOM company as planned.

To make things worse, WOM Chile, which had been a cash cow in terms of profitability, changed as the capital expenditure investments increased dramatically and cut into the cash flows that could be depended on for the group. This was mostly a worry for me in relation to Colombia, as I had expected to recycle Chilean cash flows into the investment there until the business broke even. WOM Chile got into trouble after going all-in on three big projects – fibre rollout, 5G network expansion and spectrum acquisition – during 2020–21. Unfortunately, these happened just as Covid-19 threw supply chains into chaos and inflation drove up costs, leading to major delays and a $200 million overspend – double the budget! Even with all that spending, the projects barely moved the needle on profits. WOM's debt levels climbed fast, and their bonds maturity was steadily encroaching from the other side.

By late 2023, things unravelled. Project delays, missing payments from deals and an impossible financing environment, with banks having turned super-conservative, ultimately left WOM short of cash. Add to that rising interest rates, inflation and a weakening peso and we couldn't refinance our looming debt. The bondholders were extremely inflexible and made exorbitant demands to restructure the dept when we tried to negotiate with them. With no way out, WOM had to file for Chapter 11 to restructure and stay afloat. It was, in my mind, the only way to negotiate with the bondholders, and through that process a Delaware judge held an open auction for who would put the most money into the company. In the end the only two offers came from me and some of the bondholders. They bid higher than me and took over the company, and I exited.

At the same time in Colombia, although the company was on track with customer and revenue growth getting to an incredible 8 million customers in four years, it was a cash-hungry machine that needed to be fed capital all the time until it broke even. This would not have been a problem if we had had the two key things we set out with at the start of the project: a minority equity capital partner and a Chinese 50/50 bank debt financing. We had these in Play and in Nova, and they had worked well. Basically, our Greek partners from Poland were meant to join us for the project, but they got cold feet during Covid and bailed out. I remember Panos telling me in a phone call that at his age he could no longer take the same risks he had taken in Eastern Europe, and that he was really worried about the economic effects of Covid-19 – 'a global situation we have never seen before'. He was right about that. Furthermore, the Chinese Development Bank had been instructed by the Chinese government to focus on China internally rather than focus on driving international expansion of Chinese companies like Huawei. This policy shift was mostly because of the trouble the Chinese banks got into during Covid. It was understandable, but devastating for us as we got a lot less debt financing from our usual and reliable banking partners. We received less than two thirds of the usual formula, and that led to the project being 70–75 per cent funded by equity in extremely difficult private equity markets. This turned out to be a double whammy, and I was left with putting up all the equity, which made my outlay 100 per cent more than in my original plan. We kept looking for equity partners, but interest in emerging markets had dried up.

When I realised at the beginning of 2024 that Chile was not going to be able to generate any spare cash to recycle to Colombia, finding a partner to put in the last bit of cash became hugely urgent, and I concentrated all year on that. After reaching out to more than 300 parties globally through an investment bank process and endless presentations from Brazil and New York to Dubai and Mexico, and despite coming close more than once, we failed to secure the right commitment on time. The key element that killed the deal was that Colombia had elected a left-wing government for the first time since the Second World War. The new government was headed by a Marxist president who had served jail time in his youth as a revolutionary guerrilla. This macroeconomic red flag really disturbed both international and local Colombian investors. Everyone liked the WOM story and the copy-and-paste strategy of rolling out a tried and tested business model from Poland, Iceland and Chile. But the big local Colombian investors simply said, 'We are going to sit this government out and not do anything new while they are in power.' If this was the local view, just imagine what the US investors thought.

I worked hard and closely with the Colombian Ministry of Telecommunications during this time. The ministry was desperate to keep us in the market, as we had massively lowered prices to consumers and had increased service quality for 8 million customers. There were also around 8,000 jobs on the line. WOM Colombia ultimately entered a voluntary creditor protection process, while the government and company kept things running and we gained more time to attract fresh capital. In the end, a consortium of US, UK and Latin American investors called SUR came in with new capital, got the company out of the local equivalent of Chapter 11 and took management control. Throughout this exercise I kept a small minority shareholding in the company, and I believe WOM Colombia will do well in the next five years – especially since the number two and number three operators are merging, bringing the competitors down from four to three. This is a huge tailwind for a great company from here on.

I wanted to build WOM into a regional telco operator that was more modern and nimble than existing ones. My expectations and plans were based on rolling out a challenger, country by country, case by case, until we became a regional player that would eventually list on Nasdaq and thereby provide an exit to the investment, just like I had done with Play.

What in fact happened was a typical macroeconomic event in the form of Covid-19. The financial and economic effects for business were artificially prolonged by the zero per cent interest 'rescue policies' of the US and European central banks. I learned from my experience in Iceland, when I had waited too long for the tide to turn, to cut my losses and not leave any loose ends. So in Latin America I decided to make a clean break to fully focus on new markets and opportunities without any distractions from previous operations.

I am not without fault here. There are a few things I should and could have done to make this less painful. The common wisdom was to get a 'local partner' to work with in a new country, and I could have taken in a partner at the beginning to share the gain and pain. That was certainly what the bankers advised, but my gut feeling was to build the first company there on our own. I had heard a lot of stories about local partners ripping off foreign investors in Latin America, and in my view that risk was too much to manage on top of the other straightforward business risks inherent in a start-up operation in any country, let alone one in an unfamiliar new place literally on the other side of the planet. But we did look for a partner for Colombia, because by that time we had our own experience and contacts in Latin America, and that was the plan for future countries where we could roll out the WOM concept.

Also I became too reliant on the debt funding of Chile in order to start Colombia, from both the international bond market and local banks. This came back to bite me when those markets turned and interest rates shot up. The common rule of thumb we had followed in our telco portfolio was not to invest in a new project with negative cash flows until the ones you already have are all cash-flow profitable. Play and Nova were highly profitable when we undertook Chile. We waited until Chile was profitable before undertaking Colombia, but Colombia was on such a large scale that we eventually needed to leverage future cash flows from Chile to manage the investments required. This became all too apparent after we had lost our intended partner and failed to secure a new one.

On a deeper level, I think what I had to deal with was a classic case of 'unknown unknowns'. The terms 'known unknowns' and 'unknown unknowns' come from risk management and decision theory but were popularised by Donald Rumsfeld in a 2002 press briefing. Known unknowns are things *we know we don't know*. We're aware of the gap in our knowledge. For example, if you're planning a project and know you don't have weather data for the construction site, that's a known unknown. You know weather could impact your timeline, but you just don't have the specifics yet. Since you're aware of them, you can plan for them, mitigate them, or gather more information. The really interesting bit, however, is unknown unknowns: things we *don't even know* that we don't know. They're the surprises, the blind spots and therefore the most dangerous pitfalls for strategic planning. They are harder to prepare for because they fall completely outside our awareness. As humans we also have cognitive bias: we're often too focused on what we already know or what we expect to learn, but we're blindsided by things outside that. The Covid-19 pandemic is a textbook example of an unknown unknown. The scale of global shutdowns, cascading economic impact and unexpected effects was and is extraordinary, and the after-effects are still trickling through everywhere.

This has taught me something. My classic way of preparing for investments in emerging market projects focuses heavily on *known unknowns*. For instance, we run financial simulations and recycle talented people and institutions with whom we have a working history, keeping ourselves as investors ready to fly out as a rapid-response team and set up camp in a country to deal with issues when they arise. However, when there is a 'black swan' event (the common term for unknown unknowns) the key factor is resilience. Resilience is about building systems that can adapt to *unknown unknowns*.

From a management or financial perspective, flexibility is always key in any crisis. This was the crux of Charles Darwin's message discussed earlier in this book, and it is something I find myself coming back to again and again when I reflect on the latest crisis I have had to navigate through. The Russian government default in 1998 and the global liquidity crisis of 2008 were both black swan events. My locations and businesses were very different in all of these storms, but they share a common thread.

One other Latin American venture is The Lost Explorer Mezcal, an alcoholic beverage made from the agave plant that encourages patrons to live and drink curiously. This venture came about through my friend the adventurer, conservationist and raconteur David de Rothschild. I first met David on a snowy glacier in Iceland in 2006 when I was hosting a group of the World Economic Forum's Young Global Leaders. Many years later at the Burning Man festival in the Nevada desert we started drinking mezcal together after David introduced me to the spirit. I was quite sceptical to begin with, but the taste of mezcal is unique and I continued to order it when I was out having a drink. Sharing a mezcal with someone is a conversation-starter and allows people to bond over something special.

Our Lost Explorer Mezcal is all about curiosity, seeking inspiration and enjoying the life journey. David and I are both motorbike fanatics and our love of the open road allows us to discover new experiences and cultures. In Mexico, David and I arrived in the agave fields deep in the countryside at dusk with Fortino, a master mezcalero. We decided to produce a special artisanal mezcal together and I remember Fortino showing us where he was going to plant the agaves. As the sun went down, it seemed a magical landscape, deep in the middle of authentic Oaxaca. We tweaked the recipe and came up with a spirit we are really proud of. Our new beverage is about trying new things, being bold and not being afraid to step out of one's comfort zone to discover what you need to evolve and progress in life.

We are advertising The Lost Explorer Mezcal under the tagline 'Get Lost,' with a narrative encouraging consumers to find themselves by first getting lost in new adventures. The call is for consumers to live and sip curiously. Mezcal is currently the fastest-growing spirits category in its target markets, and we believe it can replicate what tequila has achieved in the past decade. Mezcal is all about adventure, exploration and discovery, and our target customers are consumers who are naturally more curious. It also epitomises my own journey, since my first business venture was in beverages all those years ago in Russia.

It's all about curiosity – that fundamental human trait that makes us discover the world and keep evolving in life. This is the stated mantra of the company and something that resonates very deeply with me. Curiosity about the world around me is what drives my thirst for new ventures in faraway lands or ground-breaking technology and the adventure that goes with them. Embracing change by venturing into the unknown has become an intrinsic part of my life.

It is now time to move on to India and the Gulf states. At this particular moment, and in my typical passion for exotic new frontiers to immerse myself in, I find this area fascinating. My journey there began in a similar way to my adventures as an investor in Russia, Bulgaria and Latin America with a 'special situation' that led Novator to put $250 million into the visual effects and animation powerhouse DNEG. This leading player in computer-generated images for movies and video is also focused on constructing complex virtual-reality worlds for the next generation of VR headsets over the coming decade.

Namit Malhotra, DNEG's dynamic and ambitious founder and CEO, reached out to me when his biggest shareholder was in a distressed situation and his banks had foreclosed on shares pledged for collateral of loans. This was both a crisis and an opportunity for Namit, as the danger was that this stake could end up with someone who could take over the company and oust him, while it was also an opportunity for him to buy this stake himself and secure control over the company and its destiny. All he needed was the money to unlock this opportunity. This was of course a very familiar situation for me, very similar to the CCP management buyout and the Balkanpharma privatisation deal. Once again, this presented an opportunity for me to back another business founder with a big vision, in a sector where I had no experience and a geography and culture I was totally unfamiliar with. I looked at this opportunity with great interest as it had the hallmarks of my previous signature deals, with all the risks and opportunities entailed. Both were firmly in my mind, but my curiosity and sense of adventure made me engage deeply immediately.

Two things were key drivers in the investment thesis for me. The first was the macroeconomic picture of the area, which is always hugely important to me. The second was the quality of the business itself and its relation to the competitive landscape. But I had to get my head around India first and the risks and opportunities involved.

My basic gut feeling, looking in from outside, was that India was in some way becoming 'the next China'. I could see incredible GDP growth numbers that were similar to China's in the early 2000s, when I started doing business with the Chinese through telecoms. I saw how Apple had chosen to move its iPhone production to India to diversify itself away from China. The world's biggest technology company trusting the complex manufacturing of its prized consumer product there was validation that high-tech manufacturing and industry in India was going to progress very rapidly. The escalating trade war between the US and China made it logical for international companies to migrate much more manufacturing to India, and the underlying boom created by that and other factors made me positive about the area. I could see the huge growth in middle-class and upper middle-class consumers and familiar signs of a rapidly changing emerging market – my usual sandbox to play in. The stock market there reminded me of how the Chinese market was before it became so huge. I saw how structural reform and changes to the financial markets were key in fuelling future growth in wealth creation. Fast-growing public ownership of listed shares and more streamlined banking rules for lending and enforcing on collateral were significant factors. And as I looked deeper I also saw an interesting emerging deep connection between the UAE and India, which reminded me of how Hong Kong and China were symbiotic in their boom times, and I wondered if this too would make this scenario more attractive.

On the core business, I asked myself how good DNEG was in terms of international competition, and I was deeply impressed by the number of successive Academy Awards it had won, the calibre of directors working with the company and the faith of major Hollywood studios in its work. DNEG has won eight Oscars, including seven in the past decade. That's an incredible accomplishment and a remarkable endorsement of their standing in the industry.

It was a relatively big deal for me in a new sector in a new region, but I hashed it out with the founder in a relatively short time. We created a convertible $250 million loan to him to buy out Anil Ambani, one of India's best known and most powerful businessmen, who owned a 33 per cent stake through his Reliance MediaWorks company. This enabled Namit to secure a solid majority of well over 50 per cent of the company he headed. I had the option to convert the loan into a shareholding in the company at a later date, but I wanted to get to know both the company and the media sector much better over the following years before taking an equity risk. Eventually I ended up trading into equity as the due date approached, as I believed the company had much more growth potential in the future.

The plan was to publicly list DNEG on Nasdaq, and preparations were well under way. We paid our investment in tranches over time, but just after we made the last payment a huge surprise came up in the industry. The Hollywood writers' and actors' strikes in 2023 caused prolonged project delays everywhere in the film industry, which in turn impacted the pipeline of VFX and post-production work. Content production, which had been increasing rapidly with streaming services like Netflix, Prime and Apple trying to outspend each other on the sheer volume of their own content, slowed globally. This led to short-term revenue pressure for DNEG, but diversification helped: DNEG and Prime Focus Technologies, which it acquired in 2024, expanded into animation, virtual production and gaming-related services and weathered the storm far better than any of their competitors. Many of those competitors, such as Technicolor, simply folded and went bankrupt. But other big guys like ILM and WETA also survived, and the rivalry between the companies continues. Interestingly, those companies were created by film directors (George Lucas and Peter Jackson respectively) who chose to diversify from content creation into tech services. Now DNEG is doing just the opposite by going into content production itself. It has already released some international hits is and working on its first 'tentpole production' – a Hollywood term for big-budget films.

Although we had to abandon the US IPO plan, we had a few chances to cash out investment in the following years with offers from private equity firms. However, I decided to stick by my original vision of this company being radically transformed over a few years instead of taking a modest profit for a short holding period. We also recognised the potential of the Indian stock market versus the US one, as it had changed dramatically over the years since our initial entry and become much stronger and more interesting. We therefore decided to have the listing in India, and it is currently listed there and trading in Mumbai.

What really excites me about this opportunity is the next level in this company's evolution – namely, how it can play a key part in the AI revolution that is taking place globally now. DNEG, as a leading VFX and CGI powerhouse, sits on an incredible treasure trove of proprietary data that is highly valuable to AI developers. DNEG's proprietary VFX data offers AI developers an unparalleled foundation for training models that aim for photorealism, emotional authenticity and cinematic quality, enabling the next generation of generative content, virtual humans and immersive visual experiences.

The end consumer product will be high-performance digital doubles that speak any language and mirror human emotions with precise facial expressions that will revolution-ise global communication and content creation. They enable hyper-realistic, emotionally engaging real-time experiences for entertainment, customer service, education and digital commerce worldwide. These digital doubles will break down language and cultural barriers, making human-to-computer and human-to-human digital interaction seamless and emotionally compelling across the globe.

All of this, however, also raises ethical considerations around consent, identity misuse (as in deepfakes) and emotional manipulation. There is a huge potential danger if this technology is used for unethical purposes such as criminal fraud or political manipulation. The FBI has publicly warned that revenge porn by deepfakes is a growing threat to individuals, and the potential for scammers and criminals to steal from people with this tech is very real. Companies adopting this technology will need robust frameworks for ethical deployment, transparent use and data privacy, but the upside is enormous: brands and creators can scale authentic human touch globally like never before.

Be brave and test yourself in new environments.

11

THIS TIME IS NEVER DIFFERENT?

That's life, that's life
That's what the people say
You're riding high in April,
Shot down in May
But I know I'm gonna change that tune
When I'm back on top, back on top in June

Frank Sinatra, 'That's Life'

I am not so foolish as to believe in new paradigms or to state that my fortunes have now turned a corner from which there will be no return. In fact I came pretty close to another financial implosion in Latin America and, as I write these updated chapters, *Forbes* is recording my wealth as having halved from $2 billion to $1 billion.

The financial crisis of 2008–9 clearly revealed a number of systemic faults – and more have been discovered since. Indeed, the continuing cost-of-living crisis is an example of our grappling with the slow death of an idea that, although singular and simple, has been a driving force in western society for at least three generations. The idea that things can only get better has informed and fed the optimism and cultural dominance of western societies over at least the past

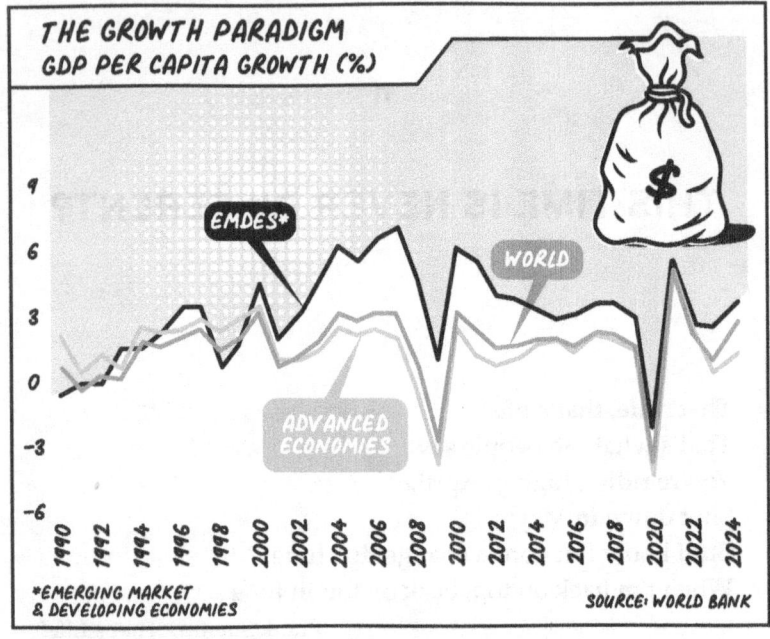

century, pausing during the horror of two world wars. It may be nonsense, but its intangible hopefulness is extremely powerful.

And it was true for quite a long period. Our parents had it better than their parents, and we have had it a little bit better than them. The GDP-per-head statistics confirm that, and major improvements in communications, technology and health-care have contributed to a general sense that we are genuinely making progress in the western world. A longer view of history, however, reinforces the common-sense dictum that such a trajectory cannot continue and that it is ridiculous to assert that western humanity is on a constantly improving curve. Logic dictates that however long economic, technological and general living improvements last, they are not ultimately and eternally sustainable. It is Newton's immutable law of physics applied to human development. Just as what goes up must come down, the idea that things can carry on improving forever doesn't wash. We think our lives will continue to get better economically, but look at Japan, which had twenty years of stagnation. Until now, there has been no western parallel, but it is easy to see one coming in Europe's sovereign debt overhang and moribund economies. Even if there is still enough progress in other short-term measures to make it seem as if we have somehow entered a new paradigm, strong reasons exist to suspect that some parts of our lives will get significantly more difficult in the next twenty years. Interestingly, studies show members of Generation Z are becoming less optimistic than their predecessors about the future. This is a disturbing trend, but Gen Z's caution may prove to be justified.

In the first edition of this book, back in 2014, I identified five major challenges for the next twenty years that would require new approaches and a new mindset. I worried about a demographic time-bomb, with the United Nations forecasting that the global population will surpass 9.3 billion people, on the way to more than 10 billion by 2100. With scientists calculating that an average of three months is being added to life expectancy every year, there could be 1 million centenarians across the world by 2030. That would clearly have major implications for a healthcare and pensions crisis, while a continued global population explosion would also create an enormous resources problem. Already the UN says that more than 1 billion people lack access to adequate food, and the health of more than half the world's population is affected by poor nutrition. Although there are signs of human longevity peaking in some western markets, this remains a major concern, with water scarcity, climate change and political and economic volatility adding to the global problem.

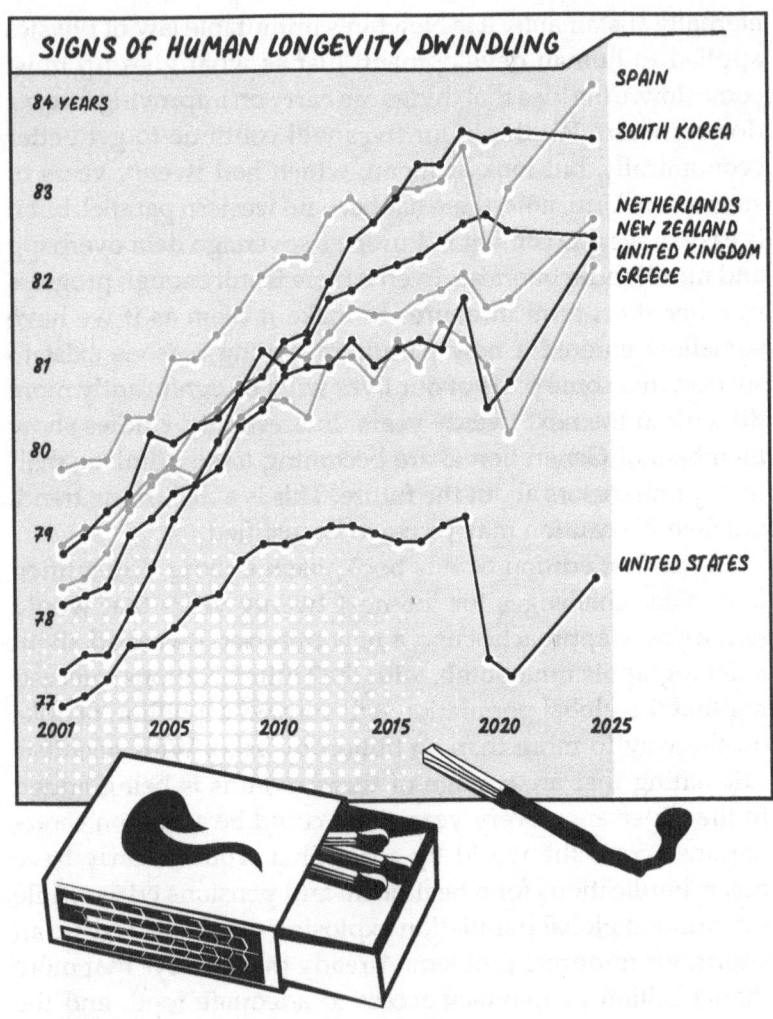

SIGNS OF HUMAN LONGEVITY DWINDLING

SPAIN

SOUTH KOREA

NETHERLANDS
NEW ZEALAND
UNITED KINGDOM
GREECE

UNITED STATES

84 YEARS
83
82
81
80
79
78
77

2001   2005   2010   2015   2020   2025

The Food and Agriculture Organisation of the UN says that for 9 billion mouths to be fed nutritiously we will have to use resources more intensively, increase productivity and use less chemicals and water. If crop yields are to match the rise in population, some of them will have to improve significantly. Indeed it has been argued that, with the world's population growing at a rate of just over 1 per cent a year, agricultural yields need to rise by 50 per cent more than that. This may not sound much, but is substantially higher than current growth rates.

Global energy supplies will also come under pressure from problems of depleting resources and security of supply.

Behind this looms the spectre of social unrest, which I witnessed at first hand in London's Notting Hill in 2011 when rioting gangs stormed into my local restaurant and began attacking the place. Angry mobs of youths were rampaging in the streets, and friends of ours had their house attacked and invaded by such a mob only 800 metres from my own house. It felt alarming to be so close to events like this. And there have been similar riots and protests in the years since, targeting austerity measures, oil and gas companies and government inaction on climate change. Social media platforms have accelerated protest organisation and outrage cycles, often pushing young people into radicalised or highly polarised movements.

Finally, I worried about a polarisation of political views, with populist governments and movements increasingly dividing peoples. This concern proved to be warranted as I, like many others, did not anticipate either Britain's referendum decision in 2016 to leave the European Union or the election of President Donald Trump in 2016 and again in 2024. I fear that much of the good work achieved with cooperation over dismantling barriers to world trade and a more collaborative global economy is being undone. One of the core underlying factors in this development is a technology-driven polarisation, in which algorithmic news feeds and echo chambers are accelerating the spread of misinformation and entrenching ideological divides at an alarming rate.

One issue I have been observing anxiously is that for young people inheriting is becoming nearly as important as working, as *The Economist* has expressed it, correctly also stating that this is dangerous for both capitalism and society. For centuries, aristocracy ruled by birthright – power and privilege passed through bloodlines. The rise of industrial capitalism and democratic ideals gave way to meritocracy, where talent and hard work – not lineage – promised success. But today that promise is fading. As wealth concentrates and inheritance surges, we're sliding into an 'inheritocracy', in which who your parents are once again matters more than what you do. The rising importance of inheritance over income is quietly but profoundly reshaping the future for young people entering the workforce. In recent past generations, education, talent and effort were generally enough to secure a decent standard of living and a path to home ownership. Today that equation has broken down. In the UK, average house prices have risen over 60 per cent in real terms since 2000, far outpacing wage growth. In the US, millennials earn 20 per cent less than baby boomers did at the same age, yet face home prices that have increased nearly 120 per cent since 2000. At the same time, inherited wealth is booming: estimates suggest that over $84 trillion will be passed down in the US alone by 2045. This means a young person's financial future is increasingly determined not by their skills or ambition, but by whether they were born into a wealthy family. For those without this advantage, it creates a sense of running an unwinnable race – working just as hard, but falling further behind. This shift doesn't just affect individuals; it corrodes social mobility, deepens inequality and risks hardening class divides into hereditary ones. If left unaddressed, it could undermine the very idea of a fair society, where opportunity is earned rather than inherited.

I have learned a lot in my rollercoaster of a life until now, and it is most often the case that the trickiest problems are the 'black swan' events that no one sees coming. My experiences in Russia in 1998 and in Iceland in 2008 showed me what it was like to watch financial market bubbles burst, but even I have been taken aback by the size and pace of the technology stocks bubble that gathered mass during Covid-19.

In the years leading up to the pandemic, tech companies became something equivalent to the promised land for investors, and every type of investor wanted a piece of the pie. This led to an overflow of cash chasing a relatively small number of opportunities, which is of course the usual seeding ground for investment bubbles. Soon we saw an overcapitalisation of the whole sector with abundant funding available even to companies with little or no sustainable business model or revenue potential. When two investor dollars are competing for every dollar needed in funding, prices take off upwards. This phenomenon was taking place for years in the venture capital arena until late 2022 when western interest rates suddenly started to go up. This led to massive 'valuation inflation' throughout the financial system and investors started overpaying everywhere.

I asked a professor at my old university how these new metrics could be justified and he said: 'Look , when it comes to valuation metrics, we have all basically thrown in the towel. It's now just based on gut feel and hope value.' A good indicator was how many 'unicorns' were appearing in the market. A 'unicorn' is a new company that reaches a valuation of $1 billion or more in a valuation round. This is a very unusual achievement historically – hence the unicorn title, because they were so rare. Now, however, they are not so rare, with the number of global unicorns jumping from 250 in 2017 to more than 500 in 2020 before nearly doubling

GLOBAL UNICORN COUNT
2017 – 2024

2017

2018

2019

2020   563   ⟶ 70%. ⟶
               INCREASE

2021

2024   1,467

SOURCE: PWC

again in a single year to almost 1,000 unicorns in 2021. During an investment bubble, there is often a disconnect between a company's valuation and its actual financial performance or potential for profitability. Valuations become inflated based on optimistic future expectations and potential, rather than on current revenue or earnings. This leads to a situation where companies with little or no profitability can achieve sky-high valuations. In hindsight this cycle, as with any bubble, was mostly driven by fear of missing out and a herd mentality.

The current situation in the market is that of a balloon slowly leaking and deflating. There are a lot of investors nursing a hangover from the overvaluation game, including me. It's interesting that I have talked publicly and indeed written a book about how to watch out for and avoid investment bubbles, and yet now I find myself with egg on my face again. This time is never different, but I felt myself drawn to

BUT... FUNDING FOR UNICORNS HAS PLUMMETED
NEW GLOBAL INVESTMENT ($BN)

300

200

100

2006   2008   2010   2012   2024

the cool tech crowd investments and disregarded my own advice. Ouch!

The main lure in all these bubbles is of course that you convince yourself you are investing alongside other investors who are much smarter than you, so you will be fine as they know much more about the situation than you do. But is it really so simple? Actually, that is just an excuse for relegating the critical thought process – in other words opting for wishful thinking as opposed to logical thinking. I guess it's no different from any mistake you make repeatedly, like drinking too much alcohol. You say to yourself: 'Damn, I'm not going to do that again,' but then lose yourself in the moment of fun and find yourself right back where you were before with a bad hangover. What you want to do and what you actually end up doing are often regrettably not closely related.

I believe that through partnership we can find new ways of managing capital, some of which may in fact be old ways, such as a return to the original partnership approach of the London insurance market. I believe the financial carnage that still exists following the 2008 crisis necessitates a change of approach. Because of capital constraints and reduced appetites for risk, the storm-riding that I used to do in financial markets has been replaced by forming partnerships with people. Rather than buying things cheaply so that one side takes a big loss and another makes a gain, people will partner up to take the risk together, sharing both benefits and pain.

Partnership is becoming my strategy. After spending most of my career largely taking my own risks, the constraints of my Darwin agreement to pay back my banking creditors, coupled with my lower risk appetite (and hopefully with a wiser head on my shoulders), mean that I am now looking for opportunities to share. Previously I would spot an opportunity, do my research and conclude that it needed perhaps £500 million, which I would fund with, say, £50 million of my own capital, borrowing the remainder. That route is now closed, so in this scenario I would aim to put in £100 million and recruit four partners to contribute £100 million each. This sort of risk sharing is what the City of London was originally built on, and I think it is on the rise again. I have redefined my business model over the last decade, including my risk profile and geographical zones of opportunity. The tools that I had in the 1990s and mid-2000s – mainly the flood of leverage that allowed a different way of thinking about business opportunities – are no longer available, so I have had to adapt my approach.

In the boom days, I was not some sort of ideologue or business guru with strict rules governing what I was doing. My business strategy in terms of all the leverage I was taking and the deals I was doing was not a model I set out with. I went to Russia, saw the opportunity and figured out the easiest way of capturing it, which happened to be leveraged deals. Then I went back to Iceland, saw that banks there and in London were throwing cash at me and wanted to find a way to put the maximum amount of cash to work, so I looked for larger deals with opportunities for higher levels of gearing. Now my world and the financial world in general have changed and this modus operandi has evolved, mostly moving to unlisted companies and technology-focused venture capital. A lot of banks, for example, still have a lot of bombed-out assets which now present opportunities. Also, as a result of the crazy zero-interest-rate environment engendered and perpetuated by Covid-19, many businesses cannot operate in a real interest-rate environment, let alone one coupled with significant inflation. I will therefore try to partner up and use the capital that's already in the system to try to revive some of these businesses. This is where the opportunities will be for my financial storm-riding in the future. We are in the midst of a major market correction, which is painful to many of my portfolio companies. I will have to try to dodge bullets again – but it will also throw up special situations, which I always find to be the best source of truly unique investment opportunities.

I am also going to focus much more intently on the

priorities in hand. When you look at too many opportunities you tend to lose focus and therefore have more opportunity to make mistakes. That's certainly what happened to me. By the time 2008 dawned, I was in too many places doing too many things. Now I want to take on fewer projects and make sure I give them my full attention. Focus is the single most important skill you need in business, along with clear vision.

I am trying to change my attitude to risk, but this is difficult because in a way it is against my nature. It's like the old fable about a scorpion asking a frog to carry him across a river. The frog's fears of being stung are allayed by the scorpion pointing out that doing this would drown them both. The scorpion climbs on the frog's back, but halfway across the river, he stings the frog anyway, dooming them both. 'But why did you do it?' asks the dying frog. 'Sorry, it's just the way I am. It's hard-wired into my nature,' are the scorpion's last words. Deals are in my nature, but nature evolves and I need to evolve as well. At Novator we have developed much longer risk matrixes and are operating on quarterly rather than annual balance sheets, which makes the risk factors much more transparent.

This sort of tightening will continue and I will force myself to do it, but there will always be the impulse to behave like the scorpion with that frog. No matter how much you think you know the risk matrix and the assets you invest in, it's always the unexpected ones that pop up and leave you with a black eye. Unfortunately, we have seen a lot of those during the past few years. With Covid-19, for example, the world shutting down for two years was a risk nobody foresaw and its repercussions are still playing out negatively all over the markets, the world economy and of course in my businesses and investments too.

I say to my people: 'Try not to be in a hurry. Try to do something constructive and make sure you do it by the book.'

But at the back of my mind I'm keen to go back and see what can be tweaked and how I can improve on the deal I've got. My instincts are always to do something radical and unexpected – break up, spin off and then look for a truly transformational deal.

Will it always be like this? Has my storm-riding of international markets ended for good? Probably not. There's a saying that a burnt child avoids the fire and the same thing is happening now. People are viewing opportunities with far more focus than before on what can go wrong. There has also been a considerable effect on my and my team's confidence. We were so badly caught out that it will take a few years to build it up again. The skill set may be there, but are we confident that we are doing the right thing, especially in this still hugely uncertain world? Inevitably, we see the downside much more than before and we are operating in a bearish world. It is partly about confidence, but it is also because we have become much more aware of how the volatility around us can affect the slightest thing. We have changed how we function internally, of course. In terms of risk management, we at Novator spend much more time on analysing risks in each project in our group than before. My job is still to try to focus on the opportunities, assemble teams and tell them what we should be looking at. It has always been that way, and if the case is good enough it gets through all the naysayers whose job is to tell us what could go wrong. It's like a debating group. You go three or four rounds, the proposal gets tweaked and the deal gets done. But our risk controller now has far more weight and authority at the table.

We will be more risk conscious, but it irritates me when it is said that people like me need to operate much more like institutional investors because smaller players in the boom times were among the main protagonists of risk. This ignores the fact that the institutions were egging us on. When we said it might be risky they would say: 'We trust you, we trust you. You figure it out but get us more risk and get us more results.' It's different with banks now, of course. When I say to them: 'We can make a double-digit return here,' they say: 'We're afraid that will fall through our risk profile.' Instead of coaxing me to take more risk, my stakeholders are doing the opposite. We are talking about different stakeholders, of course. The ones who invested with me in the boom times did so because they knew I was a risk-taking special situations operator and they were of the same mindset, though they were one step removed. If anything went wrong, they could always blame it on me. Now it is the opposite. My stakeholders in Darwin wanted almost no risk at all – and I cannot blame them for that.

There are deals that I did in the past that I wouldn't do now. I wouldn't attempt to do the deal we tried with Amer Group and I certainly wouldn't go anywhere near that dreadful Allianz investment. I would still do most of the successful deals, however, particularly the Czech Republic and Bulgarian telecoms deals. I would also still do the Actavis leveraged buy-out. The reason I made money is that other people did not get the risk assessments right – they overemphasised some risks and misunderstood the opportunities of others.

I cannot see myself investing in a bank again. My fingers have been burnt badly enough. I will be more cautious about leverage and banks are the most leveraged, most complex institutions in the world. Nathan Rothschild, who made a fortune buying in the panic after the Battle of Waterloo in 1815, is credited with saying: 'Buy when there's blood in the streets, even if the blood is your own.' But 17 years after one of the biggest bank crashes in history, I wouldn't do it today or even in a few years' time. And after another period of big banks like Silicon Valley Bank and Credit Suisse going bust over a weekend, the most famous Swiss bank of all, we can see clearly that no matter how much players try to learn from past mistakes, they simply don't. This time is never different. We always come full circle back to the same point. I also believe the traditional banking model is fundamentally broken, as the rise of the 'neobanks' (the online internet banking apps) shows. I have been an active investor in those, making a handsome profit from Monzo and taking a longer-term outlook on US mortgage company Better.com, where I found myself at the crossroads of two powerful forces: a market high on tech euphoria, and a personal curiosity about a financial tool I had never used before – the special purpose acquisition company (SPAC). My vehicle was named Aurora, alluding to my arctic roots, and was my first venture into this world. SPACs were everywhere, promising speed, flexibility and the chance to participate in what felt like the next chapter of innovation. This actually turned out to be two bubbles that would soon converge.

Better.com wasn't just another pitch deck full of dreams. It had just reported more than $200 million of net profit in its latest year – real numbers, not projections. More impressively, it was fundamentally changing how people got a mortgage: instead of the usual multi-week ordeal, it had developed technology to approve a loan in a single day. This wasn't incremental innovation. It was groundbreaking. No one had done it before. I would also be teaming up with the most prominent tech investor in the world, SoftBank, who had been championing this company before I entered the picture, and I took great comfort from their enthusiasm and willingness to put huge amounts more capital to work than they had already invested in the previous two years. I was captivated. Here was a profitable, fast-growing disruptor, and I had the means to bring it to the public market. It felt like the perfect alignment of opportunity, timing and ambition. But beneath the excitement, a quieter force was at play: fear of missing out. And afterwards, as one banking analyst put it succinctly: Better ended up being 'the exact wrong company at the wrong time'.

Blinded by my fascination with a game-changing product and the thrill of my first SPAC, I ignored the fragility of the moment, underestimated the brutal impact of rising rates and shaky leadership, and paid the price when the market collapsed and the stock crashed over 90 per cent on day one. Thankfully the public investors that had backed me in the SPAC did not lose money, as almost all of them got their cash back by redeeming before the merger consummated. I still stood by a true disruptor then and am still backing them now in my belief that they will manage to flourish once the US mortgage market recovers from its current low level.

The neobanks will disrupt the fragile old models further, and the crypto landscape of the future will do so even more, once it has had its Armageddon moment separating the weak unsustainable players from the few strong ones that will dominate the sector. That scenario is inevitable, as Darwin's law of evolution clearly tells us.

Will the sort of storm-riding I did in the past still be possible? I believe that it will be, but in different ways. There will be more special situations but in a much wider array of sectors and geographies. And there may even be more opportunities, although it will be more difficult to crack them. It's just going to be different. Evolution is at work, and Darwin famously said that it's not the strongest or the smartest that survive but rather those that are more adaptable to change. So if I can adapt to new ways of doing things, I think there could be more, rather than less, action for me.

There will always be a lot of opportunities created by various crises like the ones I have recounted here. Although black swan events by definition entail the completely unknown and its unexpected effects, we know these events will keep happening. And I believe they will actually become more frequent over the coming decades.

It seems to me that my biggest and best deals over the last three decades have all happened inside a failed process of some kind or other. The successes have come not in times of stability, but in the aftermath of collapse. If there's a philosophy that runs through my career – and my life, really – it's this: systems fail, but resilience creates opportunity. Time after time, I've seen it play out in the world around me, and in my own story. When the established order breaks down, whether in politics, in markets, or in personal fortunes, it feels like the end. But it's not. If you can hold your nerve, if you can see past the fear and the noise, you realise that failure is only a phase. On the other side of collapse is creation.

When communism crumbled in eastern Europe, the fear was palpable. Entire economies were coming apart, familiar structures were vanishing overnight. But beneath that surface, something new was taking shape. I didn't run from that chaos – I ran towards it. In Russia, I found opportunities where others saw only risk, and I managed to create a start-up business in the rubble of the old system there. The same was true during the eastern European privatisations. Governments were offloading valuable assets, often at fire-sale prices, like in Bulgaria in the pharma and telecoms assets, simply to survive the transition. These were moments not of destruction, but of reinvention. And they rewarded those who dared to act.

This pattern has played out in my own life as well. I've made a fortune, lost it, and built it back again. Each time, I've learned the same lesson: collapse isn't the end. It's an invitation to rebuild – smarter, stronger and with a clearer understanding of what really matters.

A perfect example of this is what happened in Iceland. The government had planned to bring in large, established Nordic banks to anchor its financial sector. When that plan unravelled, many saw only failure. But I saw a door opening. I stepped in and acquired Landsbanki, the country's oldest and largest bank. What was meant to be a routine privatisation turned into one of the defining moves of my career. I wasn't the obvious candidate, but I was willing to act when the conventional players hesitated. The ups and downs of that deal would of course become the core of this book and of my story as a whole.

This way of thinking has become second nature to me. I don't chase collapse for its own sake: I respect its dangers deeply. But I've learned to trust that in the ashes of old systems lie the building blocks of new success. It's a mindset that has shaped my investments, my strategies and my outlook on life itself. Conversely and importantly, others have found opportunities in some of my failures, like in Colombia. That is the circular way of the world, and just as I can time my entry into failed projects of one kind or another, I too can fail. Often spectacularly so, but that crisis becomes the other side of the coin for another opportunity.

If you're prepared to act when others hesitate, you can turn collapse into creation. I've seen it happen across countries, industries and cycles. And I believe it will continue to be true in the future. Resilience isn't just surviving the storm. It's about learning to see opportunity in the wreckage, and having the courage to build again. That is the story of my career. And, in many ways, it's the story of who I am.

One new direction I found myself drawn to is historical property and land – not a sector I have dabbled in much before. I have always had a passion for historical architecture which probably stems from my time as a young man spending many weekends walking the grand streets of St Petersburg, immersed in the greatest architecture of that imperial era. I have never taken on a full-time project in that arena, although I did spend a few years carefully reconstructing a period London house from scratch, and the same in my apartment on the Fontanka Canal in St Petersburg. These were more like hobbies at the time. Over ten years I also rescued my abandoned ancestral family home in the centre of Reykjavik after a long battle with planning authorities. But I have never before attempted anything on the scale of my latest project, the Bramshill estate in Hampshire, England.

Kristin and I looked for years for a sizeable project in the British countryside to work on together, combining her passion for nature and outdoor living and my semi-addiction to rebuilding wrecked grand buildings. The idea was for the building to be redesigned to create something complex that would provide real-time experiences for the family in finding a broken gem and unleashing its full potential through meticulous and time-consuming work.

Our opportunity came about in 2022. Bramshill is a Grade I listed, Italian Renaissance-style country house described by English Heritage as being 'a great Jacobean palace' and one of the largest and most important mansions of this period in England. Set in 400 acres of listed formal and informal gardens, farmland and sports grounds, it has a rich history, with the land featuring in the Domesday Book. The original house on the site, dating back over some 900 years to 1096, attracted owners including Henry VIII and Edward IV but was replaced in the early 1600s by Edward la Zouche, 11th Baron Zouche of Harringworth, and then rebuilt during the reign of Charles I after being partly destroyed by fire. It features a great hall displaying 92 coats of arms on a Jacobean screen, an ornate drawing room and a 38-metre-long gallery, all abounding in columns, friezes and large tapestries. After the Duke of Wellington defeated Napoleon in 1815, he was offered his house of choice and visited Bramshill, but instead chose the nearby Stratfield Saye. No fewer than fourteen ghosts are reputed to haunt the house, including that of a bride who accidentally locked herself in a chest on her wedding night and was not found until fifty years later. In more recent times, the 2022 movie *Matilda the Musical* was partly shot at Bramshill.

The grounds, laid out in the eighteenth century by Sir John Cope, 6th Baronet of Hanwell, are no less grand, with walks, drives and copses threaded through a farmed landscape. The Cope family lived at Bramshill for 236 years, expanding the deer park. The estate then went into decline in the early twentieth century, but was restored by the 2nd Baron Brocket after he acquired it in 1935. During the Second World War, the mansion was used by the Red Cross as a maternity home and then became the residence of the exiled King Michael and Queen Anne of Romania. After the war, the estate was acquired by the British government, handed to the Home Office and developed as the National Police College. Over the next half century, tens of thousands of British police officers were trained there, and an extensive series of modern buildings was constructed in the grounds to house the operation. Bramshill also housed the European Police College from 2005 until 2014, when the house and estate were sold to heritage property developer City & Country, which planned 350 new homes in the grounds. Planning permission was never granted, however, and lengthy legal battles ensued.

I became aware of these legal tussles, saw that the estate was decaying amidst this conflict between development and historical preservation, and identified an opportunity to approach this project from a completely different angle.

Although the estate was not on the market, I reached out to the owners and offered them a deal that would work for all parties, eventually purchasing the entire estate. A strategy was developed in collaboration with English Heritage and the National Trust to return the property to its former glory. Under my direction from abroad, teams are restoring the 4,088 square-metre mansion and demolishing the old college campuses in 80 buildings of almost 30,000 square metres, separate from the mansion and the other historical buildings.

Today, Bramshill House stands at a crossroads of the past and future. Its grand facade and empty classrooms remind us of its remarkable journey: from a medieval manor of Norman knights, to a Jacobean palace of courtiers, to a country seat of baronets and barons, to a cradle of modern policing expertise – and now, hopefully, we can find a new purpose for this amazing historical jewel. Gamekeepers have started rebuilding the wildlife, and are busy installing new eco-friendly heating systems and upgrading utilities and land management in order to totally revitalise the whole estate.

While people of my age typically take up golf or gardening, I am full of energy to resurrect and rejuvenate this once proud part of British history. This is a long-term project which Kristin is as invested in and as passionate about as I am. Originally, one of the conveniences of Bramshill was its proximity to Wellington College, where our children were being educated, so they could work on the estate alongside their studies. This is less relevant now that they have mostly completed their UK education. This is a project that has given both Kristin and me new vigour and enthusiasm, and we feel privileged to be able to rescue Bramshill and unleash its potential as well as reveal its unique beauty. We have many ideas for how the estate could eventually function as a community again and how it can have meaningful purpose once more. Many of my friends are surprised by my reply to their expected question of 'When will it be finished?' The answer is simply never – it goes on for ever. It is an endless project. If, when and how we will live there as a family is almost irrelevant, as we are very much on a mission now and are concentrating on the journey instead of the destination. There is also a new spanner in the works for our project there, as our foundations for living in the UK have recently undergone enormous change.

In April 2025, Britain radically changed its tax regime for foreigners living in England. It abolished a system that has been developed over hundreds of years to deal with people who have, like me, built their fortune elsewhere but who wish to spend it in England. The key principles are known as 'trusts' and 'non-domiciled residency'. Trusts began in medieval England when knights went off on crusades, leaving their land in the care of trusted people. Courts enforced these arrangements to protect the knight's family, creating the legal concept of a trust, in which one person holds property for another's benefit. Over time, trusts became a powerful tool for managing wealth, passing it on to heirs and protecting assets. They were later used to hold money and property overseas, often for tax or privacy reasons. Britain's non-domiciled tax regime started in the 1800s. It let people who lived in the UK but had their permanent home elsewhere avoid UK tax on foreign income – unless they brought it into the UK. Together, trusts and 'non-dom' status made the UK attractive both to wealthy people from around the world and to Brits who made money abroad. These systems helped protect wealth and reduce taxes, and over time became key parts of Britain's appeal as a global financial hub. They were a key reason why I chose to live in England and why I have built my family life there. But these new changes make it absolutely impossible and impractical, for many reasons, to continue our residency in the UK. I have moved our residence to another country, with the rest of the family to follow. I continue to have all trust and tax matters managed through international advisers. It's a major disruption but also a chance to immerse myself in yet another foreign culture and make an adventure out of the whole exercise.

In terms of the family project of Bramshill, these new realities disrupt not only financial planning but also the stability and continuity you need to run something on this scale. We are in many ways doing what landowners of past centuries did: investing long-term in the cultural and physical fabric of Britain. But we're doing so in a policy environment that is far less accommodating of that role. Bramshill is more than a country house: it is a symbol of Britain's living history. The systems of trust and domicile that once protected estates like this evolved for good reason – so that national treasures could survive war, exile and economic upheaval. As those systems are reshaped, there is an urgent need to ensure that the law continues to support those who are willing and able to restore and protect Britain's heritage. Our current restoration of Bramshill House reflects a centuries-old tradition: a private individual devoting time, capital and expertise to safeguard a part of Britain's national story. But this effort is now being undertaken in a climate of rising fiscal and regulatory complexity which threatens the long-term viability of large-scale restorations. Without legal frameworks that respect both the public value of such projects and the private commitment they require, many historic estates will either fall into disrepair or be repurposed in ways that permanently erase their cultural identity.

*

As for me, it has been a remarkable journey, and who knows where it will take me and my family who give me so much joy all the time? Now when I look back, I feel only gratitude, and when I look forward I feel a strong sense of hope. I hope I am humbler, wiser and more sanguine about the surprises and setbacks that life can throw up. I'll take Rudyard Kipling at his word, and 'meet with Triumph and Disaster and treat those two impostors just the same'. Whatever happens in the future, I intend to stick to that.

If you can keep your head when all about you
Are losing theirs and blaming it on you,
If you can trust yourself when all men doubt you,
But make allowance for their doubting too;
If you can wait and not be tired by waiting,
Or being lied about, don't deal in lies,
Or being hated, don't give way to hating,
And yet don't look too good, nor talk too wise:
If you can dream – and not make dreams your master;
If you can think – and not make thoughts your aim;
If you can meet with Triumph and Disaster
And treat those two impostors just the same; ...

... Yours is the Earth and everything that's in it,

from Rudyard Kipling, 'If'

EPILOGUE

Cattle die and kinsmen die,
thyself too soon must die,
but one thing never, I ween, will die, –
fair fame of one who has earned.

from Havamal, 'The words of Odin'
(c. AD 900–1200; translated by Olive Bray)

I sit here putting the finishing touches to my story in the house in Iceland that my great-grandfather built with such ambition and with his portrait hanging above me. I can't help smiling at the irony of him watching over my shoulder, as I find myself repeating so many of his endeavours, and, yes, his mistakes. The same can be said of my father's journey too. The lesson of how history repeats itself stares me starkly in the face. My great-grandfather went bankrupt twice, yet each time he drew on his boundless entrepreneurial spirit to rebuild from scratch and repay every debt. My father, too, lived through dizzying highs and devastating lows. I don't need to look generations back to find the drive to pick myself up again – my father was just as powerful a role model in that regard. In their lives, as in their legacies, they built far more than businesses. Both left behind monuments to their ambition and vision – monumental buildings in central Reykjavik, each far ahead of its time. My great-grandfather's bold structure still stands as a testament to the spirit of a man who dared greatly. Exactly a century later, my father would do the same with Harpa, now one of the city's proudest landmarks. Whatever I do next, it will be with deep respect for – and inspiration from – what they both built, not only in concrete and glass, but in character, conviction and courage.

On the day in early 2025 when I delivered the eulogy at my father's funeral in Reykjavik's Harpa concert hall, sunlight streamed through its vast glass windows, revealing the old port beyond, where he started out as a young deckhand and rose to lead a shipping company whose vessels once filled the entire harbour. But my father's story doesn't merely surround Harpa; in many ways, Harpa is his story. It was his brain-child – an audacious, heartfelt vision brought to life through Portus, the company he founded to compete for the development of this site. What began as a bold proposal became one of Reykjavik's most iconic landmarks: a modern master-piece with a shimmering glass façade, now as emblematic of the city as its towering cathedral. A world-class concert hall was always to be at its heart, surrounded by shops, apart-ments, hotels and the headquarters of Landsbanki. My father assembled a powerhouse team – visual artist Ólafur Elíasson, maestro Vladimir Ashkenazy, and Henning Larsen Architects of Copenhagen Opera House fame – and lobbied tirelessly, knowing that only the most ambitious design could symbolise the rebirth of a nation. He poured everything into it.

Born into one of the poorest countries in Europe, my father saw Iceland transform within his own lifetime into one of the wealthiest per capita. Nothing ever ignited his passion like Harpa did. By 2008, the foundation was ready, but then came the financial crash, and construction halted. The half-built shell stood like a ghost of a grand idea. Many urged the government to bury it and move on. But wiser voices prevailed, and the state chose to complete it, paying in full for what was meant to be funded over 35 years. For that, my family remains deeply grateful. Harpa rose again, reborn from crisis, and today it stands not just as a concert hall but as part of the city's soul – Reykjavik's own Sydney Opera House, a symbol of national pride to Icelanders and visitors alike. Yet, as the old Icelandic proverb goes, few get to feel the warmth of the fire they lit. My father visited Harpa only once after its completion, when my mother dragged him to a concert. I often wonder what he felt, walking through the building he had imagined in such intricate detail, down to the deep red hue of Iceland's Eldborg volcanic crater, which he specified personally for the walls. He never truly received the recognition he deserved. But for me, Harpa is more than architecture – it is a monument to a man whose ideas were as fearless as they were beautiful. Nothing was too grand, too strange or too impossible, if it carried even the faintest spark of vision. And what a monument to leave behind. Dad always aimed higher, built bigger and dreamed further than most dared.

Resilience is the key to not only surviving but prospering. Obstacles and challenges are simply a road to the next phase of progress for us, however painful they might be. I also share an ultimate irony with my ancestors regarding their and my own biggest failures: they all seemed like great ideas at the time.

APPENDICES

APPENDICES

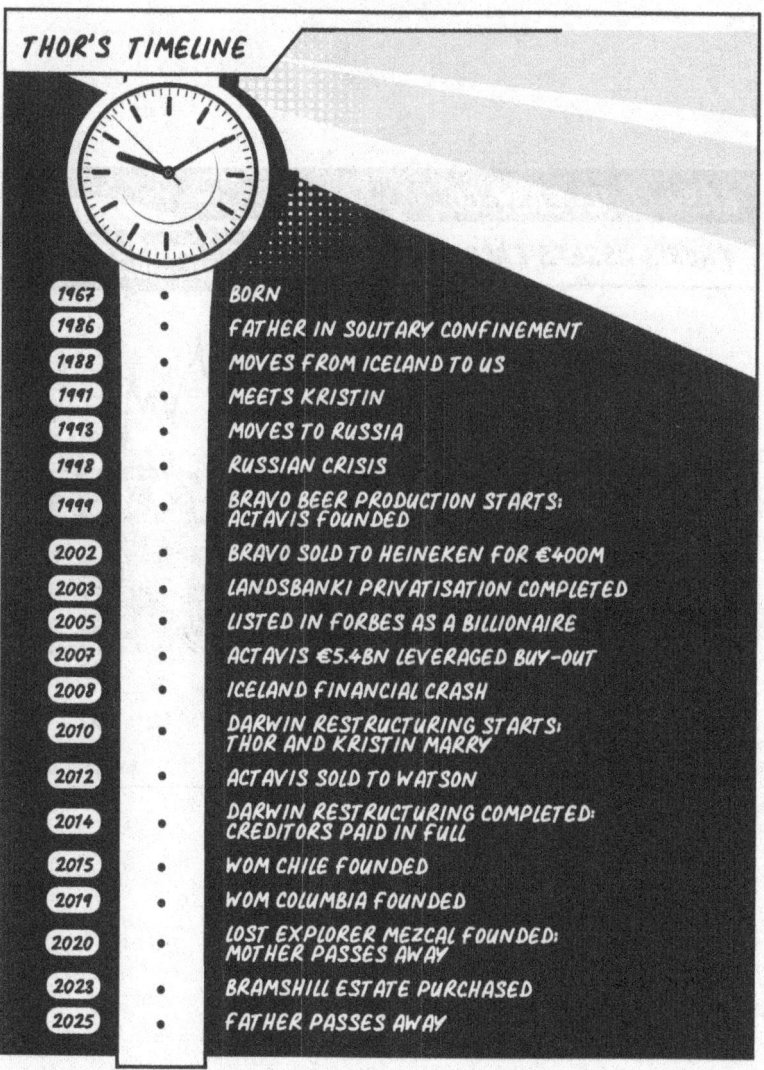

THOR'S TIMELINE

1967	•	BORN
1986	•	FATHER IN SOLITARY CONFINEMENT
1988	•	MOVES FROM ICELAND TO US
1991	•	MEETS KRISTIN
1993	•	MOVES TO RUSSIA
1998	•	RUSSIAN CRISIS
1999	•	BRAVO BEER PRODUCTION STARTS; ACTAVIS FOUNDED
2002	•	BRAVO SOLD TO HEINEKEN FOR €400M
2003	•	LANDSBANKI PRIVATISATION COMPLETED
2005	•	LISTED IN FORBES AS A BILLIONAIRE
2007	•	ACTAVIS €5.4BN LEVERAGED BUY-OUT
2008	•	ICELAND FINANCIAL CRASH
2010	•	DARWIN RESTRUCTURING STARTS; THOR AND KRISTIN MARRY
2012	•	ACTAVIS SOLD TO WATSON
2014	•	DARWIN RESTRUCTURING COMPLETED: CREDITORS PAID IN FULL
2015	•	WOM CHILE FOUNDED
2019	•	WOM COLUMBIA FOUNDED
2020	•	LOST EXPLORER MEZCAL FOUNDED; MOTHER PASSES AWAY
2023	•	BRAMSHILL ESTATE PURCHASED
2025	•	FATHER PASSES AWAY

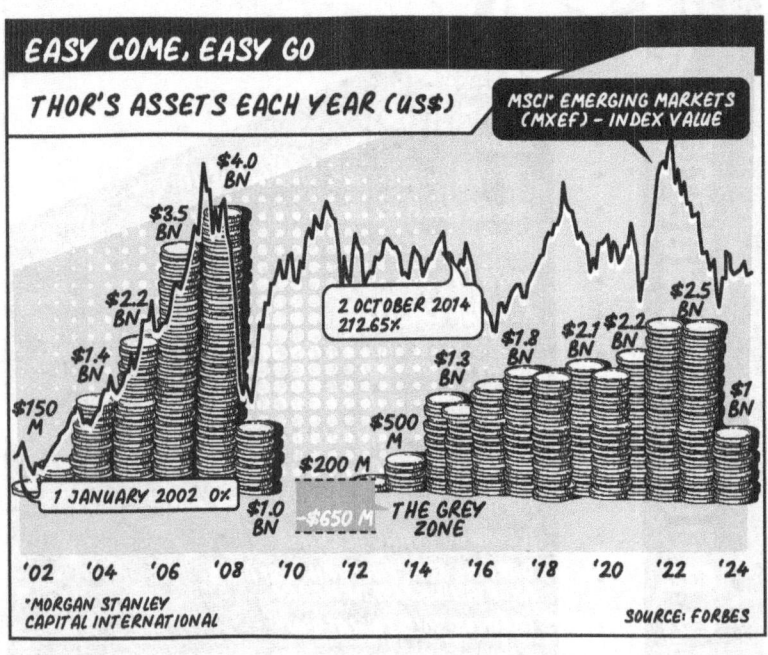

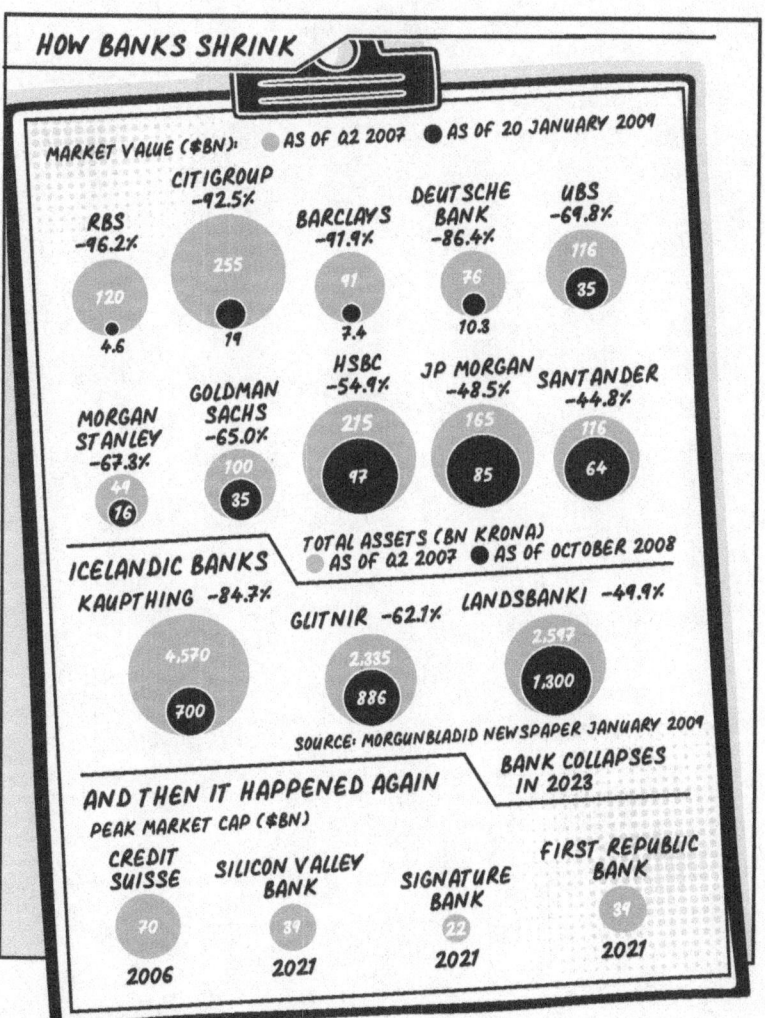

HOW BANKS SHRINK

MARKET VALUE ($BN): ● AS OF Q2 2007 ● AS OF 20 JANUARY 2009

CITIGROUP
-92.5%

RBS
-96.2%

BARCLAYS
-91.9%

DEUTSCHE
BANK
-86.4%

UBS
-69.8%

120

255

91

76

116

4.6

19

7.4

10.3

35

MORGAN
STANLEY
-67.3%

GOLDMAN
SACHS
-65.0%

HSBC
-54.9%

JP MORGAN
-48.5%

SANTANDER
-44.8%

49

100

215

165

116

16

35

97

85

64

ICELANDIC BANKS

TOTAL ASSETS (BN KRONA)
● AS OF Q2 2007 ● AS OF OCTOBER 2008

KAUPTHING -84.7%

GLITNIR -62.1%   LANDSBANKI -49.9%

4,570

2,335

2,597

700

886

1,300

SOURCE: MORGUNBLADID NEWSPAPER JANUARY 2009

AND THEN IT HAPPENED AGAIN

BANK COLLAPSES
IN 2023

PEAK MARKET CAP ($BN)

CREDIT
SUISSE

SILICON VALLEY
BANK

SIGNATURE
BANK

FIRST REPUBLIC
BANK

70

39

22

34

2006

2021

2021

2021

275

ACKNOWLEDGEMENTS

Special thanks to Kristin for all her support and advice, and to Matthew Anderson, Matthew Bishop, Andri Sveinsson, Birgir M. Ragnarsson, Ragnhildur Sverrisdottir, Emma Barton and Bjork Eidsdottir for their time and help.

Thanks also to Thomas Hoegh, Birgir Bielvedt, Anna Meleshina and Peter Henry for support and encouragement; to Gunnar Smari Egilsson for ideas and provocative thoughts; to Stephen Brough and Paul Forty at Profile Books for their belief and diligence; and to Andrew Cave for his endless patience and faith.

A special thank-you to my children, Daniel, Lorenz and Bentina, whose unquestioning love has helped see me through, and to my late sister Magga, who inspired me to think differently and always hold on to my principles and values, no matter what other people think and want.

Finally, I would like to thank my detractors, whose comments made me want to write my side of the story. I wouldn't have written this book without you.

Bjorgolfur Thor Bjorgolfsson

Mercury © 1976, reproduced by permission of Queen Music Ltd/Sony Music Publishing Ltd, London N1C 4DB.

'Just an Illusion' by Imagination. Words and music by Ashley Ingram, Lee John, Steve Jolley and Toby Swain © 1982, reproduced by permission of Associated Music International Ltd/ Broadley Music International/Sony Music Publishing Ltd, London N1C 4DB.

'Ace of Spades' by Motorhead. Words and music by Edward Clarke, Ian Kilmister and Philip Taylor © 1980, reproduced by permission of Motor Music Ltd/Sony Music Publishing Ltd, London N1C 4DB.

'Everybody Knows' by Leonard Cohen. Words and music by Leonard Cohen and Sharon Robinson © 1988, reproduced by permission of Sony/ATV Songs LLC/EMI April Music Inc., London N1C 4DB. Written by Leonard Cohen and Sharon Robinson © 1988 Sharon Robinson Songs (ASCAP) admin. by Wixen Music UK Ltd. All rights reserved. Used by permission.

'Eye of the Tiger' by Survivor. Words and music by Frank Sullivan and Jim Peterik © 1982, reproduced by permission of Sony/ATV Melody, London N1C 4DB. Words and music by James Michael Peterik and Frankie M., III Sullivan © 1982 WB Music Corp. (ASCAP) and Easy Action Music (ASCAP). All rights on behalf of WB Music Corp. and Easy Action Music administered by Warner/Chappell North America Ltd.

'Livin' La Vida Loca' by Ricky Martin. Words and music by Robi Rosa and Desmond Child. A Phantom Vox Corp. (BMI). All rights on behalf of A Phantom Vox Corp. administered by Warner Chappell Artemis Music Ltd. Words and music by Desmond Child and Robi Rosa © 1999 Desmophobia and A Phantom Vox Publishing. All rights for Desmophobia administered by BMG Rights Management (US) LLC. All rights for A Phantom Vox Publishing administered by Warner Chappell Artemis Music Ltd, London W8 5DA. All rights reserved.

INDEX

Captions for colour plates are indicated by *col. pl.*
Page numbers in *italics* indicate captions in the text.

3 (mobile phone provider) 206
9/11 terrorist attacks 102

AbbVie (pharmaceutical company) 209
Abramovich, Roman 48
AC Milan football club 28
Actavis (previously Pharmaco) 76, 101,
    112, 190–91, 208, 212
    Thor becomes chairman (2000) 150
    growth of 5–6, 76, 145, 150
    hostile bid for Pliva 88, 95, 197
    and Deutsche Bank 88, 95–7, 144–9,
        190–92, 196–9, 211
    Thor's buy-out (2007) 6–7, 95–7, 128,
        144–5, 148, 165, 256
    and SIC report 128–9
    quality issue 145–6, 153, 191
    fall in valuation (2009) 10
    restructuring 147–8, 192
    FDA and 146, 191
    Olafsson as CEO 196, *col. pl.*
    bought by Watson Pharmaceuticals
        (2012) 88, 196–200, 209, *col. pl.*
    Bisaro becomes chairman (2014) 88
    recent successes 209
Advent International 76–7, 88
agency problem 149
AI (Artificial Intelligence) 204, 241–2
AIG 84, 144, 154
Akranes, Iceland 31, 32
alcopops 51–3
Alibaba 89
Aliber, Robert 123
Allergan 209
Allianz 87, 153, 165–6, 256
Althing (national parliament of Iceland)
    115
Ambani, Anil 239
Amer Group 86–7, 256

Amer Sports 165
America Movil 221
American Nazi Party 18
Amgen 112
Andriy (Russian police colonel) 64
Anitsev, Viktor 44–5
Anne, Queen of Romania 262
Apple 150, 238, 240
Argentina 220, 226
Asgrimsson, Halldor *col. pl.*
Ashkenazy, Vladimir 268
Association of Co-operatives (SIS) 26–7
Atlanta (airline and logistics group) 108
Aurora Innovation 257
Avantel (later WOM Colombia) 225, 228

Bagus, Philipp and Howden, David:
    *Deep Freeze: Iceland's Economic
    Collapse* 126
Balkanpharma 72–4, 112, 238
Baltic Bottling Plant 40–45, 52
Baltic Financial Industrial Group 63–4
Baltika 56
Bank of America 151, 191, 201
Bank of England 175, 178
bankers' bonuses 149
Bannister, Chris 222, *col. pl.*
Barger, Sonny 164
Barr Pharmaceuticals 88, 95
Baugur 100, 112, 121, 155–7
Bayerische Landesbank 177
Beckham, David *col. pl.*
Beijing Olympics (2008) 9
Belgrade, Serbia 85
Better.com (US mortgage provider)
    257–8
Bisaro, Paul 88, 197, *col. pl.*
Bjorgolfsdottir, Bentina (Thor's
    daughter) 199, *col. pl.*

Bjorgolfsdottir, Evelyn Bentina (Thor's half-sister) 20–21, *col. pl.*
Bjorgolfsdottir, Margret (Magga; Thor's half-sister) 15, 20, 38, *col. pl.*
Bjorgolfsson, Bjorgolfur Thor 41
  born in Reykjavik (1967) 1, 16, 19
  childhood 13–15, 21–6, *col. pl.*
  family 14–15, 20–21, 34, 140, 164–5
  lifestyle ix, 94, 129, 164
  personality 17, 94
  health 164–5
  relationship with his father 14–15, 35, 50, 161–3
  caricatures of 109, 117
  earliest deal (aged 10) 1–2
  entrepreneurial from childhood 2, 22–3
  makes his first fortune working in Russia 2, 59, 69–70, 171
  Iceland's first billionaire 2, 9–10, 119
  approach to investment 4–6
  and his father's bankruptcy 10, 163
  visits San Francisco (aged 11) 15–16
  sudden end to his childhood 13–14, 24–5, 35
  at University of California in San Diego 34
  attends New York University 34
  sells books door-to-door in Iceland 38–9
  works for nightclubs in Reykjavik 39, 41
  and Baltic Bottling Plant 40–46, 52
  Bravo founded 46–7
  managing director of Bravo 50–51
  and security in Russia 48–9, 60–65
  Icelandic consul in St Petersburg *col. pl.*
  chairman of Balkanpharma 74–5
  established in Bulgaria 76
  Pharmaco–Delta merger (2002) 75–6, 101
  telecoms and 76–86, 203, 205–6, 220–23
  private jets 91, 129, 212, *col. pl.*
  yacht 93–4, 129, 212
  Landsbanki privatisation (2003) 98–110, 210, *col. pl.*
  40th birthday celebrations in Jamaica ix–xi, *col. pl.*
  Actavis buy-out (2007) 6–7, 95–7, 128, 144–5, 148, 165, 256
  believes his investment in Iceland is risk-free 10–11, 104, 110–11

blamed for financial crash in Iceland 129–31, 138, 141, 175, 186–7, *col. pl.*
  hostility in Iceland after the crash 131–2
  loses 99 per cent of his $4 billion fortune 10–11, 153–4, 160, 170
  avoids bankruptcy 158–60
  personal guarantees 10, 129, 138, 146, 210
  repays his creditors 159–60, 200–201, 212–13, 252
  restructuring settlements 212, 219
  birth of children 132, 160, 165, 199
  marries Kristin 195–6, *col. pl.*; *see also* Olafsdottir, Kristin
  changing attitude to risk 140–41, 203, 252–3
  revival in fortune 200–210
  and Play 86, 200–201
  invests in technology sector 201–5
  Grand Commander of the Order of the Phoenix 208
  apologises for part played in financial crash 211–12
  invests in South America 220–37
  sells Latin American investments 229–34
  invests in India 237–41
  Reykjavik family home 261
  and Bramshill estate 261–5, *col. pl.*
Bjorgolfsson, Daniel (Thor's elder son) 160, *col. pl.*
Bjorgolfsson, Hallgrimur (Halli; Thor's half-brother) 15, 20, *col. pl.*
Bjorgolfsson, Lorenz (Thor's younger son) 132, 165, *col. pl.*
Black Power movement 19
Black–Scholes derivative formula 126
'black swan' events 235–6, 249, 258–9
Blackstone Group 90, 144
Bogotá, Colombia 227, *col. pl.*
Bolivia 220
Bordeyri, Iceland 30–31
Borgarfjordur, Iceland 30
Borgarnes, Iceland 30
Borislavova, Tzvetelina 79
Borisov, Boyco 80
Botchkarev beer 56–7, 59, *col. pl.*
Botox 209
boxing 204
Boxmeer, Jean-François van 69
Bramshill estate, Hampshire 261–5, *col. pl.*
Branson, Sir Richard 26, 89

Bravo International 221–2, *col. pl.*
  founded (1996) 46–7
  krysha 47–8
  problems in first year 50
  alcopops and beer 50–54
  legal wrangling 53
  brewery in St Petersburg 55–9, 61
  success of 57–9
  sale to Heineken (2002) 5, 67–9, 108
Brazil 220, 226
Brexit 247
BRICS (intergovernmental organisation) 220
Brezhnev, Leonid 15
Brin, Sergey 89
British Virgin Islands 43, 53
Britvic 44
BTC *see* Bulgarian Telecommunications Company
Buiter, Willem H. 172
Bulgaria 2, 72–5, 79–81, 84, 87–8, 107, 256, 259
  Thor's bodyguards in 65, 87
  Balkanpharma 72–4
  Thor established in 2–3, 76–7
  telecommunications privatisation 77–82, 206
  Turkish lobby 77
  internet revolution 81
  Thor's role in 81–2
  Thor sells his companies 84, 95, 128, 130, 144, 165
Bulgarian Telecommunications Company (BTC) 3, 76–81, 84, 130, 165, 200
Bunadarbanki (later Kaupthing) 99–100, 105–6, 109–10
Burning Man festival, Nevada desert 236, *col. pl.*
'Business Club', Belgrade, Serbia 85
'BVI guys' *see* Ingimarsson, Ingimar Haukur; Lardner, Bernard

Cable & Wireless 86
California, USA 15, 34
Cambridge, England 205
Campelli, Fabrizio *col. pl.*
Campidoglio fortress, Rome 195–6
Canada, Icelandic settlers in 113
Capital Research 54–5, 57, 67–8
capitalism 248
Carlsberg 56, 67
Carnegie (bank) 88, 152
Carrera 77
carry trading 102, 124–5

Cazoo 205
CCP Games 202–3, 212, 238
  EVE (online game) 202–3
Central Bank of Iceland 7, 136, 152, 172, 179, 184
  high interest rates 102
  tries to nationalise Glitnir 121
  exchange rate policy 124
  and Thor's plans for Straumur 152
  takes over Straumur 132–3
  bankruptcy 103, 156
  Landsbanki and 179–80
Ceske Radiokomunikace (CRa) 81
Cetin, Serdar *col. pl.*
Charles I, King of England 261
Cheadle, Don *col. pl*
Chechen gang 61
Chicago, USA 86
Chicago University 123
Chile 220–26, 228–32, 234
China 89, 206, 231–2, 238–9
  Beijing Olympics (2008) 9
  and telecoms infrastructure 206
  trade war with US 238
China Development Bank 206–7, 231
Church of Our Saviour of Spilt Blood, St Petersburg *col. pl.*
Citibank 78–9, 145
Citigroup 172
City & Country property developer 262
City of London 252
Claro 221, 225–7
Clausen, Haukur 18
Clausen, Orn (Thor's half-brother) 15, 20, *col. pl.*
Clifford Chance (law firm) 192
climate change 90, 245, 247
Clinton, Bill 213, *col. pl.*
Clooney, George *col. pl.*
Cohen, Leonard: 'Everybody Knows' 169, 170
Cold War 91–2
Collins Stewart 152, 156
Colombia 225–34, 260
  Ministry of Telecommunications 232
comic books 1–2, 22–3
Commission for the Regulation of Communications (Colombia) 228
communism 259
Connery, Sean xi
Cope, John, 6th Baronet of Hanwell 262
Copenhagen, Denmark 32, 54
cost-of-living crisis 243

'Costs and recovery of the Treasury from the collapse of the banks' report 213

Courchevel, French Alps 86, *col. pl.*

Coventry, England 172

Covid-19 pandemic 204, 226, 228–33, 235, 239, 249, 253, 254

Credit Suisse 157–8, 256

Croatia 88, *col. pl.*

Cruz, Jose de la 204

cryptocurrency 170, 258

Cyprus 54, 68

Czech Republic 3, 75, 81, 151, 152–3, 256
    privatisation of Ceske Radiokomunikace 81
    Thor sells his companies 84, 95, 128
    and Straumur 151

Damon, Matt *col. pl.*

Darling, Alistair 179

Darwin, Charles 188–9, 235, 258

Darwin restructuring agreement 192, 200, 201, 252, 256

Davos, Switzerland 89–90, 226, *col. pl.*

day-traders 170

Daytona Bike Rally, Florida, US: motor-cycling (2008) *col. pl.*

deCODE Genetics 111–12

deepfakes 24–21

Deliveroo 202, 205

Delta 75–6, 101

Denmark
    Thor Jensen migrates to Iceland 30
    as a colonial power 30
    Icelandic independence from 32
    Thor's father's photo-processing shops 26
    brewery experts in 57
    Straumur opens in 151

Deposit Guarantee Directive 175

Deutsche Bank 78, 112–13
    advises Bulgarian pharmaceutical companies 72–3
    and Balkanpharma 73–5, 112
    and Ceske Radiokomunikace 81
    and Actavis 88, 95–7, 144–9, 190–92, 196–9, 211
    and credit markets crash (2008) 97, 157–8
    and Play 201

Deutsche Telekom 84, 205, 221

Dimon, Jamie 201

DNA 205

DNEG (visual effects and animation studios) 237, 239–41

Dominican Republic 220

dotcom bubble (2001) 101, 102, 111, 143

Durrant, Mark 173

DV (Icelandic newspaper) *182*

e-commerce 205

eBay 166

EBITDA (earnings before interest, taxes, depreciation and amortisation) 96, 145

Economic and Investment Bank (Bulgaria) 79

Economist, The 60, 62, 248

Ecuador 220

Edward IV, King of England 261

EEA *see* European Economic Area

EFTA *see* European Free Trade Association

EIBank 130

Eimskip 113–17
    Iceland's oldest and largest shipping group 27
    Jensen not allowed to be chairman 33, 113
    emblematic of Iceland's renaissance 33
    'University Fund' 113–14, *col. pl.*
    sale of Eimskip stock 113
    buys Hafskip 114
    growth of 115
    Thor becomes chairman 33, 116
    Thor breaks the company up 33, 116

Einarsson, Sigurdur 112, *182*

Element (Thor's yacht) 93–4, 129

Elíasson, Ólafur 268

Elisa (Finnish telecom company) 82, 86, 165

energy supplies 247

English Heritage 261, 263

Enskilda Bank 99

Entel 221, 225

environmental, social and governance (ESG) 205

European Court of Human Rights (ECHR) 183

European Economic Area (EEA) 101–2, 175
    law 175

European Free Trade Association (EFTA)
    court, Luxembourg 136, 175–6
    EFTA countries 185

Surveillance Authority 175
European Police College 262
European Union (EU) 174, 185–6, 213, 247
Eusébio 28
EVE (online game) 202–3

Facebook (later Meta) 202
Fall, William 152
Fantastic Four comic 23
FAP (security firm) 48
50 Cent xi, *col. pl.*
film industry 240
    writers' and actors' strikes (2023) 240
Financial Services Authority (FSA) 172, 178, 180
Financial Times 68, *col. pl.*
Finland 82–3, 151
    alcopops in 51, 52
    telecoms 82–3, 86–7
    Straumur's franchises in 151
Fjarmalaeftirlit (FME) 121, 133
Fontanka Canal, St Petersburg 261
Food and Drug Administration (FDA) 146, 191
Footsteps on the Wind (film) *col. pl.*
Forbes magazine
    estimates Thor's wealth 3, 9–10, 243
    Thor on its cover 3, 82, 89, 118, *col. pl.*
    Forbes list 118–19, 160, *col. pl.*
force majeure 54–5
Foreign Office (Iceland) 172
Forest Laboratories 209
Fortino, Don 236
France Telecom 205
Frankfurt, Germany 198
Frettabladid newspaper 211
FSA *see* Financial Services Authority
Fury, Tyson 204

Gardarsson, Gisli Orn *col. pl.*
Generation Z 245
Georgiou, Tony 43
Germany 68, 87, 191
    law 147
    government 148, 174
    'fortress Germany' 87, 148
    banks 95, 148–9, 177
    German government 174
Germanos, Panos 207–8, 231
Glitnir (previously Islandsbanki) 134
    renamed (2007) 100
    crashes (2008) 121, 130, 155–7, 172, 180

government support 136
    shareholders 138, 157
    post-crash criminal cases 181
    recovery 184
global economic crisis (2008) 7–11, 112, 120–31, 135, 152–8, 172, 179–80, 186, 235
    aftermath 169–70
    lessons learned 170–71
Gnupur (investment company) 135
Google 90
Gorbachev, Mikhail 48–9, 91–3, *col. pl.*
Great Depression 135
Greece
    Greek consortium and Balkanpharma 72, 74
    financial collapse 207
    bailed out as a PIGS economy 191
Greece Telecom 84
Green Cross humanitarian organisation 92
Grimsson, President Olafur 85, 135–6, *col. pl.*
Groundhog Day (film) 142
growth paradigm 243–5
GRU (Russian army intelligence service) 48–9
Guardian newspaper 51, 69
Gudmundsson, Albert 27–9
Gudmundsson, Bjorgolfur (Thor's father) 16, 34–5, 109, 138–40, 162–3, 267, *col. pl.*
    family background 19–20
    education 34
    marriage 19, 20
    alcoholism 12–14, 16–17, 163
    relationship with Thor 35, 161–3
    and Thor's earliest deal 1–2
    arrested and imprisoned 20, 23–4, 34
    in solitary confinement 24–5, 33
    managing director of factory 25
    chief executive of Hafskip 25–6, 114
    Hafskip court case 29
    and Baltic Bottling Plant 41–4
    and Bravo 46–7, 50, 53
    and Landsbanki 99, 108, 130, 154, 161–3, 168, *col. pl.*
    and Eimskip 114
    accusation over the crash in Iceland 130, 140, 162–3
    invests in West Ham United 161–2
    bankruptcy 10, 138, 162–3, 210
    as a role model for Thor 267

Harpa concert hall, Reykjavik and 268–9
Gudmundsson, Magnus *182*
Gulf States, 237
Gunnarsdottir, Thorgerdur Katrin *col. pl.*
Haarde, Geir H. 62, 120, 131, 156–7, 172, 174, 178, 183, *col. pl.*
Habib brothers 204
Hafskip 25–30
    Thor's father as chief executive 25–7
    logo 26
    vibrancy of 26
    unable to be a competitive player in Iceland 27
    seeks business abroad 27
    bankruptcy 28–9, 34
    bought by Eimskip 114
Haig Club House, London *col. pl.*
Halldorsson, Magnus and Juliusson, Thordur Snaer: *Island Ehf* 178
Hallgrimsson, Hallgrimur (Thor's maternal grandfather) 17, *col. pl.*
Hallgrimsson, Margret Thora (Thor's mother) 16–17, 21, *col. pl.*
    education 18
    previous marriages 16, 18
    lives in US 18–19
    marries Thor's father 19
    and her husband's alcoholism 13–14
    personality 21
    death 19
Hamley's toyshop, London, 149
Hariri, Saad 84
Harley-Davidson 164
Harpa concert hall, Reykjavik 268–9
Hartwall 56
Havamal: 'The words of Odin' 267
Hazelton, Minnesota 14
HBOS 179
healthcare technology 205
Heineken 68, *col. pl.*
    Bravo brewery sale (2002) 5, 45, 67–9, 108
Heineken, Freddy 68
Helgason, Egill 177
Hells Angels 164
Helsinki, Finland 83, 86
Henning Larsen Architects 268
Henry VIII, King of England 261
Heritable Bank 173–4, 178, 184
Höfdi, Reykjavik, Iceland 91
Hoffman, David 47

Hollywood writers' and actors' strikes (2023) 240
Homski, Gennady 41, 46, 47–8
Hong Kong 239
Hornstrandir, Iceland *col. pl.*
Hotel Hassler, Rome 195
Housing Financing Fund (Iceland) 102, 133
Howard, Trevor 18
Howden, David 126
HSBC 99
Huawei 206, 231, *col. pl.*
Humperdinck, Engelbert: 'Release Me' 192–3
Hutchison Whampoa 206
Iceland 15–16, 34, 98, 101–4, 141
    Thor Jensen becomes the richest man in 20
    a closed society 15–16
    economic problems in 1970s 16
    herd mentality 9, 130
    treatment of children 22, 175
    fishing industry 27, 32–3, 115–16
    sheep farming 31–2
    independence from Denmark 33, 101
    cronyism 34, 101
    Thor sells books door-to-door 38–9
    advertising law 40
    telecoms privatisation 83
    population 8, 173
    European Economic Area member 101–2
    free market and 101–2
    economic crash (2001) 102, 104, 111
    privatisation of its banks 102–10, 210–11
    economic boom 6–10, 101–3, 110–11, *111*, 120–21, 126–7, 130, 138, 148–9, 152, 156, 167–72, 187, 211
    liberalisation 104–5
    oligarchies 8
    Thor as its first billionaire 2, 9–10, 119
    currency (krona) 150–51, 179, 217
    economic crash (2008) 7–11, 103–4, 107, 112, 117–18, 120–31, 135–7, 143, 143, 152–8, 170–78, 187, 213–18, 260, *col. pl.*
    emergency law passed (2008) 176–7
    Thor blamed for the crash 128–31, 140–41, 186–7, *col. pl.*
    lessons from the crash 169–71, 215–17
    deposit insurance scheme 174–6
    foreign creditors 177–8

and EFTA 175–6
post-crash criminal cases 181–3, *182*
bank recovery figures 184
referendums on debt repayment 175, 177, 186
economic recovery 215–18
tourism 217–18
Icelandair 116
Icelandic Stock Exchange 103, 114, 123
Icesave 136–7, 173–7, 179, 184n, 185–7, 213
'Icesavestein monster' 185
Iliad Group 208
ILM (visual effects company) 240
Imagination: 'Just An Illusion' 120
Independence Party (Iceland) 26–8, 105, 115–16
India 237–41
Indian Motorcycles 164, *col. pl.*
ING Barings 77
Ingimarsson, Ingimar Haukur (one of the 'BVI guys') 40, 43–4, 47, 50, 52–3
Ingólfscafe nightclub 41
inheritance 248
Instagram 202
Interbrew 67–8
Intermediate-Range Nuclear Forces (INF) Treaty (1987) 91
International Monetary Fund (IMF) 56, 134
iPhone 89, 150
Iraq 185
Ireland 174
Iron Curtain 91
Islandsbanki (later Glitnir) 99–100
Israeli consortium and Balkanpharma 72, 74
Italy: bailed out as a PIGS economy 191

Jackson, Peter 240
Jakovlev, Vladimir *col. pl.*
Jamaica: Thor's 40th birthday celebrations ix–xi
Jamiroquai xi
Japan 245
Jensen, Thor Philip Axel (Thor's maternal great-grandfather) 17, 20, 30–32, 98, 267
a Danish-born entrepreneur 17
raised in Copenhagen 32
attachment to UK and 17
becomes the richest man in Iceland 20
loses and regains fortunes 30

as Thor's guiding light 30
sheep business 31–2
fishing industry 32–3
not allowed to be chairman of Eimskip 33, 116
his villa in Reykjavik 267, *col. pl.*
Johannesson, Jon Asgeir 100, 112, 155
Johannesson, Thordur Mar 134
Jónsson, Ásgeir and Sigurgeirsson, Hersir: *The Icelandic Financial Crisis* 184, 213
JP Morgan 178, 201
Juliusson, Thordur Snaer 178

Kapysh, Pavel 64
Karic, Bogoljub 85
Karolinudottir, Karen Erla 127
Kaupthing (previously Bunadarbanki) 106, 112–13, 134–5, 179
renamed 100
privatisation 100, 109
government support 136, 180, 183–4
crashes (2008) 130, 181
shareholders 138
post-crash criminal cases 181, *182*
recovery 184
KBC (Belgian bank) 80
Keflavik international airport, Iceland 13
KGB 61
Khrushchev, Nikita 2, 37, 171
King Jr, Martin Luther 19
Kipling, Rudyard: 'If' 266
KKR (private equity firm) 144
Klang Games 204
Seed (online game) 204
Klebnikov, Paul: *Godfather of the Kremlin: Boris Berezovsky and the Looting of Russia* 36–7, 67
Klimas, Egis 204
knowns and unknowns 234–6
Kors, Michael 192
Kremlin, Moscow 45
Kroll (investigations agency) 88
Kronstadt naval base, Gulf of Finland 48
krysha (Russian protection gangs) 47–8
KSF (British bank) 184

Landsbanki 99, 112, 129–30, 135, 150, 260, 268
investment in 10, 99, 168
and SIS 115
stock company (from 1997) 99

privatisation (2002) 10, 98–9, 104–8,
110, 148
Thor's father as chairman 108, 154,
161–2
share-price rise 110
put into receivership 121
and SIC report 128–9
lack of support from government
136–7
and efforts to rescue Actavis 146
most of business done abroad 151
proposed merger with Straumur
151–2, 154–5, 157
UK and 174–5, 178
refused loan 138, 178–80
crashes (2008) 153–5, 172–6, 180,
183–7
and Icesave 136–7, 173–6, 184n, 185–7
and post-crash criminal cases 183,
183n
seized by the government (2009) 10
recovery 184, 184n
and the UK government 175–6
Lapthorne, Richard 86
Lardner, Bernard (one of the 'BVI guys')
43–4, 47, 50, 52
Latifah, Queen 164
Latin America 220–29, 233–4, 236–7,
243
Lebanon 84
Lehman Brothers 84, 145, 150, 152–3,
158, 173, 179, 191
Leslie, Thomas *col. pl.*
life expectancy 51, 245–6
loan-to-value ratio 180
Loggins, Kenny: 'Danger Zone' 36
London 131, 137, 140, 165, 190
social scene 18
capital markets 54
Thor in 55, 68, 98, 164–5
Thor's Park Lane penthouse office
suite 129, *col. pl.*
house in Notting Hill 129, 164, 247
insurance market 252
City of London 252
London Olympics (1948) 19
London Stock Exchange 166
London Venture Partners 204
Long-Term Capital Management
(LTCM) hedge fund 56
Lost Explorer Mezcal, The (alcoholic
beverage) 236–7, *col. pl.*
Lowenbrau 40, 67–6
Lucas, George 240

Lucky (Nigerian nightclub owner in St
Petersburg) 62

Ma, Jack 89
Malcolm X 19
Maldives 196
Malhotra, Namit 237–9
Malone, John 223
Marley, Bob xi
Marley, Ziggy xi
Mars 42
Marseille football club 28
Martin, Ricky: 'Livin' La Vida Loca' 219
Marvel comics 1–2, 22–3
'massively multiplayer online' (MMO)
game 202
Matilda the Musical (film) 262
McInroy, Bruce *col. pl.*
Merck 95–6, 144
Merkel, Angela 148, 174
Merrill Lynch 68, 135, 191, 201
Meta (was Facebook) 202
'Metaverse' 202
Metropolitan Hotel, London 55
Mexico 232, 236
mezcal 236–7, *col. pl.*
Michael I, King of Romania 262
Michelangelo 195
Microsoft 90
Mikhalovits, Nikita *col. pl.*
Ministry of Commerce (Iceland) 185–6
Ministry of Finance and Economy (Ice-
land) 213
Ministry of Foreign Affairs (Iceland)
175–6
Ministry of Information Technologies
and Communications (Colombia) 228
Mobtel 84–6
Monaco Grand Prix 164
Monzo (internet bank) 257
Moscow, Russia 37
Bravo's customers 55–6
Morgunbladid 116, *col. pl.*
Motorhead: 'Ace of Spades' 143
Movistar 221, 225, 227
Moynihan, Brian 201
Mumbai, India, 241
Murdoch, Rupert 90–91
Musin, Valery 45
Mussolini, Benito 196

Nall-Cain, Ronald, 2nd Baron Brocket
262
Nasdaq 112

Naspers 166
National Police College 262
National Spectrum Agency (Colombia) 228
National Trust 263
NATO: bombing of Serbia 2, 72
'neobanks' 257–8
Netflix 202, 240
Netherlands
  Icesave depositors in 174–6
  Landsbanki branches 175–6
  repayment to Dutch Icesave savers 176, 185–7
Netia 206
New York 22, 40
New York Stock Exchange 104
New York Times 40
New York University 22, 34
  Stern School of Business 187–90, *col. pl.*
Newton, Sir Isaac 245
Nextel Chile (later WOM) 220–21, 223
Nextel Corporation 220
Niel, Xavier 208
Nikki Beach bar, St Tropez 97
Nokia 89–90
NordVPN 204–5
Northern Rock, collapse of (2007) 173
Norway 185
Notorious B.I.G.: 'Mo' Money, Mo' Problems' 71
Notting Hill, London 129, 164
  riots (2011) 247
Nova 222, 231, 234
Novator 86, 94, 161, 192, 197–9, 200, 204, 207–8, 212–13, 222, 228–9, 237, 254–5, *col. pl.*
Novgorod, Russia 56

Oaxaca, Mexico 236, *col. pl.*
Observer newspaper 129
Ocean's Thirteen (film) *col. pl.*
Oddsson, David 9
Office of the Special Prosecutor (Iceland) 138–9
Oger Telecom 84
Okman, Tom 204
Olafsdottir, Kristin (Thor's wife) 9, 41, 93, 135, 160, 164–5, 210, *col. pl.*
  meets Thor 39–40
  in Russia 61, 65
  birth of Daniel 160
  sense of danger in Iceland 110, 131

and hostility in Iceland after the crash 131–2, 141
  birth of Lorenz 132, 165
  and Thor's 40th birthday celebrations in Jamaica ix–xi
  marries Thor 165, 194–6, *col. pl.*
  and Thor's Stern Business School speech 188, 190
  birth of Bentina 199
  co-chair of Serpentine gallery film committee *col. pl.*
  and Bramshill estate 261, 263, *col. pl.*
  50th birthday celebrations *col. pl.*
Olafsson, Olafur 100, 181, *182*
Olafsson, Sigurdur (friend of Thor) *col. pl.*
Olafsson, Sigurdur Oli ('Siggi')
  CEO of Actavis 196, *col. pl.*
  and Watson–Actavis merger 197
oligarchies 8, 45
Ollila, Jorma 89
Omega Pharma 75
OMON (Russian elite police units) 49
Onca 181
Orange (France Telecom) 205, 221
Oscars, The (Academy Awards, Hollywood) 164, 239

Pacquiao, Manny 204
Page, Larry 89
Palace of Heavenly Peace, Beijing 206, *col. pl.*
Paris
  Icelandic embassy 28
  Thor's first visit 21
pension funds 74, 102, 133, 180, 202
Pepsi 40, 42, 46, 61
Peru 220, 226
Pfizer 209
Pharmaco (later Actavis) 112
  a pharmaceutical business 41
  bottling equipment used in Baltic Bottling Plant 41, 72–3
  reverse takeover of Balkanpharma 73–5
  Pharmaco–Delta merger (2002) 75–6, 101, 108
  Thor's father on the board 160–61
  Thor as chairman 160–61
  change of company name (2004) 76
Piatko, Viktor 52
PIGS economies (Portugal, Italy, Greece and Spain) 191
Pitt, Brad *col. pl.*

Play mobile telecoms company 86, 146, 200–201, 205–9, 212, 221–23, 228, 231, 233–4
Pliva generics company, Croatia 88, 95, 144, 197
Poland: telecoms 86, 201, 206–8, 221–2, 231–2
Polaris Industries 164
political polarisation 247
Polkomtel 205, 221
population growth 245–7
Portugal: bailed out as a PIGS economy 191
Portus 268
Prime 240
Prime Focus Technologies 240
Progressive Party (Iceland) 26, 28, 105–6, 114
property investment 260
Putin, Vladimir 45–6, 92, col. pl.

Queen: 'Bohemian Rhapsody' 98
QXL (online auction site) 166

Radio City Music Hall, New York 188
Ragnarsson, Birgir Mar col. pl.
Ramos, Don Fortino col. pl.
RBS see Royal Bank of Scotland
Reagan, Ronald 48, 91–3
Rebag (online retailer) 205
Reliance MediaWorks 239
Reykjavik, Iceland 16, 91
    Thor born in 1, 16, 19
    Norwegian embassy 18
    nightclubs 39
    Thor Jensen's villa 131, col. pl.
    Harpa concert hall 268–9
    Geir Haarde's office col. pl.
Reykjavik cathedral 17
Reykjavik summit (1986) 48
Ritchie, Guy col. pl.
Rockefeller, John D. 112
Rockwell, George Lincoln 18–19
    This Time the World 18
    White Power 18
Rome, Italy: Thor's and Kristin's wedding (2010) 195–6, col. pl.
Romeo and Juliet (theatre production) col. pl.
de Rothschild, David 236, col. pl.
Rothschild, Nathan 256
Royal Bank of Scotland (RBS) 145, 179
Royal Dutch Shell 89
Rumsfeld, Donald 234

Rusinov, Nikolai 61, 64
Russia 7, 41–3, 59–66, 88, 92, 171, 253, 259
    oligarchies 8, 45
    societal change in 36–7
    Baltic Bottling Plant 40–46, 52
    Putin and 45–6
    alcohol intake and life expectancy 50–51
    alcopops 51–3
    beer 54, 57–8
    economic crisis (1998) 7–8, 55, 66–7, 96, 110, 171, 235
    aftermath of the crisis 171
    the Wild East 2, 59
    security and violence 48–9, 60–65
    Thor makes his first fortune working in Russia 2, 59, 69–70, 171
    murder rate 67
    job creation in 80
    Thor's role in 81
    Thor sells his companies 128
    see also Soviet Union
Russian mafia 59–65, 70

S-Group 99–100, 106, 181
SAB Miller 67–8
Sabaliauskas, Eimantas 204
Saigon, Vietnam: falls to North Vietnamese army (1975) 97
St Moritz, Switzerland col. pl.
St Petersburg, Russia 37, 42, 47, 58, 60, 261, col. pl.
    Bravo brewery 55–9
    Bravo's customers 55–6
    Thor as Icelandic consul col. pl.
St Tropez, France 9, 97
Salomon sports brand 86
Samson Holdings 99, 100, 107, 129–30, col. pl.
San Francisco, USA 15–16, 22, 34, 38, 163
Sanbar, Maya col. pl.
Santiago, Chile 221, 227
Sants, Hector 178
Schiffer, Claudia 90
Schwarzman, Steve 90, 95–7
Scientific American 25
Scotland
    and sheep farming 31–2
    Eimskip trades with 33
Seattle, USA 86
Second World War 17, 101, 262
Seed (online game) 204

Serbia
  bombed by NATO 2–3, 72
  telecoms 84–6
Serpentine gallery, London *col. pl.*
Sexton, John 187–8
Shell Oil Company, Iceland 17
SIC *see* Special Investigation
  Commission
Sidekick Health (digital therapeutics
  company) 205
Sigurdsson, Hreidar Mar 112–13, *182*
Sigurgeirsson, Hersir 184, 213
Silicon Valley Bank 256
Simmons, Jean 18
Sinatra, Frank: 'That's Life' 243
SIS (Association of Co-operatives)
  114–15
Skulason, Pall *col. pl.*
Sky TV 179
Slim, Carlos 221
Slovakia 75
Smith, Terry 156
social media 186, 203, 247
social unrest 25, 247
Sofia, Bulgaria 73, 80
SoftBank 257
Songs of the Young (radio programme)
  15
South Africa 25
South Korea: in crisis (1998) 56
Soviet Union
  collapse of 2, 92
  see also Russia
Spain, bailed out as a PIGS economy
  191
Special Investigation Commission (SIC)
  report on the Iceland crash 128
special purpose acquisition company
  (SPAC) 257–8
Spotify 201
Sprint (telecoms company) 220
Starovoytova, Galina 62
Steel City Interactive (gaming com-
  pany) 204
Stod 2 TV station 130
Stratfield Saye estate, Hampshire 262
Straumur Investment Bank 112, 150–51
  stake in Carnegie 88
  Thor as chairman 128, 134–5
  revenues 151
  proposed merger with Landsbanki
    151–2, 154–5, 157
  and Collins Stewart 156
  equity to debt ratio 157

and Play 207
crashes (2009) 153
taken over by Central Bank of
  Iceland 132–3, 210–11
bought out by Novator 208
Sturgis, South Dakota 164
subprime crisis (2008) 113
Sunday Times 160
SUR consortium 233
Survivor: 'Eye of the Tiger' 194
Sveinsson, Andri *col. pl.*
Sweden 88, 151–2
Switzerland 185

T-Mobile (Deutsche Telekom) 205, 221
Talermo, Roger 86–7
Talking Heads: 'Once In a Lifetime' 1
Tambov gang 47–9
Tatura, Valentin 64
tech companies 201–4, 249–51
Technicolor 240
Telefonica 221
TeleNor 86
Terziev, Peter (Bulgarian entrepreneur)
  72
Teva Pharmaceuticals 209, *col. pl.*
Tevez, Carlos 162
al-Thani, Sheikh Mohammed Bin
  Hamad 181
Thor (Norse god) 20
Thorisdottir, Hulda 127
Thors, Margaret (Thor's maternal
  grandmother) *col. pl.*
Thors, Thor (Thor's maternal great-
  uncle) 19
Thorsteinsson, Magnus 40, 105, *col. pl.*
  Baltic Bottling Plant 41, 44–5
  Bravo 46, 50
  and Landsbanki privatisation 99, 130,
    col. pl.
  and Atlanta 116
  and Samson 99
  bankruptcy 138
Thorvaldsson, Armann 113
  Frozen Assets 113
Tigo 227
Tomlinson, David 18
Touchlight (healthcare tech company)
  205
trade co-operatives 30, 32, 114
Treasury (Iceland) 172, 213, 215
Trump, Donald 247
Turkish Telecom 84
Tuscany, Italy *col. pl.*

Tzvetansky, Georg (Bulgarian entrepreneur) 72

UAE (United Arab Emirates) 239
Uber 201
UBS 158
Ukraine 46
UN *see* United Nations
'Undisputed' (boxing game) 204
'unicorns' 249–51
United Kingdom
    Thor's grandfather's attachment to 17
    Thor's mother educated in 18
    Cable & Wireless 86
    Landsbanki and 174–6, 179
    Icesave depositors 174
    deposit protection scheme 175–6, 178
    anti-terrorism legislation 179–80, 213
    repayment to UK Icesave savers 176, 185–7
    house prices 248
    non-domiciled tax status 264–5
United Nations (UN) 245
    Food and Agriculture Organisation 246
United States (US)
    Thor's mother lives in 18–19
    Thor moves to 22
    murder rate 67
    Federal Reserve 56
    Food and Drug Administration (FDA) 146, 191
    trade war with China 238
    inherited wealth 248
University of California, San Diego 34
University of Iceland 118, 123, 127, 184
    grants from Eimskip 113–14, *col. pl.*
    Psychiatry and Sociology Department 9
US Air Force 18
Usyk, Oleksandr 204
Utvegsbanki 27

'valuation inflation' 249–51
Venezuela 226
Verne Holdings 212
Vesturport (Icelandic theatre company) *col. pl.*
'Viking raiders' 128
Viking religion 20
Virgin 26
Virginia, USA 220

Vivendi 205
Vodafone 205, 221

Waldorf Astoria Hotel, New York 197
Wall Street, New York
    1929 crash 135
    Thor's internship 40
    bails out LTCM 56
Walton, Sam 118
Warner Chilcott 209
Warsaw Stock Exchange 208
Washington Post 47
Watson Pharmaceuticals 88, 196–200, 209, *col. pl.*
weapons of mass destruction (WMD) 185
Weiner, Eric: *The Geography of Bliss: One Grump's Search for the Happiest Places in the World* 120
Weintraub, Jerry *col. pl.*
Wellesley, Arthur, 1st Duke of Wellington 262
Wellington College, Berkshire 263
Wellington, Duke of *see* Wellesley, Arthur, 1st Duke of Wellington
West Ham United football club 161–2
WETA (visual effects company) 240
Wikipedia 17
Wilson sports brand 86
Wired magazine *col. pl.*
WOM Chile 222–5, 227, 230–31, *col. pl.*
WOM Colombia 225–8, 232–3
World Bank 51
World Economic Forum, Davos, Switzerland 89–91, 236, *col. pl.*
    Young Global Leaders 236

X-Men comics 1–2, 22–3

Y2K bug 185
Yeltsin, Boris 36, 45, 62
Young Vic theatre, London *col. pl.*
youth associations 30

Zashita 48
Zoom 226
Zorilla, Alberto 21
Zorilla, Sonja 21–2, *col. pl.*
la Zouche, Edward, 11th Baron Zouche of Harringworth 261
Zuckerberg, Mark 202
Zwift (indoor cycling programme) 203–4